Is God past his sell-by date?

Is God past his sell-by date?

John Blanchard

EVANGELICAL PRESS

EVANGELICAL PRESS
Faverdale North Industrial Estate, Darlington, DL3 0PH, England

Evangelical Press USA
P. O. Box 84, Auburn, MA 01501, USA

e-mail: sales@evangelicalpress.org
web: http://www.evangelicalpress.org

First published 2002

British Library Cataloguing in Publication Data available

ISBN 0 85234 500 3

Other books by John Blanchard:

Does God Believe in Atheists?	*Right with God*
How to Enjoy your Bible	*Ultimate Questions*
Meet the Real Jesus	*What in the World is a Christian?*
Pop Goes the Gospel	*Whatever Happened to Hell?*
Read, Mark, Learn	*Where was God on September 11?*

Printed and bound in Great Britain by Creative Print & Design Wales, Ebbw Vale

Contents

		Page
Preface		7
Introduction		9
1.	Cards on the table	13
2.	For the undecided	30
3.	'Goodbye, God'?	44
4.	The science thing	57
5.	Maria got it right	73
6.	From protons to people	90
7.	Is ANDi one of us?	114
8.	Signs of significance	134
9.	Where was God on September 11?	157
10.	One solitary life	187
11.	The beginning?	218
Notes		237
Index		259

Preface

A few years ago, I set out to write a fairly small book specifically intended for atheists, agnostics and others with serious doubts about the existence of God. I failed.

What eventually appeared was *Does God Believe In Atheists?* It ran to over 650 pages, which went far beyond the scope and depth I first had in mind, but the remarkable response it generated — five printings in the first eighteen months and a national 'Best Book' award — encouraged me to go 'back to the drawing board' and tackle the smaller book it was originally intended to be. This is it.

As with most of my recent books, I have asked an *ad hoc* team of capable friends to critique the material for me. On this occasion Trevor Archer, Andy Ball, Ian Coffey and Richard Gibbons agreed to do this, and I am grateful to them for their time and effort and for their many helpful suggestions.

Joy Harling, now in her twenty-second year as my secretary, has once again risen superbly to the task, never missing a deadline, even when under severe pressure from an author who constantly insisted on going through the whole thing 'one more time'.

It has been said that a person with an experience is never at the mercy of one with an argument. Although that statement needs to be treated with care, I am thankful to the ten people

who have made a significant contribution to this book by allowing me to share their stories.

Many other friends, too numerous to name, continue to join
me in praying that these pages will have a life-changing impact
on many of their readers. I owe them a debt I shall never be
able to repay.

John Blanchard
Banstead
Surrey
February 2002

Introduction

Thank you for reading this book — or at least for getting this far! From time to time, philosophers, scientists, authors and other movers and shakers have hit the headlines with claims that God is non-existent, irrelevant or 'past his sell-by date'. The famous nineteenth-century German thinker Friedrich Nietzsche shocked Europe with his dramatic announcement: 'God is dead! God is dead! And we have killed him!'[1] The twentieth-century British biologist Julian Huxley once claimed, 'Operationally, God is beginning to resemble not a ruler, but the last fading smile of a cosmic Cheshire cat.'[2] Writing in *The Times* in January 2000, the author and broadcaster Sir Ludovic Kennedy noted the current decline in the Church of England's attendance figures and added, 'But why do we bother to keep it alive, when we know that God is dead?'[3]

This book has been written specifically for those who take a similar line, who think that God is non-existent or irrelevant, or who are in some way sceptical about the whole issue.

I am going to assume that you are in one of these categories, and I do appreciate your willingness to read what follows. I want to write honestly and fairly, yet with a genuine concern to get across a message which I believe to be the most important that anyone can ever hear.

- You may never have had a serious interest in religion. On the other hand, you may have had a very strict religious upbringing, but have long since rejected all you were once taught to believe.
- You may have 'tried religion' in some shape or form without finding anything that convinced you of God's existence or relevance.
- You may have attended church on a fairly regular basis, but eventually found it boring and pointless — or you may know regular churchgoers who claim to believe in God but whose lives seem no different as a result.
- Life may be going so well for you at the moment that you fail to see why believing in God would improve things. On the other hand, life may be going so badly for you, physically, emotionally, financially, or in some other way, that you have given up on the idea of a God who is supposed to care what happens to people and to have the power to change things for the better.
- You may at some time have had a very traumatic experience which turned you against the whole idea of God. Trevor Bayliss, the inventor of the clockwork radio, says that being sexually abused as a child completely destroyed what faith he had.[4]
- Natural disasters such as earthquakes, floods and volcanoes, and other tragedies which hit the headlines, may have led you to agree with BBC journalist Michael Buerk who, after reporting the Ethiopian famine in 1984, told the *Daily Express*, 'When you have seen two million people starving through no discernible fault of their own, you cannot sign up to the premise of an all-seeing and all-sustaining deity any more.'[5]
- Perhaps the sudden or lingering death of a family member or friend has made you bitterly cynical when people talk about a loving God. On the other hand, the

seeming health and prosperity of people who totally ignore God may have convinced you that he is surplus to
requirements.
• You may have come to the conclusion that science
can explain everything, and that there is no point in looking for any kind of supernatural being.
• Perhaps you go along with the popular idea that the
entire natural world, human beings included, evolved from
some primitive life-form over millions of years, and that
this alone rules out a supernatural Creator.
• You may be deriving such satisfaction from 'doing your
own thing' that you are reluctant to think too deeply about
the possibility of there being a God who sets moral standards for mankind and to whom you might one day be
answerable.
• You may be what the British surgeon Bernard Palmer
calls an 'unconscious atheist',[6] someone who has not totally rejected all belief in God but who regards him as
nothing more than an optional extra who might come in
useful in an emergency.
• You may be confused or frustrated about the bewil-
dering variety of religious ideas on offer, or turned off by
public squabbles among those who claim to believe in
the same God, and as a result you have decided to reject
religion altogether. You might even have turned your back
on it because you have come to the conclusion that over
the centuries it has done more harm than good.
• You may feel that it is either difficult or impossible to
know whether God exists at all, and have therefore settled for being an agnostic.

If any of these scenarios, or anything like them, rings a bell,
this book is for you! I know it asks questions you need to face;
I hope it provides answers you will want to find.

1.

Cards on the table

Before we go any further, let me put my cards on the table, face upwards. I have been convinced of God's existence since I was in my early twenties, having faked my way through years of formal religion which had no inner reality. Yet even this statement needs fine-tuning, because without clear definitions there can be a tendency to generate more heat than light. In this case, the crucial question is the meaning of the word 'God'.

Some people think of God as an impersonal life force, cosmic dust, universal energy woven into the fabric of the universe, or a remote mystery 'outside' of material reality. Dictionaries of philosophy or religion list hundreds of other ideas, but it will clear the decks for all that follows if at this point I set down what I mean when I use the word 'God' in this book.

The next sentence may seem very complex, but it is vitally important. Put in a nutshell, when I speak of God I mean a unique, personal, plural, spiritual, eternally self-existent, transcendent, immanent, omniscient, immutable, holy, loving Being, the Creator and Ruler of the entire universe and the Judge of all mankind. Let me elaborate a little:

- By *unique*, I mean the one and only, as opposed to all other objects or ideas given that name.

• By *personal*, I mean that God is not an inanimate 'thing' or 'power', or some kind of influence or energy, but a living Being who thinks, feels and acts.

• By *plural*, I mean that there are distinguishable persons (usually called the Father, the Son and the Holy Spirit) within a single Godhead.

• By *spiritual*, I mean that God has no physical attributes or dimensions, that he does not have a body or any characteristics that can be defined in terms of size, shape or matter.

• By *eternally self-existent*, I mean that he always has within himself the power of 'being', and has neither beginning nor end.

• By *transcendent*, I mean that he is over and above all things, outside of time and space, completely distinct from the universe and not to be confused with it in any way.

• By *immanent*, I mean that while remaining separate from the universe in being and essence he permeates every part of it.

• By *omniscient*, I mean that he knows everything, including the past, the present and the future.

• By *immutable*, I mean that he is unchangeable in every aspect of his being.

• By *holy*, I mean that he is utterly without fault or deficiency in his being, essence and actions.

• By *loving*, I mean that he cares for all the universe, and that in a very special way he demonstrates particular love for humanity and communicates this to individuals.

• By *Creator*, I mean that by his own choice and power he brought into being all reality other than himself.

• By *Ruler*, I mean that he is in sole and absolute control of everything that exists or happens, and that nothing can prevent him from doing as he pleases.

- By *Judge of all mankind,* I mean that he alone deter-
  mines the eternal destiny of every member of the human
  race.

This is not meant to be a complete definition, but it will give
you a good idea of what I mean when I use the word 'God'
from now on.

Database

Let me turn up another card. The words I have just used to
identify God are not plucked out of thin air, nor are they a
haphazard collection of ideas that have accumulated over the
centuries. Instead, the concepts which they convey are all taken
from a single source — the Bible.

At this point you may not want to read any further, believing
that the Bible has long since been shown to be nothing more
than a patchwork of fantasy and folklore, a mishmash of super-
stitious ideas now discredited by modern science and virtually
irrelevant in our technology-driven twenty-first century. If this is
how you feel, let me ask you two straightforward questions.
Have you read the Bible through for yourself? If so, did you
read it with an open mind, or with a built-in prejudice against
it? These are critically important questions — and require honest
answers. They also lead to a number of other questions, which
may help you to see the Bible in a very different light.

Firstly, did you know that we have in existence today *more
copies of manuscript biblical material* than of any other ancient
document? For example, whereas we have only nine or ten
copies of Caesar's *Gallic War* (58 – 50 B.C.), ten copies of
works by the Roman historian Cornelius Tacitus (born *c.* A.D.
52), twenty copies of Livy's *Roman History* (59 B.C. – A.D.

17), and just eight copies of the works of the Roman historian Suetonius (c. A.D. 60 – 140), we have 100 large scrolls of Old Testament material and nearly 25,000 copies of all or part of the New Testament. The closest that any other ancient document can get to the Bible in terms of handwritten copies is Homer's famous *Iliad*, with just 643.

Secondly, were you aware that these copies are *much more textually accurate* than anything else in existing ancient literature? To give two examples, some 10% of *Mahabharata*, the national epic of India, is textually corrupt, while Homer's *Iliad* has twenty times more instances than the Bible in which the words are in doubt. Sir Frederic Kenyon, one-time director and principal librarian of the British Museum, summed up his assessment of nearly 2,000 years of investigation into the Bible's integrity as follows: 'It cannot be too strongly asserted that in substance *the text of the Bible is certain... This can be said of no other ancient book in the world*'[1] (emphasis added).

Thirdly, had you realized that the Bible manuscripts we now possess are *much closer in date to the originals* than in any other case? The gap is over 1,000 years in the case of Caesar's *Gallic War*, 900 years for the writings of Cornelius Tacitus, and 800 years for the works of Suetonius, but when we come to examine the Bible manuscripts we are presented with a very different picture. Although there is a gap of 300 years between the earliest major manuscripts of the New Testament and the events they claim to record, some papyri (papyrus was a cheap form of writing material) narrow this to just over 170 years. Smaller documents get this down to less than 100 years, while some fragments have been dated to less than fifty, and were written by eyewitnesses of the events they describe.

No other known piece of ancient literature, religious or otherwise, has anything remotely approaching the Bible's credentials in this area. For example, nobody doubts that Julius Caesar came to Britain in 55 B.C., but there are only nine or ten manuscripts to support this, and the earliest was written 900 years after he came! As far as the New Testament is concerned, Kenyon came to this conclusion: 'In no other case is the interval of time between the composition of the book and the date of the earliest manuscripts so short ... *and the last foundation for any doubt that the Scriptures have come down to us as they were written has now been removed'*[2] (emphasis added).

Fourthly, do you know *how accurately the manuscripts were copied*? It is one thing to say that we have thousands of biblical manuscripts, but quantity is no substitute for quality, and in this case counts for little unless the manuscripts were accurately copied over the centuries. As they had none of our modern technology, but did everything by hand, how can we be sure that the copyists got it right? One example of how they went about their work will go a long way towards answering the question.

From A.D. 50-100, the task of transcribing the Old Testament fell to a group of people called the Talmudists, whose work was governed by minutely detailed regulations. The text had to be copied on to ceremonially clean animal skins, prepared and fastened in a particular way. When it came to writing, each skin had to contain a prescribed and equal number of columns. Each column had to be between forty-eight and sixty lines in length, and each line had to consist of exactly sixty letters. Only black ink, prepared to a meticulously prescribed recipe, could be used. No word or letter, not even a *yod* (the tenth and smallest letter of the Hebrew alphabet) could be written from memory and without reference to the document from which the scribe was copying. There had to be the breadth of a hair or thread between consonants, the breadth of nine consonants between sections, and three lines between books. In addition, the copyist had to sit in full Jewish dress, having washed his whole body before beginning his work. He was forbidden to write the name of God except with a pen newly dipped in ink, and should anyone, even a king, talk to him while writing that name, he was forbidden to take any notice. These and the many other rules may strike us as carrying things much too far, but such meticulous care is not only impressive, it is unique in the history of literature.

The experts

Did you know that *contemporary evidence provides outstanding confirmation of the Bible's historical details?* For the last 200 years or so it has been fashionable in some circles to deny the Bible's historical accuracy, but rigorous scholarship has shown this to be a lost cause. Here are two examples, one relating to the Old Testament and the other to the New.

Robert Dick Wilson, one-time Professor of Semitic Philology (the language and literature of the Middle East) at America's Princeton Theological Seminary, set himself an astonishing forty-five-year schedule of research into the subject. When he had finished, he declared, 'I have come to the conclusion that no man knows enough to assail the truthfulness of the Old Testament.'[3] At one stage he focused on the Bible's record of kings who had lived during a period of about 1,600 years, and eventually came to this conclusion: 'There are about forty of these kings living from 2,000 B.C. to 400 B.C. Each appears in chronological order ... with reference to the kings of the same country and with respect to the kings of other countries ... *no stronger evidence for the substantial accuracy of the Old Testament record could possibly be imagined* than this collection of kings. Mathematically, it is one chance in 750,000,000,000,000,000,000,000,000 that this accuracy is mere circumstance.'[4] The contemporary expert Allan Millard, Professor of Hebrew and Ancient Semitic Languages at the University of Liverpool, goes so far as to say, 'We affirm that *nothing has been found which can be proved to contradict any statement of the Old Testament.* Archaeological research is a welcome aid to a richer knowledge of the Bible's message'[5] (emphasis added). So much for the idea that the Bible is a collection of myths and fables!

As far as the New Testament is concerned, we can call on Sir William Ramsay, widely recognized as one of the greatest archaeologists of all time. A founder member of the British Academy, he was knighted for his outstanding services to the world of scholarship. In his student years, Ramsay swallowed the trendy idea that the New Testament narratives were largely make-believe, rather than accurate, contemporary historical records. One particular target was the book entitled the Acts of the Apostles, which claims to have been written by a first-century physician called Luke. Ramsay was convinced that Acts was seriously flawed, and was in any case written not by Luke, but by an anonymous storyteller about a century after the events it claimed to record. However, after painstaking on-site research in Asia Minor he became convinced, not only that Luke did in fact write Acts, but that he was 'a historian of the first rank' who 'should be placed along with the very greatest of historians'.[6] He eventually concluded, 'You may press the words of Luke in a degree beyond any other historian's and they stand the keenest scrutiny and the hardest treatment.'[7]

At the end of 1974, *TIME* magazine ran an article entitled 'How True is the Bible?', discussing its integrity after 200 years of critical attack. With no religious axe to grind, the article came to this conclusion: 'The breadth, sophistication and diversity of all this biblical investigation are impressive, but it begs a question: Has it made the Bible more credible or less? ... After more than two centuries of facing the heaviest scientific guns that could be brought to bear, the Bible has survived — and is perhaps better for the siege. Even on the critics' own terms — historical fact — the Scriptures seem more acceptable now than they did when the rationalists began the attack.'[8]

History in advance

Have you ever realized *the part that prophecy plays in authenticating the Bible?* The American author Dave Hunt has pointed out that there are no prophecies in Islam's *Qur'an*, in the Hindu *Vedas* or *Bhagavad-Gita*, in the sayings of Buddha or Confucius, or in the Book of Mormon.[9] By contrast it has been estimated that about 30% of the Bible consists of prophecy of one kind or another, making it unique in religious literature. It is impossible even to summarize such a vast amount of biblical prophecy here, but a modern scientist's evaluation of one small sample should be sufficient to get your attention.

In his book *Science Speaks,* Peter Stoner, Professor Emeritus at Westmont College, California, and charter member of the American Scientific Affiliation, identifies eleven prophecies about Israel taken from the writings of four Old Testament prophets, Isaiah, Jeremiah, Ezekiel and Micah, each of whom claimed to be speaking God's words. These prophecies related to the land as a whole, the destruction of Jerusalem, the rebuilding of the temple and the later enlargement of the city — *and every one came true.* Calculating the probability of all eleven prophecies being fulfilled by chance to be one in 8×10^{63}, Stoner then gives an illustration of what this means. He says that if we were to scoop together a pile of coins equal in size to 100 billion stars in each of two trillion galaxies in just one second, add to the pile at the same rate every second, day and night, for twenty-one years, then ask a blindfolded friend to pick out one marked coin from this incomprehensibly massive pile, his chances of doing so would be the same as the likelihood that these four prophets could have got these things right by guesswork.[10]

This in itself is mind-boggling, but it still tells nothing like the full story, as it involves just eleven Bible prophecies out of several hundred which scholars agree were fulfilled to the letter. What do you make of this? Surely it is in a completely different league from horoscopes, crystal balls, tea leaves and tarot cards? These prophets all claimed to be God's spokesmen: do you know of an alternative explanation for their infallible track record? We shall see other marks of the Bible's integrity in the course of the next chapter, but the ground we have already covered shows that to write it off without detailed study and careful thought is to play fast and loose with the facts.

Finding flaws

Not even the most enthusiastic believer would claim that every statement in Scripture is crystal clear, or that it is perfectly easy to see how it all fits together, but unsolved problems are not necessarily errors, and nobody without total and final light on every issue involved is in a position to say that he has found the Bible to be flawed. An unanswered question is not the same as proof of a mistake. In the twentieth century alone, countless so-called 'errors' and 'contradictions' were cleared away by modern discoveries, and the comparatively tiny number that remain, *none of which affects the Bible's message or substantive meaning*, is being steadily whittled away.

In assessing the integrity of any document, literary critics still begin with a principle laid down by the Greek philosopher Aristotle over 2,500 years ago: 'The benefit of the doubt is to be given to the document itself, not arrogated by the critic to himself.' Simon Greenleaf, Royal Professor of Law at Harvard University, and one of the world's greatest experts on legal evidence, gives the following as his first rule in this kind of case: 'Every document apparently ancient, coming from the proper repository or custody, and bearing on its face no evident marks of forgery, the law presumes to be genuine *and devolves on the opposing party the burden of proving it to be otherwise*.'[11] The Bible certainly fits the bill; if you say it is fatally flawed, it is up

to you to prove your case. Are you prepared — and qualified
— to do this?

The little matter of miracles

In spite of what you have just read, you may still be inclined to
write the Bible off because its storyline is littered with miracles.
Many people have done this, especially since the eighteenth
century, when the Scottish sceptic David Hume mounted a fierce
attack. He said that the laws of nature were based on the highest degree of probability, whereas miracles had the lowest degree of probability; so a wise person should never believe in
them. The subject of miracles is fascinatingly complex, though
a friend who suggested that I write a book on it is almost certainly going to be disappointed! Instead, the bottom line can be
reached in a couple of pages.

Although they are mainly clustered around a few people and
events spread over some 2,000 years of recorded history, there
is no point in denying that the Bible records many miracles.
One writer has listed 232,[12] but even this is an open-ended total
as the Bible also says that there were many others the details of
which are unrecorded. Quite apart from those surrounding the
creation of the universe, the Old Testament tells of a wooden
staff being turned into a serpent (and then turned back into a
staff),[13] 'bitter' (perhaps poisoned) water being made drinkable,[14]
a supply of food that did not dwindle with use,[15] a child re-
stored to life[16] and an iron axe-head made to float on water.[17]
These are just samples, and by no means the most spectacular
(Hollywood has long since cashed in on films featuring events
such as the nine plagues which devastated Egypt), but they are
standard ammunition for atheists. The New Testament is another stamping-ground for the sceptic, with a raging storm being
stilled in an instant,[18] evil spirits migrating from people to pigs,[19]

ten lepers healed at once (leprosy was incurable at the time)[20] and a crowd of five thousand fed with a handful of loaves and fish,[21] to say nothing of people being instantaneously healed of a wide range of physical, mental and psychological diseases. What do you make of all this? Was Hume right when he suggested that the only real miracle was that anybody should believe in miracles?

The word 'miracle' literally means 'something to be wondered at'. One dictionary defines a miracle as 'an event or act which breaks a law of nature',[22] and for some people this is precisely the problem: anything which seems to contradict the scientific laws governing our world of time and space cannot be genuine. Yet this idea has long since breathed its last, and the following statements by modern scientists should help you to arrange its funeral.

- In *Quarks, Chaos and Christianity*, John Polkinghorne, one-time Professor of Mathematical Physics at Cambridge University and President of Queen's College wrote, 'The question of miracles is not primarily scientific, but *theological*. Science simply tells us that these events are against normal expectation. We knew this from the start. *Science cannot exclude the possibility that, on particular occasions, God does particular, unprecedented things.* After all, he is the ordainer of the laws of nature, not someone who is subject to them'[23] (emphasis added).
- In *God, Science and Evolution*, Edgar Andrews, Emeritus Professor of Materials Science in the University of London says, 'The truth of the matter is, of course, that *miracles lie outside the terms of reference of science, so that science can, in and of itself, make no contribution to an understanding of the miraculous...* Science studies that which already exists in this universe, and must concern itself with the habitual and universal behaviour exhibited

by nature. It cannot consider any unusual or altered behaviour that may take place'[24] (emphasis added).

• In a letter to *The Times* in 1984 thirteen prominent
scientists, most of them university professors, joined Professor R. J. Berry, president of the Linnean Society, in
saying, 'It is not logically valid to use science as an argument against miracles. To believe that miracles cannot
happen is as much an act of faith as to believe that they
can happen ... miracles are unprecedented events. Whatever the current fashions in philosophy or the revelations
of opinion polls may suggest, *it is important to affirm that
science* (based as it is on the observations of precedents)
can have nothing to say on the subject' [25](emphasis
added).

These statements make it clear that rejecting miracles on
scientific grounds is decidedly unscientific! The right approach
is to begin with an open mind and then to ask the right questions. If God is personal and wants to communicate with us, it
is at least possible that he might from time to time do so in
unique or unusual ways, and once we accept the idea of an
independent, omnipotent and all-wise God there is no philosophical, scientific or logical reason for refusing to accept *any*
of his actions. To rule God out from the start is to put the cart in
front of the horse; it shortens the discussion, but makes no useful contribution to it.

The Bible never speaks of its miracles as changes or devi-
ations from the laws of physics, but as events in which, consistently with his nature and purposes, and as a sign of his presence and power, God has acted in unique or unusual ways.
The question to ask is not, 'Can miracles happen?' but 'Did
they happen?', and each case must be examined in the light of
the evidence. If they happened, they demand an explanation
— and if God exists there is no need to look any further for

one. When we grasp who God is, the question as to whether miracles can happen disappears.

The case for God rests on four solid foundations that cannot easily be shaken — history, revelation, reason and experience. We have already touched on the first three. Now, and at the end of the following nine chapters, I want to appeal to experience, the testimonies of people whose stories represent millions of others over thousands of years.

Call Monty White

A one-time atheist, and a graduate of the University of Wales, where he was awarded a Ph.D. for his research in the field of gas kinetics, Dr A. J. Monty White held a number of university posts before his appointment as Chief Executive of Answers in Genesis.

My parents met and married during the Second World War, and I was born two years later. My father was a committed atheist, and at a very early age I was given the full treatment: there was no God; Jesus Christ was not the Son of God; the Bible was nothing more than a collection of fairy stories.

I can still remember the first spiritual conversation I had with my parents, even though I was just three years old. My grandmother had written to tell us that her pet canary had died and as we were crying together (I loved that canary!) I asked what would happen to us after we died. My mother told me that our bodies would simply rot in the ground and that would be the end of us. I remember being saddened and shocked.

When I began to attend school, the teachers taught me stories from the Bible. I was particularly impressed by one about a young boy, Samuel, who, when he sensed that God was calling his name, replied, 'Speak, for your servant is listening.'[26] I wanted to believe that there was a God, and that he would speak to me, and I used to pray

Samuel's prayer every night, but nothing happened and my parents told me that, as God did not exist, I was wasting my time.

When I was six years of age we moved to north-east Wales and for the next five years I regularly attended the local Anglican church in the hope of discovering the truth about God's existence. I got no-where; the church was very 'high', with elaborate rituals, incense, and prayers for the dead, and the vicar had no time for a poor kid like me from the local council estate. By the time I had passed my eleven-plus examination and begun attending the local Grammar School I had given up on the church and I gradually came to agree with my parents' views: I became an atheist.

In spite of this, I occasionally read the Bible, but only so that I could argue with people about its contents, and especially with those who claimed to be Christians and who looked to the Bible for their basis of faith. I had three main targets. The first was *Bible prophecy*: I would argue that the prophecies were so general that you could interpret almost anything from them. The second was *the person of Jesus Christ*: I refused to accept that he was the Son of God, or that he could pos-sibly have risen from the dead after he had been crucified. The third was *the whole miraculous element*: if Christianity was a religion of miracles, why did we not see them today?

There was an interesting twist to my atheistic stance. A Church of England clergyman suggested that I should get confirmed, as I would then receive the Holy Spirit and know that God had come into my life. I attended preparation classes and the day came when the Bishop of St Asaph laid his hands on my head, but all to no avail. When I got home I told my mother that I was now a confirmed atheist!

I went to university at Aberystwyth in 1963, and started attending meetings of the Christian Union and the Anglican Society so that I could get into discussions with the members and try to show them that they were deluded. However, I soon ran into students who were very different from the so-called Christians I had met before. Here were people who said they knew God, and some of them spent many hours trying to explain how their experience tied in with what the

Bible teaches. Before long, I began to find that my three major lines of attack were crumbling in the face of the facts.

The first concerned *prophecy*. For all my bluster, I had been reluctantly impressed by Micah's prophecy concerning the destruction of Samaria:

> Therefore I will make Samaria a heap of rubble,
>   a place for planting vineyards.
> I will pour her stones into the valley
>   and lay bare her foundations. [27]

These four specific predictions were made in the latter half of the eighth century B.C., but it was almost two thousand years later that they began to be fulfilled. One could hardly argue that Micah saw these things happening, wrote about them, then pretended that he had written a few decades beforehand! Exactly as Micah predicted, Samaria was totally destroyed in A.D. 1265, when Muslims defeated the Crusaders, and it has never been rebuilt. In order to use the site for agricultural purposes, Arabs living in the vicinity cleared most of the ruins away and, when digging up the foundations, they piled the rubbish up in heaps or dumped it in the valley below. Today, grape-vines can be seen growing on the site — exactly as prophesied by Micah about 2,700 years ago.

My second attack had concerned *the deity of Jesus Christ and his resurrection from the dead*, but I now began to see that these were linked with the first. I became increasingly impressed with the way in which events in Christ's life fulfilled Old Testament prophecy to the letter, but could the New Testament be trusted? What if its writers had deliberately falsified the accounts to fit in with what the Old Testament had said? How reliable were the New Testament documents? I began to study the question with great care, and in the course of my research I came across Professor F. F. Bruce's book *The New Testament Documents,* in which he wrote, 'The evidence for our New Testament writings is ever so much greater than the evidence for many writings of classical authors, the authenticity of which no one dreams of questioning. And if the New Testament were a collection of secular writings their authenticity would generally be regarded as beyond all doubt.' I could sense that my second line of attack was being firmly closed down. There was every reason to believe that the New Testament records were accurate; and if they were, Jesus Christ did exist, he was who he said he was, and he did rise from the dead.

At about the same time, my attack on *miracles* was being countered by one testimony after another of remarkable happenings in the lives of contemporary Christians. Try as I might, I found it impossible to dismiss them all as unlikely coincidences. I gradually began to realize that the three major strands in my atheism were beginning to look decidedly thin: there *was* a God; I *could* trust the Bible; Jesus *was* God's Son; he *did* rise from the dead, and miracles *did* occur. Needless to say, my father was far from happy about my involvement with what he called 'religious nutters'. He told me that he had sent me to university to study chemistry, not theology, so I decided to leave theology to the Christians and concentrate on chemistry.

Some time later, right out of the blue, a friend asked me to go to church with him. As the service progressed I began to be painfully aware of something I had virtually ignored in the course of all my arguing — my sin. I began to remember words and actions that had caused hurt to my parents, my sister, other family members and friends. Most of all, I became aware that all my sin offended against a pure and holy God before whom I would one day stand and who had said that on the Day of Judgement the wicked would 'go away to eternal punishment'.[28] Sitting there in the church, I could see this happening, especially when the preacher quoted the Bible in speaking of hell as a 'lake of fire'.[29] The impression became so strong that I thought I might be going mad. Perhaps my father had been right about the dangers of religious mania!

I returned to my lodgings determined to put all this stuff about sin and judgement out of my mind, but I found I could not stop thinking about it. I could not sleep or work, I lost my appetite, and all I could think about was my sin and God's holy hatred of it. Although I was unaware of it at the time, God was answering my childhood prayer. A few days later, my friend asked if I had enjoyed the service. I told him what I was going through and asked him a question straight from the pages of Scripture: 'What must I do to be saved?'[30] He carefully explained the meaning of Christ's death on the cross and showed me that I could be made right with God by trusting in that wonderful means of salvation that he had provided. There and then, on 25 February 1964, I repented of my sin and put my trust in Jesus Christ as my own personal Saviour.

Shortly after my conversion, I took a degree course in geology and, as a result, came to the conclusion that the origin of the universe and everything in it can best be explained in terms of creation rather than evolution. I have had the privilege of speaking about God's creation of the universe in schools, colleges, universities and many other settings both in the United Kingdom and in a number of European countries. I have written many articles and several books on the subject of creation and can say with confidence that my scientific studies have powerfully underlined my conviction of the Bible's authenticity as 'the living and enduring word of God'. [31]

2.
For the undecided

If you are an out-and-out atheist, you may be tempted to skip this chapter altogether, as it is expressly written for agnostics. However, as it tackles a number of issues equally relevant to those who are convinced that God is non-existent, I suggest you read straight on.

The word 'agnosticism' was coined in 1869 by the British biologist Thomas Huxley, who was a passionate advocate of Charles Darwin's ideas about the origin and evolution of species. Huxley produced the word by adding the prefix 'a' (without) to the word 'gnostic', which translates the Greek *gnosis* (knowledge). The basic meaning of 'agnosticism' is therefore 'to be without knowledge' — in our present context, without knowledge of God. Agnosticism comes in two different brands, which we can label 'soft-core' and 'hard-core'.

Why opting out is difficult

To put it simply, soft-core agnostics are not sure whether God exists, or whether it matters in the slightest one way or the other. The British journalist Bernard Levin may be a good example. In an article in *The Times* published in 1994 he wrote, 'For the

thousandth time I tell you that I am not a Christian, though for
the life of me I couldn't say what I am, if anything. (Probably
nothing.)'[1]

If this is your position you need to consider the major challenge posed by the distinguished American psychologist and
philosopher William James. In his book *The Will to Believe*, he
discussed the question of options, the decision between two
hypotheses, which he said might be living or dead, forced or
avoidable, momentous or trivial. On the existence or non-
existence of God, James showed that, in the light of the issues
involved, this particular question is 'living, forced and momentous'[2] — in other words, that it is inescapable.

The soft-core agnostic's response to this is to sit on the fence,
but there is no way to avoid the point James is making, because every debate about human life and death, and about the
universe in which we are all living and dying, ultimately re-
volves around the question of the existence or non-existence of
God. Those who take sides on this matter are not merely arguing about some interesting but irrelevant point of science, philosophy or religion, but about the ultimate issue of all. The British philosopher C. Stephen Evans hits the nail on the head
when he says that believing in God is not like believing in the
Loch Ness Monster: 'The Loch Ness Monster is merely "one
more thing"... God, however, is not merely "one more thing".
The person who believes in God and the person who does not
believe in God do not merely disagree about God. *They disagree about the very character of the universe.*'[3]

Soft-core agnosticism is not the avoidance of an option; *it is
an option*. It is deciding to be undecided — but is this sensible
in the light of what is at stake? The question asks what kind of
universe we live in. This is a real question, and it must have a
real answer. What is more, the answer will obviously tell us
whether the way we choose to live is of any relevance

whatsoever. This being the case, soft-core agnosticism is out of touch with reality. If you are a soft-core agnostic, let me ask you the following questions:

- Is it sensible for you to remain undecided about a question which involves the nature of the universe and the significance of your own part in it?
- If you are not making any effort to pursue the question, how can you ever hope to get the matter settled?
- How can you claim that being undecided has a sound basis when by definition agnosticism admits its inbuilt ignorance?
- Are you seriously interested in discovering whether or not God exists?
- Have you honestly examined and considered the claims of those who say that he does?
- Are you deliberately avoiding getting to grips with the question in case you come face to face with a God who may revolutionize your thinking and challenge your lifestyle?
- If having to give an account of yourself to a holy and just God who will determine your eternal destiny is even a *possibility*, would it not make sense to do everything you can to sort the issue out — and to do so urgently? Would you honestly be happy to die in the dark and risk whatever consequences would follow if you were wrong?

Firm but flawed

Hard-core agnostics take a very different line. Not only do they say they are not sure whether God exists; they claim it is impossible for anyone to know. Theism, which represents the God we identified in the previous chapter, says that he is by definition outside the natural, material world; hard-core agnostics say that this puts him out of the reach of human knowledge.

This tells us that we would be technically correct to say that agnosticism is a form of atheism (one of Karl Marx's colleagues called the agnostics of his day 'shamefaced atheists').[4] As *theism* is belief in God, *atheism* is everything outside of this, and therefore includes hard-core agnosticism, which neither asserts nor denies God's existence. This is not the same as saying that an agnostic is a non-believer. In 'You've Gotta Serve Somebody', Bob Dylan sings, 'You've either got faith or you've got unbelief; there ain't no neutral ground,' but this misses the point that while there are believers and unbelievers, *there are no non-believers*. This may seem a strange thing to say, but the hard-core agnostic is a good example of what I mean, because his creed says, 'I believe it is impossible for finite human beings to know whether an infinite God exists.' The hard-core agnostic is not denying the possibility of God's existence, but he is denying that we shall ever be able to answer the question.

It is exactly at this point that he overreaches himself, because while sounding humble and reasonable, he is neither. Think about it. A hard-core agnostic can hardly claim to be humble, because he claims that knowledge of God is impossible. But how can he know the limits of human knowledge? Nor is he being reasonable, because he says that on the issue of God's existence we must accept as certain truth the fact that there is no such thing as certain truth — in other words, that there can be no agnosticism about agnosticism! Agnosticism insists on being dogmatic about the fact that it is impossible to be dogmatic, and asserts as a matter of objective truth that there is no such thing as objective truth. In other words, the only way to claim ignorance is to claim all available knowledge. Does this make sense? If you are a hard-core agnostic, let me ask you the following questions:

• As you do in fact have a belief, what is the evidence on which you are basing that belief?

• How do you know that it is impossible to know, and how can you be certain that we must for ever remain uncertain?

• How can you say that ultimate reality (God's existence or non-existence) is unknowable unless you know everything it is possible to know? More simply put, how can you rule God out unless you know everything?

• Have you sensed nothing in the nature of the universe which even vaguely suggests the possibility of a transcendent Creator?

• Have you never, in person or indirectly, come across people whose behaviour backs up the claim that their lives have been transformed for the better because of a dynamic relationship with God? Do you have a credible reason for rejecting the testimonies of millions of people over thousands of years?

• Are you honestly open to the evidence on the issue, or are you so locked into your agnosticism that you refuse to let the evidence speak for itself? The story is told of a man who thought he was dead, and was persuaded by a friend to visit a psychiatrist. After assessing this most unusual case, the psychiatrist decided to solve the problem by convincing his patient of one simple fact — that dead men do not bleed. After several weeks, the message seemed to have got through, but when the psychiatrist then punctured the patient's arm with a needle and blood seeped out, the man shouted, 'I knew I was right! Dead men do bleed after all!'

• Do you have a vested interest in remaining an agnostic? Would you be prepared to believe in God if doing so were to lead to a transformation of your world-view and a moral revolution in your lifestyle?

- Can you confidently rule out any possibility that you might be wrong?

Back to the book

Agnostics also face the awkward issue of the Bible. Sir Isaac Newton, universally acknowledged as the father of modern science, called it 'a rock from which all the hammers of criticism have never chipped a single fragment'. The significance of its integrity for the agnostic (and of course for the atheist) is that it is saturated from cover to cover with the claim that is not a collection of religious ideas, but 'the living and enduring word of God'.[5]

Phrases like 'God said', 'God spoke' and 'the word of the LORD came' occur about 700 times in the first five books, and the Old Testament alone makes nearly 4,000 claims to divine authorship. The New Testament writers are so emphatic in making similar claims for their own words that the American seminary professor Harold Lindsell says about them, 'No writer gives the impression that what he writes is not to be taken as though it came from the very lips of God himself.'[6] Lindsell is not exaggerating. Not only did one of the New Testament writers describe the Old Testament as 'the very words of God',[7] but another had no hesitation in calling his own contribution to Scripture 'not ... the word of men, but ... the word of God'.[8] That God should speak to human beings in this direct way may seem startling or strange, but it is perfectly consistent with the concept of a personal and caring Creator choosing to reveal himself in a way we can understand. He has not left us wondering who he is, what we are, or whether we have business with each other. He has spoken.

Sceptics may argue that to call the Bible the Word of God because the Bible says it is the Word of God is to argue in circles, and on the surface this seems fair comment, but the argument is seriously weakened when we put it alongside the impressive evidence we have already seen for the Bible's fundamental integrity. This evidence is a powerful indication that the Bible's overall message can be trusted; yet that message is meaningless unless it is the Word of God. As the contemporary American theologian R. C. Sproul points out, 'If the Bible is trustworthy, then we must take seriously the claim that it is more than trustworthy.'[9] If we can trust the Bible to be true — and no sceptic has yet proved it to be otherwise — we must trust the thousands of statements it makes about its divine origin. The most emphatic and concise of these claims says, 'All Scripture is God-breathed.'[10] This tells us, not that the human writers were *inspired*, but that the words they wrote were divinely *expired* — that God breathed out the very words they wrote down. Where does that leave agnosticism?

The message; the man

In *Young Pillars,* a selection of Charles Shultz's famous Peanuts cartoons, a teenage boy on the telephone to his girl friend tells her, 'I've begun to unravel the mystery of the Old Testament — I've started to read it.' Have you got that far? Have you read either the Old or the New Testaments with an open-minded interest in discovering what they say? If not, let me give you a very brief overview of their message.

The Old Testament is a collection of thirty-nine separate books written by some thirty authors over a period of about 1,500 years. The first seventeen books are *history*, written by Moses and others, and they begin with God's creation of 'the heavens and the earth',[11] a Hebrew phrase meaning all reality outside of God himself. They then go on to tell of humanity's disastrous rebellion against God and spell out its appalling aftermath: the

whole of the cosmos wrenched out of sync, all human experience degraded and the onset of environmental and personal
decay, disease, pain and sorrow. Just as radically, this revolt
also brought about human mortality: 'In this way death came
to all men.'[12]

The Bible then records that, in spite of humanity's deliberate rebellion, God planned to bring into a living relationship
with himself 'a great multitude that no one could count, from
every nation, tribe, people and language'.[13] The earlier books
major on the lives of men chosen by God as key players in
putting his plan into action — people like Abraham, Isaac, Jacob
(later called Israel) and Joseph. Then comes the story of the
miraculous release of God's people from 400 years of slavery
in Egypt, followed by forty years of erratic progress through the
Sinai Peninsula until they reached the land of Canaan, which
God had promised Abraham he would give to his descendants.

In the course of their wanderings, God gave his people the
Ten Commandments, in which he revealed his own character
and told them how they should live. The rest of the history
books outline their conquest of Canaan and what followed.
After the land had been divided among the twelve tribes, God
led them to establish a monarchy, and for many years the nation
flourished under the leadership of King David and his son Solomon. Then came a bitter civil war, which led to ten rebellious
tribes establishing the northern kingdom of Israel and the remaining two forming the southern kingdom of Judah. An almost
unbroken succession of corrupt rulers led to the downfall of
both nations, which were eventually dragged into exile, Israel
by the Assyrians in 722 B.C. and Judah by the Babylonians in
587 B.C. The northern kingdom was wiped off the map for
ever, but God miraculously intervened to end Judah's exile
after just fifty years.

Woven into this historical tapestry are five books of *poetry*
— Job (which deals with the vast topic of God's role in a world

of evil and suffering), Psalms, Proverbs, Ecclesiastes and the Song of Solomon.

The remaining seventeen Old Testament books consist of *prophecy*. Before and after the exiles of Israel and Judah, and in spite of all their unfaithfulness and idolatry, God continued to speak to his chosen people through a succession of prophets, warning them of the consequences of their sin and urging them to live God-centred lives. The prophets also specifically predicted ways in which God would intervene in both national and global history. Above all, they told of a time when God would break into time and space in the person of the Messiah ('the Anointed One'), who would be his people's Saviour, Deliverer and King. They predicted the time and place of his birth, the quality of his life, the trend of his teaching, the scope of his miracles and the manner of his death. They also went one stupendous step further and said that he would rise again from the dead and establish a universal and eternal kingdom of 'justice and righteousness'.[14] Malachi, the last of the Old Testament prophets, summed up all that had been said by his predecessors and confirmed, 'Surely the day is coming...'[15] This was the last God-given prophecy for 400 years.

The New Testament has twenty-seven books, divided into three groups, the first of which records *history*. Matthew, Mark, Luke and John give us a biography of Jesus of Nazareth, who fulfilled to the letter the Messianic prophecies which had ended four centuries earlier. His own claim to do this was so confident that he had no hesitation in saying, 'These are the Scriptures that testify about me.'[16] Later, in talking to two of his followers, we are told that 'Beginning with Moses and all the Prophets, he explained to them what was said in all the Scriptures concerning himself.'[17]

The last book in the historical section is Acts (sometimes called the Acts of the Apostles) which, in the words of his followers, tells of the founding of the Christian church by Jesus and traces its dynamic expansion into the Middle East, Asia and Europe. From a despised and ridiculed handful of people dismissed as cranks, it grew to the point where some of their enemies complained that they had 'turned the world upside down'.[18]

The second group of New Testament books consists of twenty-one *letters*, some written to individuals, some to specific groups of Christians, and others to believers in general. They set out basic Christian doctrine, tackle teething troubles in the emerging churches, warn against the dangers of false teaching and give consistent and comprehensive guidance on such things as worship, human relationships, marriage, sexuality, work, money and a wide range of other social issues.

The last book in the New Testament, Revelation, is *prophecy*. Mainly through a series of spectacular visions, it anticipates a day when Jesus will return to the earth and usher in God's ultimate and universal triumph.

This has been nothing more than a quick aerial overview of Scripture, but it helps to establish that the Bible is much more than a history book or a code of ethics. To put it in one sentence, it claims to be God's revelation of himself, crystallized in the identity, character and relevance of one particular human being — Jesus Christ. This is the fundamental key to understanding what the Bible is all about, and the people who share their stories in the following pages show that his identity, and what he accomplished in his life and death, were critical factors in their approach to Scripture and in their coming to living faith in God. Towards the end of the book, we shall devote an entire chapter to Jesus, and we shall see there that as a historical figure, open to thorough investigation, he poses an extremely serious problem for atheists and agnostics.

Call Peter Sammons

Peter Sammons is a South African. After matriculating, he embarked on a sixteen-year career in the pump industry before entering full-time Christian ministry. With his wife and two children, he makes his home in Germiston, South Africa.

I was born in Johannesburg, the youngest of four children. My mother's family was Roman Catholic and my father's Anglican, but both in name only. Although it ruffled a few feathers in my mother's family, my parents were married in the Anglican Church and had all their children christened there. We attended Sunday School in our early years, and the odd service when my brothers sang in the choir, but our interest soon wore off, and before long we went to church only for christenings, weddings and funerals. My father described us as 'not religious, but not irreligious', but even this may have been going too far. I had no idea what my brothers and sister believed, and it never bothered me one way or the other.

My father was a successful and well-respected man in our community, serving on numerous community committees and boards including Johannesburg City Council. I respected him immensely (I still do) and his opinions powerfully affected my own thinking. I remember him telling me that when he and a friend enlisted in the army prior to World War II, his friend described himself as 'agnostic', whereas my father put down 'Anglican'. When I asked him what 'agnostic' meant, his answer told me that this would have been a better description of his own position.

My father certainly believed in the existence of a transcendent power who (or which) was responsible for the whole of creation, and possibly for holding it together. When I put forward the case for atheism he would point to the natural world as evidence for intelligent design and tell me in no uncertain terms that 'Only a fool says there is no God.' However, he also believed that the person (or thing) commonly called 'God' was so infinitely great as to defy description or definition — in other words that it was impossible to know who or what this 'God' was.

One obvious implication of this position is that all religion is redundant. It is impossible to worship, serve or please an unknowable deity, nor can he (or it) hold you morally responsible in any way. The best you can do is to treat creation — everything from fauna and flora to humanity — with respect. This was not discussed in any depth within the family, but it was the very atmosphere of my upbringing, the subconscious philosophy of my early years.

My position hardened when I became a teenager and, as my natural scepticism was fuelled by my doubts about all brands of religion, I soon reached the point where I rejected the supernatural altogether. As far as I was concerned, unless something could be verified by one of the five senses, or tested and proved scientifically, it simply didn't exist. Although I never set out to become one, I was gradually turning into a full-blown atheist, and I distinctly remember when I realized that this had happened. As an eighteen-year-old doing my national service in the South African Navy, I was required to attend church services, but I found myself treating religion as nothing more than superstition, a crutch for emotional and intellectual cripples in need of what I jokingly called 'an invisible means of support'. For me, God had become as unreal as the Easter Bunny and the Tooth Fairy. Those who claimed to worship him were slaves to superstition, and I found myself cursing God and using his name as a profanity without the slightest qualm.

I had some interesting discussions with my father at this time. Looking back, I can now see that his arguments were far more logical and reasonable than mine, not least his insistence that if God did not reveal himself, nobody could discover him. Yet like many atheists, when I was faced with having to choose between intelligent creation or chance, I always chose chance, even though I sensed that existence by chance was impossible. My father, on the other hand, argued against chance and in favour of an intelligent creator who was nevertheless beyond our knowledge.

My conversion was the result of a process that began when, to my great surprise, a friend who had been a professional musician in a rock-and-roll band invited me to attend a church service. This seemed so strange that I went out of curiosity, to see what kind of church an ex-rocker would attend. It could not have been more traditional and, in a way, old-fashioned. An elderly lady played the organ; they sang hymns, took up an offering and listened to a sermon. I can't now remember exactly what the preacher said, but I do know that for the first time it made sense to me. Even more surprising was the way in which the church members accepted a typical hippie look-alike. With hair past my shoulders, and a full beard and moustache, I was dressed in a tee shirt, ragged old bell-bottom denims and sandals, yet these formally dressed Christians showed genuine interest in me as a *person*, and not just as a visitor.

I was so impressed that I found myself attending regularly, and over the next few months the faithful teaching of Scripture gradually exposed the fallacy and folly of my atheism. Logic, the lives of the church members and the change taking place in my life were becoming powerful pointers to the reality of God's existence. One series of three sermons made a particular impact. The first, 'Why I believe there is a God', was very convincing, but during the following week other doubts arose. How could I be sure that Christianity was the right religion and that Jesus Christ was unique? On the following Sunday, the sermon was: 'Why I believe that Jesus is God's Son'. Again, the evidence seemed overpowering, but I had further questions: all I was being taught came from the Bible, but how could I trust it to be true? As if the preacher had been reading my mind, the final sermon in the series was: 'Why I believe the Bible is the Word of God'. A year earlier, those sermons might well have left me cold, but in God's providence they became powerfully clear and relevant.

Belief in God has given cohesion to my view of life, the world and everything around me. Things are the way they are and work the way they do because of his transcendent design, his perfect plan and his wise purpose. The universe in which we live, nature, mathematics, physics, chemistry, music — everything makes sense because it has been designed to do so by an intelligent Creator, and everything is part of an integrated whole. As an atheist I lived in a world of accidental and fragmented realities, and I could never give a logical reason why anything in the cosmos could be related to anything else. Things were they way they were just because they were. Now, in spite of many discordant notes, I see a basic harmony in nature that can find its explanation only in a wise and purposeful Creator.

3.
'Goodbye, God'?

Having noted two brands of agnostic, we can now identify three brands of atheist, and label them 'muted', 'moderate' and 'militant'. If you claim to be an atheist, this chapter will show which of these best describes your position.

The *muted* atheist comes pretty close to being an agnostic, and may be the kind of person the British philosopher A. J. Ayer had in mind when he wrote, 'It is characteristic of an atheist to hold that it is at least probable that no god exists.'[1] The muted atheist has no great interest in arguing the pros and cons of God's existence; he is happy to 'go with the flow' and get on with life on the assumption that vague religious ideas are good enough. Giving the 1996 Eric Symes Abbott Memorial Lecture at Westminster Abbey, the playwright David Hare had people like this in mind when he spoke of those who 'have some generalized religious belief' but who would be at a loss to 'actually say what it is'.[2]

The *moderate* atheist takes things a lot further, and the astronomer and author Isaac Asimov provides a good example of what I mean: 'I've been an atheist for years and years, but somehow I felt it was intellectually unrespectable to say one was an atheist, because it assumed knowledge that one didn't have. Somehow it was better to say one was a humanist or an agnostic. I finally decided that I'm a creature of emotion as well as of reason. Emotionally, I'm an atheist. I don't have the evidence to prove that God doesn't exist, but I so strongly suspect that he doesn't that I don't want to waste my time.'[3]

The *militant* atheist takes a much stronger line. To quote Etienne Borne, one of atheism's modern advocates, 'Atheism is the deliberate, definite, dogmatic denial of the existence of God... It is not satisfied with approximate or relative truth, but claims to see the ins and outs of the game quite clearly — being *the absolute denial of the Absolute*'[4] (emphasis added). In her book *What on Earth is an Atheist?*, Madalyn Murray O'Hair, founder of American Atheists Inc., asserted, 'There are no supernatural forces, no supernatural entities such as gods, or heavens, or hells, or life after death. There are no supernatural forces, nor can there be.'[5] Ludovic Kennedy is equally militant and dogmatic. In the opening pages of his book *All in the Mind* he endorses the statement: 'The quest for God may be likened to a blind man in a darkened room, looking for a black cat that isn't there.'[6] He explains in the introduction that he chose the title *All in the Mind* to emphasize that the God worshipped by those he calls 'the orthodox' is 'entirely a creature of their imaginations', and goes on to say that 'Arguments ... as to whether God does or does not exist are futile.'[7]

To nail down the point being made, it is worth quoting one other militant atheist. The British zoologist Richard Dawkins is Simonyi Professor of the Public Understanding of Science at Oxford University, and so fervently atheistic that he calls historian Paul Johnson's theistic belief system 'ignominious, contemptible and retarded'.[8] When a 1993 issue of the *Independent* carried a leading article commending author Susan Howatch's endowment of a Cambridge University lectureship in science and theology, Dawkins let fly in a letter to the editor: 'What has theology ever said that is the smallest use to anybody? ... What makes you think that theology is a subject at all?'[9] During an edition of BBC television's *Soul of Britain* in June 2000 he said,

'I am unhappy to be living in a society where I think the majority of people are deluded. I'd love to do something about it, which is why I write the books I do.' This makes it clear that, far from being honestly scientific, open to following where the evidence leads, Dawkins' writings have a passionately atheistic agenda, something that came across loud and clear when he added, 'I devoutly wish that we did live in a post-God society.'[10]

Proof or prejudice?

Many of today's militant atheists have hitched their wagons to ideas endorsed by the British philosopher Bertrand Russell, who in turn took on board theories put forward by the French philosopher Auguste Comte. The big idea popularized by Comte and Russell became known as logical positivism, which says that only statements which can be verified by one or more of the five senses have any meaning. According to logical positivism, anything which cannot be scientifically proved by this so-called 'verification principle' does not qualify as reality or knowledge but can be written off as being purely subjective and essentially meaningless. The British philosopher Peter Williams gives a simple example of this in his excellent book *The Case for God*: 'To "verify" something means to check it out with the senses. In other words, the statement, "This is a book", is meaningful because you can verify it by touching and reading the book; but the statement "God exists" is not meaningful because you can't verify it by touching or looking at God.'[11] This is the line of thinking behind Ludovic Kennedy's statement that God 'does not exist in any meaningful way and like all previous gods, therefore, must be an invention of the human mind'.[12] Quite apart from the bizarre claim that 'God' is a very recent idea, Kennedy shoots himself in the foot, because the very assertion he makes is itself not part of eternal reality or knowledge, but (to use his own phrase) an invention of the human mind.

Positivism runs into enormous problems, especially in trying to explain why anything exists at all. A. J. Ayer, whose book *Language, Truth and Logic* strongly promoted positivism, later confessed that it led down a blind alley, and in an interview for *The Listener* in 1978 admitted, 'Nearly all of it was false.'[13] Over twenty years later, Ronald Nash, Professor of Philosophy at Western Kentucky University, wrote, 'Today, it is quite difficult to find any philosopher who is willing to claim publicly the label of logical positivism. The movement is dead and quite properly so.'[14]

In *The Atheist Debater's Handbook* we are told, 'Atheism … is an intellectually respectable viewpoint … the atheist may know that God does not exist.'[15] Yet with logical positivism dead and buried, what is the basis for such a claim? The question is important, because, as Birkbeck College's Anthony Grayling pointed out on *Soul of Britain,* atheism flourishes, not as a fact but as an article of faith: 'The point about atheism is that it's a deliberate choice. You have to think it through. It is a definite commitment.'[16] Some atheists try to blur this, and to suggest that atheism is not belief in the non-existence of God, but the absence of belief in his existence. In *Atheism: The Case Against God,* George Smith argues, 'Atheism … is the absence of theistic belief … in its main form, it is not a belief; it is the absence of belief.'[17] This is a nifty sidestep, avoiding the need for atheism to explain or prove anything about itself, but it falls foul of its own verification principle, because *the claim itself cannot be verified.* The modern American scholar Robert Morey turns the screw: 'If it is true … that a word or an idea is nonsense if it is not capable of falsification or verification, then atheism is nonsense and should be dismissed as meaningless.'[18]

This confirms that, in common with all other human beings, atheists are believers. People can choose *what* to believe, but not *whether* to believe; believing is wrapped into the whole business of being human. As author Martin Robinson points out, 'Those who characterize themselves as "unbelievers" do not believe in nothing. On the contrary, they often have a very definite set of beliefs, which may be held just as passionately as so-called "believers" hold to the tenets of their faith.'[19]

Let me personalize the question we asked earlier: if you claim to be an atheist, what is the basis for your belief? At this point, some atheists do even more wriggling, and claim that the burden of proof falls exclusively on those who believe God *does* exist, while the atheist has no such responsibility. The Australian philosopher Michael Scriven claims, 'We need not have a proof that God does not exist in order to justify atheism.'[20] But why not? According to Scriven, we must presume that theism is wrong unless or until it can be proved to be right, but are to presume that atheism is right unless or until it can be proved to be wrong. This is hardly a level playing field! Theism clearly *is* a belief system, and those who hold to it can properly be asked to produce their reasons for doing so. But atheism is also a belief system — 'the deliberate, definite, dogmatic denial of the existence of God'— and atheists can also be asked to explain why they believe as they do. As Ronald Nash insists, 'The sensible person will reject the claim that theism should be presumed guilty until proved innocent';[21] by the same token, we should reject the claim that atheism should be presumed innocent until proved guilty.

Reduced to its simplest terms, atheism says, 'There is no God,' but even this collides headlong with the fundamental fact that it is impossible to prove a universal negative. Let me illustrate. I was born on the Channel Island of Guernsey, just off the coast of France. I may be slightly prejudiced here, but I believe that Guernsey produces the finest tomatoes, milk, butter and flowers in the world — and I am sorely tempted to add to the list! Yet for all its rich resources, I am not aware that anyone has found gold in Guernsey (other than in the tax-free temptations in its jewellers' shops). Yet I dare not claim that there is none to be found. To do this, I would have to excavate every inch of the island's twenty-five-square-mile surface, and keep digging until I had reached the centre of the planet (or, perhaps, come out on the other side). Only if I then came up empty-handed would I have a basis for claiming, 'There is no gold in Guernsey.'

If you are an atheist, are you not in a similar position? Unless you have been everywhere in the universe (simultaneously!), existed throughout all of time, and now know everything it is possible to know, how can you be *certain* that God does not exist? To know this with absolute certainty you would need to be in possession of total knowledge about all reality. If even one fact was unknown, God's existence could not be ruled out, as it might be the fact in question. Nobody can deny that God is a *possible* fact, and to rule him out is to claim infinite knowledge that there is no infinite Being. Can you seriously do that?

Darkness and light

The Bible addresses the issue of atheism head-on. In the Old Testament, David begins two of his psalms by saying, 'The fool says in his heart, "There is no God." ' [22] This is not intended as a definition of a 'fool'. The phrase, 'There is no God,' could literally be translated, 'No God for me' — in effect, 'I am not having God in my life.' It speaks of someone who chooses to live as if God were non-existent or irrelevant. Such a person never praises him, thanks him, prays to him, confesses his faults to him, or asks for his help. As far as this individual is concerned,

'God' is nothing more than a word, sometimes useful as a general-purpose expletive. Does this ring a bell?

Yet, as David shows by his use of the phrase 'in his heart', external behaviour has an internal source. Jesus endorsed this when he said, 'The things that come out of the mouth come from the heart.'[23] The words we say, the things we do and the attitudes we adopt are all indications of what we are at heart. We may deceive some people — and even ourselves at times — but our conscious or unconscious deceit does nothing to change the biblical statement that the heart is 'the wellspring of life',[24] the driving force behind all we do.

The practical atheist follows the desires of his heart — and David says that in so doing he is a 'fool'. The word has nothing to do with a person's IQ. It translates the Hebrew *nabal*, which in context means a perverse lack of wisdom. The issue here is not intellectual, but moral and spiritual. By biblical definition, atheism is never neutral; it is a wrong-headed determination to shut God out of one's life.

The New Testament elaborates, and at one point the apostle Paul says this of atheists: 'For although they knew God, they neither glorified him as God nor gave thanks to him, but their thinking became futile and their foolish hearts were darkened. Although they claimed to be wise, they became fools.'[25] The word 'thinking' translates *dialogismos*, from which we get our English word 'dialogue', while 'futile' means 'empty, vain or worthless'.[26] Those who refuse divine revelation are reduced to human speculation, to tossing around religious and philosophical ideas in the futile hope of finding something that will be intellectually and morally coherent and satisfying.

Paul then goes an important step further and says of such people that 'Their foolish hearts were darkened.' Here, 'foolish' translates the Greek *asunetos*, which means 'without insight or understanding'.[27] The Bible takes no prisoners here. It says that when people reject God their thinking is distorted, their wills are subject to bias, and their emotions cannot function properly. With God sidelined, their entire world-view is out of focus, with their own independent ideas about reality automatically flawed by their fundamental presupposition that no supernatural Being exists. As a result (and as we shall see in later chapters) they have to explain existence without creation, design without planning, a universal ethical code without a transcendent lawgiver, and life without a supernatural origin. As an example of this last point, they are reduced to agreeing with evolutionist Sidney Fox's breathtaking suggestion that 'In the beginning, life assembled itself.'[28]

The moral and spiritual ignorance of the people Paul had in mind was compounded by the fact that 'They claimed to be wise.' Nothing has changed. In an article published in the *Independent* in 1996, Richard Dawkins claimed the intellectual high ground by asking, 'Have you ever met an uneducated atheist?',[29] while in the course of an Oxford University debate in the same year his fellow atheist Peter Atkins, a lecturer in physical chemistry, deplored the fact that the university had a professorship in theology and dismissed it as 'a chair in the study of fantasy'.

There is a tragic irony here. Far from being able to make such dogmatic statements about ultimate reality, man is incapable of valid, independent insight about anything, because he is turning his back on the one who alone 'gives wisdom to the wise and knowledge to the discerning'.[30] The atheist can deny the existence of God only by ignoring the very basis of rationality on which he does so. Nobody has made this point more clearly than the universally respected scholar and author C. S. Lewis. After pointing out in one of his famous *Broadcast Talks* that if there was no creative intelligence behind the universe, the human brain was never designed to come to any rational conclusions, he went on, 'It is merely that when the atoms inside of my skull happen for physical or chemical reasons to arrange themselves in a certain way this gives me, as a by-product, the sensation I call thought. But if so, how can I trust my own thinking to be true? And if I can't trust my own think-ing, I can't trust the argument leading to atheism, and therefore *I have no reason to be an atheist.* Unless I believe in God, I can't believe in thought, *so I can never use thought to disbe-lieve in God'* [31] (emphasis added).

Do you have an answer to this? Can you sensibly be certain that God does not exist while admitting that your convictions are produced by a mechanism that was never designed to come to intelligent conclusions but which came about by accident? Is logic nothing more than a shuffling of atoms inside human skulls? Even Charles Darwin admitted, 'With me the horrid doubt always arises whether the convictions of man's mind, which has been developed from the mind of the lower animals, are of any value or at all trustworthy.' [32] Are you any more certain than Darwin was?

The article in *The Times* by Ludovic Kennedy referred to in the introduction was headed: 'Goodbye God, we can get along just fine without you.' [33] In the letters that followed one cor-respondent wrote, 'Whatever view one has of religion, may we know what amazing powers your correspondent acquired to *"know* that God is dead"?' Over the last 30 years we have been made aware of some of Sir Ludovic's attributes, but I did not realize that omniscience was one.' [34] How can atheism avoid this response? To argue against the existence of God is to argue against the existence of the one who alone gives the ability to argue for or against anything. Unless God exists, no atheist can rationally argue that he does not!

The Bible sums up the issue we have discussed in this chap-ter by affirming that while 'God is light', [35] atheists' hearts are 'darkened' [36] — not because the light is not shining, but because they have deliberately drawn the blinds: 'Light has come into the world, but men loved darkness instead of light.' [37] The same verdict holds good today. Have you got the blinds drawn, or are you open to the truth?

Call Julian Evans

Julian Evans, OBE, is Professor of Tropical Forestry at Imperial College, London, and holds an honorary chair of forestry at the University of Wales, Bangor. He is a director of Tearfund and the author of seven books and some 100 scientific and technical papers.

I grew up in a caring and loving family but not one that was Christian in the religious sense. Though I never went to Sunday School my parents were happy for me to attend monthly church parades as a Boy Scout and to join in acts of worship at school. Both of my parents had a great interest in English language and literature, my father as a Fleet Street journalist, my mother as a Cambridge graduate in English and later as a teacher and O-level examiner.

Natural history was my father's other great love and he much admired the Darwins. He had many of the great works on evolution, including most of Erasmus Darwin's writings and many by Charles Darwin, Alfred Russell Wallace, the Huxleys, and more recent evolutionists such as Ernst Mayr. Between literature and natural history we once estimated that our three-bedroom semi in south-east London held close on 5,000 books! It was an active, intellectual environment, but an agnostic one.

Born in 1946, I grew up believing that I was named after the evolutionary biologist Julian Huxley. However, on my recently asking my mother to confirm this she could not now remember. She felt it could well have been so, but said that the medieval female mystic, Julian of Norwich, may also have come into the reckoning!

As a teenager, I inclined towards a science career, but I also began to think seriously about religious things. It was not a passion, nor did it fill my time between rowing and playing chess for the school, but I particularly remember a very earnest discussion with a fellow sixth-form student at the City of London School, and his remark, 'Oh, I'll worry about it when I'm older,' has remained with me. My wife-to-be was also an influence, and as the one doing the courting I felt I should join her in attending church.

Wholly appropriately, God used a book — *Who Moved the Stone?*, by the British lawyer Frank Morison — to begin drawing me to himself. For the first time, I began to weigh the evidence of the historic facts surrounding Christianity. I was enthralled and, as a nineteen-year-old student reading forestry at the University of Wales, Bangor, devoured the book in one long night, finally getting into bed at five in the morning. It really made me think. Did the Bible's recorded facts stand up to scrutiny, or were they simply legends embellished by much retelling and wishful thinking? Over the next couple of years I gradually became convinced that the Bible as history was true. I can even recall trying to convince someone of this when travelling around North America on Greyhound buses! This conviction has never left me.

A second book completed my conversion, thanks to my wife's aunt Joyce. She had emigrated to South Africa in 1948 to work as a midwife in the African township now known as Soweto. In 1968, I began research in Swaziland as fieldwork for a Ph.D., looking at the growth of successive crops of pine trees — what we now call sustainability — and while there I spent my first Christmas away from home with Joyce and her friends in Johannesburg. On Christmas morning old Mr Durston (he lived to over 100) gave me C. S. Lewis's *Mere Christianity* as a present. As I read it on the tedious train and coach journey back to Swaziland, it changed my life. Here were not new facts in the historic or scientific sense, but facts interpreted, explained and revealed, and realization began to dawn. I knew the historicity was important; *Mere Christianity* began to show me *why* it was. I was so engrossed on the coach that people in the seat behind saw what I was reading and asked if I was a missionary. I squirmed at the very thought, but a few days later I knelt down and asked God to show me my need of a personal Saviour.

Immediately after this I wrote two letters, one to Joyce to tell her that I hadn't realized before how much Jesus had done for us, and the other to my parents owning up to certain teenage misdemeanours. Some years later, Joyce died suddenly in her sixties, right in the midst of another selfless act of kindness, arranging for her dear African friend, Maria, to visit England for the very first time. Joyce had kept my letter, and we found that across the back of the envelope she had written, 'Julian saved'. I treasure it still — tucked inside *Mere Christianity*! When I wrote to tell my parents my father replied, explaining why he could not believe in the God of the Bible. He was able to accept a force beyond the universe (a form of pantheism) but not a God who would intervene in the natural order.

After I had completed my Ph.D. I began to work with the Forestry Commission in South Wales. My career since then has been a mix of university teaching, research and work with development-aid charities. In the 1970s, four years were spent at the Papua New Guinea University of Technology in Lae, after which I became a research project leader with the Forestry Commission, and subsequently the Chief Research Officer responsible for their southern research station near Farnham. The Swaziland research has also continued to flourish. Commitment to Third World development has been both voluntary, with Tearfund since the early 1980s, and for a time as an employee of the International Institute for Environment and Development. All this has led to the usual researchers' and academics' output of papers and books and to acquiring a D.Sc. along the way, together with the unexpected honour of an OBE.

As a scientist, being a Christian has opened my eyes to God's remarkable world. Science helps us understand its workings; in the Bible God answers why we are here. Science does not explain God, just as it cannot fully explain man's inclination to selfishness, pride and sin. Being a Christian also helps me ask the right questions, including questions about Jesus. His name proclaims his saviourhood, he claims to be 'the way and the truth and the life'[38] and his own life utterly supports his testimony. Scientists who dismiss his claims are guilty of the very thing of which they accuse Christians — they don't look at the evidence objectively. Are the records in the Bible true? Did Jesus exist? Did he die and then return to life? When these questions are asked honestly (scientifically, if you like) I believe the conclusion is inescapable: it is often the scientist who wilfully ignores evidence. Genes or no genes, facts are facts and that is where Richard Dawkins' explanation falls down. Any reasonable scientific enquiry surrounding the life, death and resurrection of Jesus Christ will, I believe, affirm the accuracy of the biblical account beyond reasonable doubt. The historicity of these events is one of the great facts of this world, and perhaps my genes made me willing to look at them impartially. A delightful irony is that I currently find myself as Professor of Tropical Forestry at Imperial College in the T. H. Huxley School of the Environment, Earth Science and Engineering!

4.

The science thing

'I love to think of nature as an unlimited broadcasting system through which God speaks to us every hour, if only we will tune him in.'[1]

'All my studies in science ... have confirmed my faith. I regard the Bible as my principal source of authority.'[2]

'Because Jesus Christ is the Son of God, he can address himself to the very issues which science highlights but cannot solve. He deals with the problem of our nature.'[3]

These statements about the reality of God, the reliability of the Bible and the relevance of Jesus Christ have one interesting thing in common — they were all made by distinguished scientists. The first is by George Washington Carver, one of the world's leading agricultural chemists and only the third American in history to have a national monument erected in his honour. The second is by Sir Ghillean Prance, one-time Director of London's Royal Botanic Gardens at Kew. The third is by Professor Verna Wright, an outstanding British medical expert who originated multi-disciplinary research in bio-engineering almost before the term was coined.

My reason for quoting them here is that we are constantly being bombarded with such sweeping statements as, 'Science has done away with the need for religion', 'Science makes God unnecessary' and 'Science contradicts the Bible.' Yet claims like

these collide with the fact that vast numbers of scientists, including many of great distinction, hold firmly to the biblical
account of creation and find no conflict between this and their
scientific knowledge.

Definitions

It would help if we defined what the word 'science' means, yet
even this is not as straightforward as it seems. As the American
scholar J. P. Moreland points out, 'No generally accepted definition of what science is is agreed on by a majority of philosophers of science.'[4] In ancient times, 'science' was synonymous
with 'knowledge', but the word now has a much broader meaning and use. In our present context, it essentially means 'pursuit
of [systematic and formulated knowledge] or principles regu-
lating such pursuit'.[5] This is the *Concise Oxford Dictionary*'s
formal way of saying that science is neither an end nor an en-
tity, but an enterprise. What is generally known as the 'scientific
method' consists of techniques of controlled observation used
in the search for knowledge. As philosopher Danah Zohar put it
in a recent television programme, 'Great science is about asking great questions… Science invites us to investigate, to look
further, beyond appearances, to see what lies behind.'[6] To put
it even more simply, science is the process of learning things.

This being the case, there seems no reason why there should
be any clash between a search for truth and any statement about
ultimate reality, yet according to Edgar Andrews, 'The divorce
between science and religion is one of the most significant of
our modern philosophical scene.'[7]

In what follows, I am not trying to relate science to ideas
such as pantheism (which says that God is everything and everything is God), animism (which says that supernatural spirits in-
habit material objects), monism (which says that there is only

one essential principle in the universe), or deism (which says God is a remote, impersonal power). Nor am I trying to see whether science is compatible with religious systems such as Hinduism (which has no fewer than thirty-three million gods), Buddhism (which is basically monistic), Islam (whose Allah has been called 'out and out deistic')[8] or Sikhism (which is a patchwork of pantheistic ideas). My main purpose in this chapter is to examine whether science rules out the sole and sovereign Creator and Sustainer of the universe who, according to the Bible, broke decisively into time and space 2,000 years ago in the person of Jesus Christ.

Trailblazers

The 'divorce' between science and biblical religion seems particularly strange when we look at the history of science. The scientific method as we know it began in the sixteenth century, and most of its pioneers were men who believed that the universe was orderly and worth studying precisely because they saw it as the work of an intelligent, divine Creator. When the Royal Society, Britain's oldest and most prestigious body of its kind, was formed in 1662, its founders dedicated this scientific enterprise 'to the glory of God'. In 1865, the manifesto of the British Association for the Advancement of Science, signed by 617 scientists, including many with outstanding reputations, made it crystal clear that it saw the natural sciences as being in complete harmony with the Bible's teaching.

Since then, many scientists who have made landmark contributions to their particular disciplines have been firmly convinced that the laws of nature were God-ordained. I have gone into this in some detail elsewhere,[9] but even a short list of names is impressive: Francis Bacon, who drew up the inductive method of scientific investigation, and eventually became England's Lord

Chancellor; the German astronomer Johannes Kepler, acknowledged as the father of modern physical astronomy; the Irish
physicist Robert Boyle, one of the Royal Society's founders
and the father of modern chemistry; John Ray, in his day the
world's greatest authority in both botany and zoology; the Dan-
ish scientist Niels Steno, the first man to trace the human lymph-
atic system and (in pursuing a secondary interest!) the founder
of modern geology; the Swedish biologist Carolus Linnaeus,
the father of biological taxonomy; the outstanding English astronomer William Herschel; the brilliant British chemist and
physicist Michael Faraday, who discovered electromagnetic in-
duction and introduced the concept of magnetic lines of force;
the British physicist William Thomson, who established the
Kelvin scale of absolute temperatures and gave precise termin-
ology to the First and Second Laws of Thermodynamics; and
the British scientist James Clerk Maxwell, the father of modern
physics.

Over the top

These men — and many other truly great scientists — made it
clear that there was not the slightest conflict between their Christian faith and their scientific knowledge. Writing in the *Daily
Mail* in 1995, Paul Johnson went so far as to say, 'The overwhelming majority of great scientists have always believed in
God and regarded adding to our knowledge of him as a central
part of their work.'[10] Today, organizations of scientists committed to belief in God are flourishing all around the world (just
one of many in the United States has about 2,500 members)
and statements by highly qualified experts in various scientific
disciplines are scattered throughout this book. Then why today's popular idea that science and religion are no longer on
speaking terms? One major factor is that increased knowledge

of the physical universe has led to phenomenal achievements in technology, which for many people have fostered the illusion that humanity is independent of nature, understands how it works and can bring it under ever closer control, all without any reference to a transcendent Creator. For example, stupendous advances in medical science can lead people to ask, 'Who needs God when we can transplant hearts, conduct keyhole surgery, manipulate genes, manufacture "wonder drugs" and eliminate diseases which proved fatal less than a century ago?'

'Science' has become one of the most dominant words in our current culture, and stupendous claims have been made on its behalf. In the middle of the last century, Jawaharlal Nehru, the first Prime Minister of India, told his country's National Institute of Science, 'It is science alone that can solve the problems of hunger and poverty, of sanitation and illiteracy, of superstition and deadening custom and tradition, of vast resources running to waste, of a rich country inhabited by starving people... Who indeed could afford to ignore science today? ... The future belongs to science and those who make friends with science.'[11] In his book *Religion and Science*, Bertrand Russell went even further: 'Whatever knowledge is attainable must be attained by scientific means; *and what science cannot discover, mankind cannot know*'[12] (emphasis added). In a 1998 debate, Peter Atkins agreed — and dumped God at the same time: 'There is no necessity for God because science can explain everything.' Not to be outdone, Richard Dawkins told the *Daily Telegraph Science Extra*, 'Religion is no longer a serious candidate in the field of explanation. It is completely superseded by science.'[13]

This all sounds very impressive, yet what we have here is not science, but scientism, which assumes that the whole of reality is composed of nothing but atoms and molecules. The formal word for this is 'reductionism', but I much prefer what the distinguished British scientist Donald MacKay called it —

'nothing-buttery'. According to this idea, even human beings, with all their amazing complexity (we shall look at this in a later chapter) are nothing but collections of biological bits and pieces, and when we have come up with a scientific description of these, we have said all that can be said on the subject. Yet this is like saying that a piano concerto is nothing more than black blobs on sheets of paper; it gives us only a fraction of the facts.

It is easy to see how scientism automatically kicks God into touch, and Richard Dawkins did so with his usual panache when he told *Daily Telegraph* readers, 'God cannot be proved by any scientific hypothesis. Therefore he does not exist.'[14] This kind of thinking is based on the verification principle, which we noted in chapter 3, yet it has at least three fatal flaws. In the first place, the principle itself is incapable of verification! How can we prove scientifically that the only reality is that which can be proved scientifically? Scientism says, 'What you see is what you get' — but how can we know this? As soon as the verification principle is applied to its own claims it self-destructs. When science says that only what can be known and proved by science is rational it is being *irrational*, because the claim itself cannot be known and proved by science! As J. P. Moreland rightly points out, 'One cannot turn to science to justify science any more than one can pull oneself up by [one's] own boot straps.'[15]

Secondly, how can science explain the origin of logic, upon which all scientific reasoning is founded? Without logic, science is stuck — but it has no idea where logic comes from. Thirdly, science itself is based on assumptions that cannot be proved by any scientific method. Science works because scientists assume the validity, consistency and dependability of the basic laws of physics — yet they can have no scientific explanation of *why* these laws exist, where they came from, or why they operate so efficiently. Keith Ward, Regius Professor of Divinity at Oxford University, uses an amusing illustration to make the point:

Suppose the basic laws of physics popped into existence for no reason at all. One day, they did not exist. The next day, there they were, governing the behaviour of electrons and atoms. Now if anything at all might pop into existence for no reason, there is actually no way of assessing the probability of laws of physics doing so. One day, there might be nothing. The next day, there might be a very large carrot. Nothing else in existence whatsoever, but there, all alone and larger than life, a huge carrot. If anything is possible, that certainly is. The day after that, the carrot might disappear and be replaced by a purple spotted gorilla. Why not? We are in a universe, or a non-universe, where anything or nothing might happen, for no reason. Why does this thought seem odd, or even ridiculous, whereas the thought that some law of physics might just pop into existence does not? Logically, they are exactly on a par. [16]

Do you have an answer to this?

Limits

A much more sensible approach than scientism is to recognize that science works brilliantly *within certain limits*. It is a superb tool, but not one capable of tackling every task and answering every question. The contemporary atheist Steve Jones, Professor of Genetics at University College, London admits, 'It is the essence of all scientific theories that they cannot resolve everything. Science cannot answer the questions that philosophers — or children — ask: why are we here, what is the point of being alive, how ought we to behave? Genetics has almost nothing to say about what makes us more than machines driven

by biology, about what makes us human.'[17] Jones hits some
hot buttons here. Here are others from a very long list:

- Science can tell us nothing about *why the universe
should have come into being*. In *Black Holes and Baby
Universes*, the British physicist Stephen Hawking confesses, 'Although science may solve the problem of how
the universe began, it cannot answer the question: why
does the universe bother to exist? I don't know the answer
to that.'[18]

- Science cannot explain *the fundamental facts about
humanity*. When the international Human Genome
Project (HGP) published its long-awaited report in February 2001, spelling out the three billion letters that make
up the human genetic code, James Le Fanu told *Sunday
Telegraph* readers that this 'impressive achievement' was
also 'devastating news for science, and in particular for
those who, for the past 20 years, have regularly promised us that once the genome is cracked, all that is currently obscure will be made clear and we will be able to
have perfect babies and cure all manner of ills'.[19] After
pointing out the vast difference between the forecasts and
the facts, he went on, 'The holy grail, the dream that
science would soon tell us something significant about
what it means to be human, has slipped through our hands
— and we are no wiser than before. *The human genome
… can tell us absolutely nothing about the really important things in life*'[20] (emphasis added).

- Sir John Eccles, a Nobel Prize-winning pioneer in brain
research, underlines and expands this failure: 'Science
cannot explain the existence of each of us as a unique
self, nor can it answer such fundamental questions as
"Who am I? How did I come to be at a certain place and
time? What happens after death?" These are all myster-
ies beyond science.'[21]

- Science cannot explain *why the mind exists and functions as it does.* Oxford biochemist Arthur Peacocke told the *Sunday Telegraph* in 1996, 'Science can investigate all the physical aspects of the brain, but there is still something about the mind — and therefore about who you really are — that it cannot get at.'[22] To give a fundamental example of this, science is unable to explain consciousness, or even to find the language to explain what it is.
- In spite of all the technological advances it has spawned, *science can add nothing to the quality of life.* The British scientist Sir John Houghton, former director of the Meteorological Office, made the following note in reviewing a 'Quality of Life' session at a 1991 conference organized by the International Council of Scientific Studies: 'Although we could largely agree on those factors which ideally make up quality of life, as scientists we could say virtually nothing (and there was considerable debate on the issue) about how to achieve it in practice. In particular, how could we overcome the inherent selfishness, greed and other undesirable characteristics shown by human beings? The problems can be described by science, as can the factors which may exacerbate them, *but science cannot solve them*'[23] (emphasis added).
- Science cannot *explain human purposes, meanings and values*, or the principles involved in human behaviour. It can say nothing about love, justice, freedom, beauty, goodness, joy or peace. Nor, for that matter, can it tell us how to distinguish between good and bad, right and wrong, or why we should choose one rather than the other. As the atheistic journalist Natasha Walter admitted on *Soul of Britain,* 'I don't think any scientist would say that it was for science to say what is ethically right to do.'[24]

These few examples are sufficient to justify this verdict by quantum theory expert Erwin Schrödinger: 'I am very aston- ished that the scientific picture of the world around me is very deficient. It gives a lot of factual information, puts all our experi- ence in a magnificently consistent order, but is ghastly silent about all and sundry that is really near to our heart ... it knows nothing about beautiful and ugly, good or bad, God and eter- nity. Science sometimes pretends to answer questions in these domains, but the answers are very often so silly that we are not inclined to take them seriously.'[25]

Bridging the gap

Another obvious limitation of science is that it cannot explain why human beings should have any kind of religious instinct. Molecular biologist Andrew Miller goes even further, and pre- pares the way for us to put an end to the supposed feud be- tween science and religion: 'To suggest that recent advances in our understanding of life rule out belief in God is only valid against a very simplistic, though once popular concept of a "God of the gaps"... *It is certainly not a scientific matter to decide whether or not there is a God*'[26] (emphasis added). Richard Dawkins was right to say that God cannot be scientifically proved, but Miller shows that neither can God be scientifically disproved, as the question lies outside the parameters of science. Having claimed that the central truths of the Christian faith 'find no support in science', Bertrand Russell frankly admitted, 'I do not pretend to be able to prove that there is no God.'[27] Debat- ing the issue at Oxford University in 1998, Peter Atkins took his usual enthusiastic swipes at religion in general and the Bible's teaching in particular, yet his opening words let a rather large cat out of the bag: 'I have to admit from the outset that science cannot disprove the existence of God.'

This is the first step in bridging the gap, as it tells us that no 'either ... or' situation exists. What is more, many experts are recognizing that modern advances in various scientific disciplines are narrowing the gap, rather than widening it. Commenting on recent discoveries in cosmology, molecular biology and neurophysiology, James Le Fanu told *Sunday Telegraph* readers in 1996, 'Science can never disprove the existence of God, but one could say it is making signposts to his existence much more obvious.'[28] Writing a year later about the certainty he felt in listening to the eighteenth-century music of Johann Sebastian Bach, he concluded, 'Thanks to the onward march of science over the past forty years, it has become ... a lot easier to be certain about the existence of a creator god than it was in Bach's day.'[29]

Others well qualified to comment have recently come to the same conclusion: 'A significant and growing number of scientists, historians of science, and philosophers of science see more scientific evidence now for a personal creator and designer than was available fifty years ago. In the light of this evidence, it is false and naïve to claim that modern science has made belief in the supernatural unreasonable.'[30]

The gap becomes even narrower when we realize that the militant atheist often sets up a rigged contest between scientism and a grossly distorted view of God. Preparing for a public debate with Richard Dawkins in 1996, William Gosling, Professor of Communications Engineering at Bath University, told *Daily Telegraph* readers, 'Like most atheists, he attacks a God so primitive that few educated believers would recognize the image. If I thought God has the characteristics Dawkins assigns to him, I would share his lack of belief.'[31]

On *Soul of Britain* Dawkins rightly called science 'a disinterested search for truth',[32] but as we saw in chapter 3, he had blown his cover a few minutes earlier by claiming that people who believed in God were 'deluded', and that his motive for writing books was 'to do something about it'. [33] Later in the programme he said, 'I think science really has fulfilled the need that religion did in the past, of explaining things, explaining why we are here, what is the origin of life, where did the world come from, what life is all about.'[34] Of course science has done no such thing — nor should we expect it to.

Dawkins went on to say, 'I've never been very sympathetic to the very fashionable view that science and religion must work side by side. Science has the answers to its questions. I don't think religion has the answers to any questions at all.'[35] This was hardly being 'disinterested'! Dawkins is not an authority on religion, or the relationship between religion and science, and his statement clashes head-on with the verdict of someone who is — Fraser Watts, Starbridge lecturer in both theology and natural science at Cambridge University: '*I do not know of any research that conflicts with religion.* The problem comes from the ideological position, *held by a minority of scientists,* that science is the only valid form of knowledge and has got all the answers'[36] (emphasis added).

Dawkins' dogmatism is also rejected by Sir Karl Popper, arguably the world's best-known philosopher of science: 'The old scientific idea of *episteme* — of absolutely demonstrable knowledge — has proved an idol. The demand for scientific objectivity makes it inevitable that *every scientific statement must remain tentative* for ever.'[37] In true science, the latest word is never the last word!

The idea that, whereas science deals with facts, religion is a matter of faith at best and superstition at worst is another atheistic anthem, but it is badly off-key, failing to grasp that true science relies heavily on faith (implicitly trusting the rationality of the universe and our ability to make sense of it) and failing to realize that nature and Scripture often overlap in presenting different angles on the same truth. What is more, to say that science can explain everything is to overlook the fundamental fact that *science cannot even explain itself*. On the other hand, biblical religion sees our ability to grasp something of the symmetry and elegance of natural law as a pointer to the existence of a transcendent, rational mind. As Elaine Storkey of King's College, London, told *Soul of Britain*, 'The reason science is possible is that we live in a law-ordered cosmos which God has created.'[38]

If your atheism is based on the idea that modern science has ruled out the possibility of God's existence, should you not have a radical rethink? Science and biblical religion are in perfect harmony with each other, and work together in giving us a true picture of reality. In the course of a lecture at the Royal Institution in London in 1919, the English physicist William Henry Bragg said, 'Sometimes people ask if religion and science are opposed to each other. They are: in the sense that the thumb and fingers of my hand are opposed to one another. It is an opposition by means of which anything can be grasped.' Another physicist said much the same thing: 'A legitimate conflict between science and religion cannot exist. Science without religion is lame; religion without science is blind.'[39] His name was Albert Einstein.

Call Boris Dotsenko

Dr Boris Dotsenko was born in Siberia. After scientific training in the then Soviet Union, and working there in the fields of rocket technology and nuclear physics, he defected to the West and pursued an academic career in North America.

As a teenager, I often found myself asking myself, 'Why am I here?' and 'What is the purpose of life?' I was impressed by the clear, logical

ideas of Greek philosophers like Plato and Socrates, but I was a convinced atheist, having absorbed Marxist thinking into the very mar-
row of my bones.

One August afternoon, while recovering from pneumonia at my
grandfather's farmhouse, I fell asleep on a pile of hay in an old barn.
When I woke, I found that I had slipped to the floor between the hay
and the back wall. As I struggled to my feet I found on the floor parts
of an old book, yellowed with age and written in Old Slavonic, with a
Russian translation. The first words I read were, 'The beginning of the
gospel about Jesus Christ …,'[40] and immediately I felt a shiver of fear.
Christians were being persecuted in my country at that time, churches
were being destroyed or closed, and preaching was a crime. Yet I
was intrigued by what I read and I smuggled the book back to my
room.

It was obviously a copy of the New Testament. As I read on, I came
to the opening words of John's Gospel — 'In the beginning was the
Word, and the Word was with God, and the Word was God'[41] — words
which came as a psychological shock to me as they contradicted everything I had been taught about the beginning of all reality. Other shocks
followed. Stalin had said, 'He who is not with us is against us'; now I
discovered that he was twisting the words of Jesus: 'He who is not
with me is against me.'[42] As I continued to read, I discovered that
Jesus also taught that the most important commandment was: 'Love
the Lord your God with all your heart and with all your soul and with
all your mind and with all your strength'[43] — but how could I love God
if God did not exist? I found myself resisting what I read, but unable to
stop reading. After two weeks of my surreptitiously reading the Bible
in this way it mysteriously disappeared from my room, yet its words
continued to burn in my heart as I moved on to study physics and
mathematics at the University of Kiev.

At that time I had a particular interest in the Law of Entropy, a
fundamental law of nature concerned with the probable behaviour of
the particles (molecules, atoms, electrons and so on) of any physical
system. This law, also known as the Second Law of Thermodynamics,

says that, left to itself, any physical system will decay as its matter becomes increasingly disorganized. As I thought it through, it occurred to me that as the universe was still intact there must be an amazingly powerful organizing force at work, keeping the universe controlled and in order. What is more, this force must be non-material, or it would disintegrate. Eventually I came to the conclusion that this omnipotent and controlling force was the God of whom the Bible speaks.

Graduating from Kiev, I enrolled in the University of Leningrad, where to my great surprise I came across another Bible in, of all places, the personal library of the world-renowned scientist Jakob Frenkel. I was shocked, yet impressed, that a man with such an intimate knowledge of the laws of nature could openly have a Bible on his shelves for everyone to see. It was at about this time that I began to reach out to God in prayer.

As one of the three best graduating students in Leningrad I was sent to Moscow's State University, where in 1954 I obtained a Ph.D. in Physical and Mathematical Sciences. After doing research in rocket technology in the Academy of Sciences of the Soviet Union, I moved to the nuclear branch of the Institute of Physics in Kiev. My religious ideas were slowly developing, but had a serious setback when I found that members of my own family were reporting regularly to the KGB (Secret Police) on my actions and beliefs. I became so distraught that at one stage I tried to take my own life.

In 1966 I was summoned to the Central Committee of the Soviet Communist Party in Moscow and told that I was to be sent to Canada as a senior member of the International Atomic Energy Agency. From there I would be expected to send back information about the achievement of nuclear researchers from other countries. The importance of the mission was underlined by a senior official who told me, 'Boris Borisobich, we will be able to reward your service greatly — up to the Nobel Prize in Physics!'

Two days later, as I unpacked my luggage in Edmonton, Alberta, I found yet another Bible — this time one which had been placed in my hotel room by the Gideons International, a group of Christian

businessmen who distribute Bibles to hotels, schools and other public institutions. To my astonishment, the Bible was open at the very
words which had struck me so forcibly in that Ukrainian barn twenty-
two years earlier: 'In the beginning was the Word, and the Word was
with God, and the Word was God.'[44] I began to read the Bible at every
opportunity, and within a very short time I came to put my trust in the
Lord Jesus Christ as my own personal Saviour.

I quickly realized that my relationship with Jesus Christ was more
important than my career, or even my beloved homeland, so I sought
political asylum and have remained in Canada ever since, where I
have pursued a busy career teaching physics at schools, colleges
and universities.

My understanding of the nature of God has grown steadily over
the years through Bible study and prayer, and I recognize him to be
the Creator of the universe and the one who controls each part that
helps to make it up. It is hard for us to conceptualize adequately his
relationship with this world, because he does not belong to this 'reality', the only one with which we are familiar. Just as the movements of
particles or iron placed in an electric field are controlled by that field,
though the field itself does not become part of the system of particles,
so God controls the entire universe without becoming a part of the
system.

As a professor, I want to train my students in science. More importantly, I want to help them to become people who realize their chief
responsibilities — to society, to the world around them, and above all
to God himself.[45]

5.

Maria got it right

Somebody once asked Bertrand Russell what he would do if (to his great surprise) he met God after death and was asked why he had not believed in him. Without hesitation, Russell replied, 'I would look him straight in the eye and say, "Not enough evidence".' Russell had a reputation for blowing hot and cold on all kinds of issues — one Cambridge professor said he 'produced a brand new philosophy every few years'[1] — but in this case his response accurately reflected his atheistic views. Russell insisted that the only realities were those that can be verified by scientific investigation, and that man was nothing more than 'a curious accident in a backwater'.[2] He claimed that morality was a matter of personal choice, and that there was no point in discussing human destiny: 'No fire, no heroism, no intensity of thought and feeling can preserve an individual life beyond the grave.'[3] Russell had no way of proving that these claims were valid, but he still insisted that evidence for God was either non-existent or so skimpy that one could safely rule him out.

If he was wrong he could not have made a more appalling or tragic mistake, and in the next four chapters we will look at some of the evidence suggesting that he did indeed get it disastrously wrong.

The fundamental fact

In his highly successful science fiction spoof *The Hitch-hiker's Guide to the Galaxy*, Douglas Adams has one of his characters declaring, 'Space is big. Really big. You just won't believe how vastly mind-bogglingly big it is. I mean you may think it is a long way down the road to the chemist, but that's just peanuts to space.'[4] This off-beat comment points us towards the first item of evidence, which is that we find ourselves surrounded by an amazing universe that demands some kind of explanation. In his best seller *A Brief History of Time*, Stephen Hawking calls Earth 'a medium-sized planet orbiting around an average star in the outer suburbs of an ordinary spiral galaxy, which is itself only one of about a million million galaxies in the observable universe'.[5] That is superbly succinct, but it is only when we start filling in the details that we begin to get some inkling of the vastness involved.

Hawking's 'medium-sized planet' has a diameter of about 8,000 miles, a circumference of nearly 25,000 miles and a total surface area of about 197 million square miles, some two-thirds of which is water. The 'average star' around which it orbits is the sun, with a volume over one million times that of Earth. Although it loses four million tons of its mass every second, the sun is so vast that it still has enough fuel to last another 5,000 million years. Yet it is only one of a stupendous number of stars (some much larger) in the outer suburbs of what Hawking calls 'an ordinary spiral galaxy', the gigantic, disc-shaped Milky Way, which stretches some 621,000 million million miles across, and contains about 100,000 million stars.

These figures are mind-boggling, but even the Milky Way is only one of about a million million known galaxies. Travelling at the speed of light (just over 186,282 miles per second) we would reach the moon in 1.3 seconds and the sun in 8.3 minutes.

Yet we know of galaxies that are more than 13,000 million light years away. Until recently, astronomers thought that the far-thest objects in space were quasars, mysterious sources of light it would take over ten billion light years to reach, but in 1996 the Hubble Space Telescope found six massive objects that appear to be fourteen billion light years away.[6]

These distances are incomprehensible, even when we try to scale them down. If Earth was the size of the full-stop at the end of this sentence, the distance to the moon would be five-eighths of an inch, the distance to the sun would be just over nineteen feet, the distance to the nearest star would be 1,005 miles, the distance to the centre of the Milky Way would be 23,380,000 miles and (to choose one of the other million million galaxies out there) the distance to the Andromeda Galaxy would be 467,600,000 miles. No serious thinker can take this on board and evade the fundamental question it raises: 'How did it all get there?' There are only three possibilities.

1. The first is that *it is eternal* — in other words, it has always been there. This seems to be what Bertrand Russell meant when he wrote, 'The world is simply there, and is inexplicable.'[7] In 1948 the British astronomer Sir Fred Hoyle helped to promote the so-called 'steady state' theory, which maintained that the universe was infinite and eternal, and that as matter 'died' through expansion it was replaced by other matter which sprang into exist-ence out of nothing, so keeping the entire cosmic process in balance. There has never been any reliable evidence to support Hoyle's idea, and in any case it contradicts the Second Law of Thermodynamics which, reduced to its simplest terms, says that any physical system becomes less ordered and more random over time. As we know the universe is becoming less ordered, it must have been more ordered in the past, and must have had a highly ordered beginning. This alone explains why philosopher William Lane Craig says that the steady state model 'has been abandoned by virtually everyone'.[8]

2. The second possibility is that *it is self-created*. The notion of spontaneous generation can be traced back at least as far as the Greek philosopher Anaximander (*c.* 610 – *c.* 547 B.C.). The idea has not always had a good press, but in the nineteenth century some scientists got very excited about it, and even went so far as to say that it could account for the existence of the entire universe. This would neatly dispose of God, but it is in direct conflict with what Isaac Asimov called 'the most powerful and most fundamental generalization about the universe that scientists have ever been able to make'.[9] This is the First Law of Thermodynamics, which states that, while matter can be converted into energy, and energy into matter, neither can be self-created or destroyed. Yet even without thermodynamics, the self-creation idea runs into another brick wall — the law of non-contradiction. For something to create itself, it would need to exist before it existed — in other words to be and not to be at the same time. Does that make scientific sense — or sense of any kind?

3. This leaves us with the third possibility — that *it was brought into being by a transcendent, eternal, self-existent power.* Science claims to take us back to the moment on which the laws on which it leans began to operate — a point one ten-millionth of a trillionth of a trillionth of a second after time began — but then it gets stuck. As Edgar Andrews points out, 'No matter how close to the instant of origin one may be able to press the scientific model of the cosmos, it remains impossible for such an explanation to be applied at or before the zero time

point. Thus it follows that science, even at its most specu-
lative, must stop short of offering any explanation or even
description of the actual event of origin.' [10]

We saw in an earlier chapter that science is restricted to only
one form of knowledge, which means there are limits to the
number of questions it can answer. To say that if there is no
scientific explanation of something there *is* no answer is neither
scientific nor sensible. As I sit revising this chapter in a friend's
home in Scotland, I have just met a couple who twenty-four
hours ago got engaged to be married. I am sure they have no
scientific explanation for what has happened, but I am equally
sure they would not thank me for saying that their relationship
has no reality or meaning! The obvious thing to do when faced
with the existence of a universe which is not eternal and did not
create itself is to acknowledge that there must be something
beyond the purely physical and material. Sir Arthur Eddington,
the British physicist who dominated the world of stellar astronomy and was one of the earliest exponents of the theory of
relativity, was right on the mark when he wrote, 'The beginning
seems to present insuperable difficulties unless we agree to look
on it as frankly supernatural.' [11] If we open ourselves to this possibility, we find that the God identified in chapter 1 meets all
the criteria necessary for bringing the universe into being. This
is not reaching desperately for a 'God of the gaps' to plug a
hole science is unable to fill. Instead, as Keith Ward puts it, 'To
grasp the idea of God is to grasp an idea of the only reality that
could form a completely adequate explanation of the existence
of the universe.' [12]

The Bible's record of divine creation is summed up in its
opening sentence: 'In the beginning God created the heavens
and the earth.' [13] The Hebrews had no single word to describe
the universe, and they used the phrase *hassamayim we'et
ha'ares* ('the heavens and the earth') to speak of all reality

outside of God himself. As the American theologian Douglas Kelly explains, ' "The heavens and the earth" is a way of saying "everything that exists", whether galaxies, nebulae or solar systems, all things from the farthest reaches of outer space to the smallest grain of sand or bacterial microbe on planet earth.'[14]

If we ask why God should do such a stupendous thing, the Bible limits itself to saying:

> You are worthy, our Lord and God,
>   to receive glory and honour and power,
> for you created all things,
>   and by your will they were created
>   and have their being. [15]

God did not create the universe because he had to, but because he chose to; it was part of his 'good, pleasing and perfect will'.[16] As God's verdict on creation was to call it 'very good',[17] we know that it reflected his majesty and glory. To grasp this is to have the foundation of a coherent and sustainable worldview.

The Big Bang and all that

If the existence of the universe is one problem for the atheist, its nature is another. Far from being a meaningless 'loose cannon', we find it governed by universal and dependable laws that enable us not only to send men to the moon but to perform millions of functions on our own planet, from boiling an egg to performing open heart surgery, and from playing football to building skyscrapers. We can do all these things because of laws the existence and dependability of which we take for granted — but surely they must have some kind of explanation?

By far the most popular current idea as to the origin of the
universe is that of the Big Bang, which says that about fifteen
billion years ago all the matter in the entire universe was con-
centrated in a speck of matter so small that it could easily have
passed through the eye of a needle, so hot that no atoms or
even subatomic particles could exist in it, and so dense that the
laws of physics would not have applied. Then came the 'bang'
in which the speck 'inflated' to the size of a football in one
million billion billion billionth of a second — and another fifteen billion years of expansion, cooling, gravity and the natural
operation of the laws of physics produced the universe as we
now see it.

Before we look at some specific questions in connection with
the Big Bang, we need to accept that, although millions of people
with little or no knowledge of cosmology take the occurrence of
the Big Bang for granted, it is in fact nothing more than a theory,
or model. What is more, it is one whose claims are seriously
questioned by leading scientists in many relevant disciplines.
This is partly because many of its key calculations are based on
estimates, not facts. For example, many claims rely on the content and behaviour of 'dark matter' and 'dark energy', which
together are thought to make up all but a tiny percentage of the
universe, but about which we know very little. The British
astrophysicist David Wilkinson confesses, 'It is somewhat hum-
bling to realize that for all our discoveries we still do not know
what 90% of the universe is made of,'[18] while Stephen Hawking admits that if the present estimates about 'dark matter' were
even 10% wide of the mark the Big Bang idea would be
worthless.

Other estimations used in the Big Bang model include those
involving distances to the furthest known galaxies, but in
Wrinkles in Time the American astrophysicist George Smoot
shows that the procedure used to estimate these is 'a risky

manoeuvre, based on the unproven assumption that all galax-ies of the same type have similar absolute brightness'.[19] The rate of the universe's expansion is another estimate on which the Big Bang idea relies, but as Berkeley professor Timothy Ferris points out in *The Whole Shebang*, there are 'troubling uncertainties'[20] in this.

In 1997 BBC Television ran a six-part series entitled *Stephen Hawking's Universe*, in which he developed his belief that we are on the verge of discovering 'the Theory of Everything', a total explanation of the universe that could be expressed in a single line of mathematics. Yet in listening to the voice-overs I noticed a lot of hesitation behind the hype: 'The *hope* is that soon we *may* be able to see the heat of the early universe in enough detail to answer our questions about how it was formed. *If* the data is detailed enough, it *could* offer observational evi-dence that *may* clarify how everything began.'[21] Reviewing the programme the following day, the *Sunday Telegraph*'s Robert Matthews said that being led to believe that science alone was on the brink of knowing the origin and nature of the universe was 'a trick that the series attempts with the skill of an estate agent [selling] a house with dodgy foundations ... while keep-ing quiet about the nasty cracks in the scientific cellar and the intellectual doors that won't shut properly'.[22]

We have space for just two major problems posed by a 'natu-ral' Big Bang, one with no place or need for God. Firstly, where did that indescribably dense speck of dust come from? The atheist says, 'It was just there', but this tells us nothing. Why was it there? Why was it not somewhere else? Was there no-where else for it to be? Was there nothing else to be anywhere else? The eighteenth-century German mathematician and phi-losopher Gottfried Leibnitz put his finger on the fundamental issue: 'The first question which should be asked will be, *Why is there something rather than nothing?* That is, why does any-thing at all exist?'[23] Not even the Big Bang can provide an answer, as every one of the vast accumulation of things which form the universe needs an explanation for its own existence. Cosmologist Edward Tryon suggests, 'Our universe is simply one of thousands which happen from time to time,'[24] but how can he possibly know this? And why and how do they 'happen'? Towards the end of the blockbuster film *Sound of Music*, Maria sings 'Nothing comes from nothing, nothing ever could.' This was hardly meant to be a serious scientific statement, but Maria hit the nail on the head. *Ex nihilo, nihil fit* (Out of nothing, nothing comes) is a fundamental fact universally accepted in scientific circles, and the Big Bang does nothing to change it. When Peter Atkins cheerfully assures us that, for all its stupendous size and brilliant diversity the entire universe is 'an elaborate and engaging rearrangement of nothing',[25] he is standing science on its head and rewriting the rules of common sense.

When we hear the sound of an unexpected explosion, we instinctively ask what caused it. Why not ask the same question when faced with the biggest explosion of all? William Lane Craig tells us where this should lead: 'Since everything that began to exist has a cause of existence, and since the universe began to exist ... the universe has a cause of existence. We ought to ponder long and hard over this truly remarkable conclusion, for it means that transcending the entire universe there exists a cause which brought the universe into being *ex nihilo*... This conclusion ought to stagger us, ought to fill us with a sense of awe and wonder at the knowledge that our whole universe was caused to exist by something beyond it and greater than it.'[26]

The second problem the Big Bang poses for atheists is that even planned explosions produce disorder, not order. The atheist says that the universe was kick-started by one that was *unplanned* — an accidental, unguided, purposeless detonation — yet he finds the result governed by elegant, dependable, universal laws of physics. Is this a fluke? Stephen Hawking tells us, 'If the rate of expansion after the Big Bang had been smaller by even one part in a hundred thousand million, the universe would have recollapsed before it ever reached its present size.'[27] The British mathematician and physicist Roger Penrose, who worked with Hawking to develop our understanding of 'black holes', computed the odds of the Big Bang producing our ordered universe by accident, and estimated them as one in $10^{10^{123}}$,[28] a number so absurdly large that it is 'too big to write down in full even if every proton in the entire universe were used to write a digit on!' Are you sure that order occurred accidentally against odds like these?

User-friendly universe

All we have seen so far nudges us towards what has become known as the argument from design. Although he flatly denied that we could argue from nature to God, the influential eighteenth-century German sceptic Immanuel Kant conceded that the argument from design was 'the oldest, the clearest, and the most accordant with the common reason of mankind',[29] while his fellow sceptic David Hume admitted, 'A purpose, and intention, or design strikes everywhere the most careless, the most stupid thinker.'[30] Kant and Hume were not exaggerating. Wherever we look in the cosmos, we find things fitting together in an amazing way, as if they had been engineered for a specific purpose. The relative strengths of gravitational and electromagnetic forces, the way in which strong and weak nuclear forces operate, the relative mass of the proton, the electron and the neutron (the three subatomic particles which form the atom) and the exact extent to which matter exceeds antimatter, all contribute to making our universe viable. To illustrate just one of these, George Smoot says that if the excess of matter over antimatter was different by about one particle per ten billion, our life-sustaining universe would never have come into being.[31]

Why is the universe precisely the way it is? How did these elegant, universal, dependable laws come into existence? Why does so much seem so well structured and interrelated? Is 'chance' really a good enough answer? Do you think that the book you are reading, with all its pages neatly held together and filled with precisely spaced words putting across a series of rational arguments, came about as the result of an explosion at the printers? There is no logical or mathematical reason why this should not be the case — but is that what you instinctively think? Logically speaking, there is no reason why random typing by a team of quick-fingered chimpanzees should not produce a gripping novel with an exciting plot and a cliff-hanging climax, but would you be prepared to bet on this ever happening? Is it any more likely that our vast, complex and coherent universe is just a gigantic fluke for which there is no explanation? Is it not more sensible (and more natural) to suppose that it owes its existence to a transcendent, intelligent Creator?

When there is no scientific explanation for the existence of natural law, should we not look for another one? Isaac Newton was convinced that the cosmos 'could only proceed from the counsel and dominion of an intelligent and powerful Being',[32] while Edgar Andrews goes so far as to call this argument 'as close to a proof for the existence of God as is possible'.[33]

In recent decades, science has fine-tuned the argument from design and uncovered a mass of evidence to suggest that the universe has in some way been specifically designed to sustain intelligent life on our particular planet. Princeton physicist Freeman Dyson writes, 'The more I examine the universe and the details of its architecture, the more evidence I find that the universe must in some sense have known we were coming.'[34] To put some of the evidence very simply, if Earth were ten per cent smaller or larger, it would be unable to sustain the atmosphere we breathe; if it were a little nearer the sun, we would fry; a little further away and we would freeze; if it were not on a twenty-

four-hour spin cycle, no life could exist on it; if it were not tilted
at exactly 23.45 degrees, we would not be alive to discuss it; if
our ozone layer were a tiny fraction thinner, no living matter
could survive.

Are you satisfied to write all of this off as yet another series
of flukes? Oxford scholar J. L. Mackie, one of the most influential atheists of our time, admits in his book *The Miracle of Theism*, 'It is ... surprising that the elements of this unique set-up
are just right for life when they might easily have been wrong.'[35]
Paul Davies, Professor of Natural Philosophy at the University
of Adelaide, goes further and says, 'If we could play God, and
select values for these quantities at a whim by twiddling a set of
knobs, we would find that almost all the knob settings would
render the universe uninhabitable.'[36] Linking our present universe to its original state, Stephen Hawking concedes, 'It would
be very difficult to explain why the universe should have begun
in just this way, *except as the act of a God who intended to
create beings like us.*'[37] Theism says that such a God exists —
one who is transcendent, eternal and self-existent, with the freedom and power to bring into being anything he wishes (including matter, time and space) and to sustain the whole of his
creation by laws of nature which he put in place.

Nothing in this chapter proves the existence of God, but
where does the evidence point? Why should the universe exist
at all? Why should it be as complex and orderly as it is? How
can we make any sense of the universe unless it *does* make
sense? Shrugging our shoulders and saying, 'These things just
happened,' gets us nowhere. As Keith Ward says, 'It seems odd
to think that there is a reason for everything except for that
most important item of all — that is, the existence of *everything*, the universe itself.'[38] We can only settle for that if we have
decided beforehand that God is not a sufficient explanation.

Ruling out creation by God without examining the evidence
is easy, but is on a par with the car bumper sticker that reads,

'My mind is made up. Please don't confuse me with facts.' Ruling out creation by God after examining the evidence is no wiser.

Call Adzo Apaloo

Adzo Apaloo was born in Ghana, where she studied medicine and specialized in anaesthesia. She has taught and practised in Ghana and Hong Kong, and is currently practising in England.

From a very early age I became familiar with fear. Living in a country with an oppressive regime and a heavily charged political atmosphere, everyone had to be careful that they were on the right side of the political divide; a careless word could cost you your job or land you in prison. Then there was fear based on superstition and the supernatural. People were afraid that their neighbours or enemies could cast a spell on them, bringing all kinds of evil their way. There were times when a conversation would be cut short abruptly because it was suspected that an informer was present; on other occasions there were whispered and cryptic conversations, which only the initiated understood.

My parents had attended church schools, and would call themselves Christians. At my mother's instigation, my brother and I sometimes went to a nearby Presbyterian church. My father was a nominal Catholic, occasionally attending church 'to do his duty'. My mother taught us to pray, and would pray with us at bedtime. She also taught us to give God thanks at mealtimes. Yet fear was lurking beneath the surface, and one day my mother decided to seek protection. She took me by night to see a man reputed to have supernatural powers. For a small fee he would call on beings from the spirit world that could allegedly protect us from those who were plotting evil against our family. When this did not seem to work, we went to another man and bought a charm, which he claimed would keep evil at bay. But this also failed, so we tried certain people said to have a ministry of prayer. Yet in spite of all our efforts we remained fearful, certain that evil was lurking around the corner, waiting to harm us if we let our guard down.

When we moved house in 1966 the church to which we had been attached was a long way off, and our attendance went from infrequent to sporadic. However, a Baptist church held morning services for children and as it was more convenient we started attending. It was at these services that I began to learn verses from the Bible. A couple of American missionaries lived up the road from our new home, and we began attending their Sunday School classes. Here, Scripture began to become real to me, and I began to learn passages, which I would proudly recite when I got home. Sunday School was fun, but it had serious competition — our favourite Sunday activity of cycling in the local park. Sunday was our only free time to do this, and we always looked forward to it, and to riding on our neighbours' new bikes. We were torn between two activities, but eventually chose the Sunday School because attendance was growing rapidly and it was 'the place to be'.

Later, boys' and girls' clubs were started during the week. I was no needleworker, but I slowly graduated from making soft toys to quite intricate embroidery. More importantly, I was increasingly drawn to the Bible stories I heard, and I eventually earned my own Bible as a prize for reciting 100 verses.

The more I read the Bible, the more its message came home to me, and at eleven years of age I came to recognize that I was a sinner and that I needed to put my trust in the Lord Jesus Christ as my Saviour. In a very simple yet definite way I asked him to forgive me and to come into my life, quite certain that he would do as he had promised. In the following months, I steadily grew to appreciate that I had become a child of God.

When I was twelve years old I went away to boarding school in Aburi, a small town in the eastern region of Ghana. Despite the excitement of a new life I was often terribly homesick, yet the prayers my mother had taught me years before were a great help and comfort to me, and I had a deepening sense of God's presence. At the same time, I was discovering who I was — a vivacious and mischievous teenager who enjoyed her popularity. There were times when I got into more than my share of trouble at school. When I was sixteen, a play entitled *Of six who died,* which portrayed people facing God's judgement, made a major impression on me. As I thought through its implications, I wondered how much of my life would count for anything. That night, I rededicated my life to God, determined to find and follow his will. This major step forward brought great joy, especially as I was reminded of God's goodness in bringing me into a living relationship with him.

Realizing that I had been living a very mediocre Christian life, I embarked on a plan. As the quiet girls at school were thought to be the good ones, I stifled my natural exuberance for a whole year. My friends wondered what had happened — and were not in the least impressed by my explanation. Through this episode, I learned that God did not want me to try to ape others, but to be myself, and to allow him to refine what he had created. The difference was remarkable, and I soon found myself an active member of a singing group, which also placed great emphasis on the value of prayer.

In 1975 I started medical training at the University of Ghana. I graduated in 1981 and completed my pre-registration year of training and experience. I then moved to the UK to gain more experience and to begin training in anaesthesia. After I gained my fellowship I had the privilege of working in Hong Kong for a few years. The experience of living and working in different countries among different peoples expanded my view of life. Naturally, I gained more experience as a doctor, but there were big lessons of life to grapple with too. I grew to understand that our worth as people comes entirely from God, with many things uniting us as human beings, and that differences that might seem to separate us were causes for celebrating the diversity which adds colour to God's creation.

In my work, I am acutely aware of how helpless some people become when sickness strikes, and I long to show them the true source of spiritual life and health. I gradually realized that I can reach my patients through prayer, asking God to touch their lives, and over the years this has become an important part of my work. In particular, I continue to be deeply moved when I have to look after patients who are suffering, and I am constantly experiencing the value of obeying the biblical command to 'mourn with those who mourn'.[39] It is a special joy to care for colleagues who are ill, some asking me to do so because they know I am a Christian. Praying with them before their surgery has been an enriching experience, and there have been many occasions when non-Christian colleagues have asked me to pray for them. In these and other ways I am learning to trust God more and more for his wisdom in doing the work to which he has called me.

I find no conflict between science and what I read in Scripture. When I observe the order and the evidence of design that exist in nature, together with the precision with which life is structured, I cannot but acknowledge that there is a creative Designer who has a purpose for his universe. The laws of nature, a part of the manual for the proper and optimum functioning of nature, pre-existed their discovery by researchers. Even now, with the enormous advances we have made in science, including the medical sciences, the paucity of our knowledge is evident as the struggle to find the cause and cure of diseases continues. For me the existence of God creates no conflict: 'By faith we understand that the universe was formed at God's command,'[40] and science must answer to him. In addition to design in the universe pointing to God I have experienced the reality of a relationship with him, a staggering reality; the Designer of the universe has chosen to have a relationship of love with me.

My personal experience of God's love convinces me of his existence, and before such undeserved and unconditional love I bow in awe. It is equally true of my life as a scientist and as a Christian that I see 'but a poor reflection as in a mirror',[41] yet I have an assurance that one day things will become perfectly clear.

As I look back on my life, I can trace God's goodness in delivering me from a situation of living in fear of life itself and what it might mete out to me, and in bringing me to trust in the living Lord Jesus Christ, who died for me and lives to bring me a liberty I could never have without him. For a deep inner sense that I have a living relationship with him, and that he is guiding my steps through this life to the glorious life which lies beyond it, I give him all the glory.

6.

From protons to people

When the Human Genome Project's 2001 report was published, spelling out the three billion letters that make up the human genetic code, the *Daily Telegraph*'s Science Editor was understandably excited: 'A new era in science began yesterday... The dark age of biology has now ended... The implications are immense.'[1] The *Daily Mail's* Science Correspondent went even further: 'The end of disease could be only 50 years away after scientists unveiled the genetic "book of life" yesterday in what was hailed as the most important discovery in the history of mankind.'[2]

One fascinating piece of new information was that instead of the 140,000 genes previously thought necessary to make, maintain and repair a human being, it takes only just over 30,000. This is only a few more than those of a mouse, a housefly or a worm, while even a tiny plant such as thale cress has 25,498. Statistics such as these led Francis Collins, head of the American arm of HGP, to tell *USA Today*, 'If you're judging the complexity of an organism by the number of genes it has, we've just taken a big hit in the pride department.'[3]

The discovery of a low human gene count raised what is probably the most intriguing question to emerge from the 'book of life': how do relatively few genes build and maintain an organism as complex as a human being, which has between

90,000 and 300,000 proteins and 100 trillion highly specialized cells? This conundrum may keep geneticists and others busy for generations to come, but atheism is faced with an even greater one — the existence of life itself. What exactly is it? How did it originate?

Accidental information?

In 1953, the British biophysicist Francis Crick walked into his local pub in Cambridge and announced, 'We have found the secret of life.' What he actually meant was that he and his colleague James Watson had discovered the now famous double helical structure of deoxyribonucleic acid (mercifully known as DNA!). Although it is a relatively simple molecule with just four basic components, it governs all biological reproduction and the transmission of all inherited characteristics.

DNA houses an amazing amount of genetic information. For example, all the data needed to specify the design of a human being, including such features as hair, skin, eyes and height, and to determine the arrangements of over 200 bones, 600 muscles, 10,000 auditory nerve fibres, two million optic nerve fibres, 100 billion brain cell nerves and 400 billion feet of blood vessels and capillaries is packed into a unit weighing less than a few thousand-millionths of a gram, and several thousand million million times smaller than the smallest piece of functional machinery ever used by man. It has been said that on the same scale all the information needed to specify the design of every living species that has ever existed on our planet could be held in a teaspoon, with enough room left over for all the information in every book ever written.[4]

To give another illustration, a single chromosome contains the information equivalent of up to 500 million words; at 400 words to a page it would take 5,435 books, each 230 pages long, to record the information contained in a single chromosome.[5] Yet one fertilized human egg contains forty-six chromosomes, and it would need a library of just over a quarter of a million of these 230-page long books to contain its information. As if that were not amazing enough, this staggering amount of information is encoded in a 'language' that has only four 'letters' and whose 'dictionary' contains only sixty-four three-letter words. I have discussed this in much greater detail in *Does God Believe in Atheists?*,[6] but it is worth noting here that DNA can make copies of itself only with the help of specific enzymes that in turn can be produced only by the controlling DNA molecule. In other words, as each is dependent on the other, both must be present before any copy can be made. Nobody has yet come up with a 'natural' (that is, atheistic) picture of how this could happen.

All of this raises a serious problem for the atheist: how did this staggering amount of highly organized information come about unless it had an intelligent source? After all, information is not a material substance, but something altogether different and, as Berkeley law professor Phillip Johnson points out, 'A theory of life thus has to explain not just the origin of the matter but also the independent origin of the information.'[7]

Francis Crick is said to understand the nature of living substances 'as well as any man living',[8] yet after years of research he came to this conclusion: 'An honest man, armed with all the knowledge available to us now, could only state that in some sense the origin of life appears at the moment to be *almost a miracle*, so many are the conditions which would have to be satisfied to get it going'[9] (emphasis added).

As a hard-line atheist, Crick inserted 'almost' in order to sidestep God, yet he was sure that life could not possibly have arisen spontaneously here on earth. Forced to look elsewhere for a solution, he eventually opted for a version of panspermia, the theory that germs of life are to be found all over the universe. In *Life Itself: Its Origin and Nature*, he promotes the exotic idea that micro-organisms first reached our planet 'in the head of an unmanned spaceship sent to earth by a higher civilization which developed elsewhere some billions of years ago'.[10] He even discusses the possible design of the vehicle! Space invaders make exciting science fiction, but relocating the first spark of life somewhere else in the cosmos leaves us stranded in space with the basic question still unanswered.

Others determined to keep God out of the frame have come to equally bizarre conclusions. Harvard scientist George Wald, winner of the 1967 Nobel prize for physiology writes, 'When it comes to the origin of life on earth, there are only two possibilities: creation or spontaneous generation. Spontaneous generation was disproved 100 years ago, but that leads us to only one other conclusion: that of supernatural creation. *We cannot accept that* ... therefore *we choose to believe the impossible,* that life arose spontaneously by chance'[11] (emphasis added). Notice that Wald comes to his conclusion not on the basis of evidence, but because his preconceived atheism forces him to rule God out regardless of where the evidence points. This is hardly the kind of thinking we should expect from a distinguished scientist.

Richard Dawkins takes the same line: 'Superficially, the obvious alternative to chance is an intelligent designer... I am afraid I shall give God very short shrift ... as an explanation of organized complexity he simply will not do.'[12] As all his thinking is pre-programmed to exclude God, he is forced to come up with an alternative. In *The Selfish Gene* he plumps for a self-replicating life form he calls 'the Replicator', which he says came into being by accident at some point in the earth's prehistory. He admits that such a thing is 'exceedingly improbable',[13] but in *The Blind Watchmaker* he sidesteps this by claiming, 'Given enough time, anything is possible.'[14]

Time as 'the hero of the plot' is a popular atheistic ploy, but it leaks like a sieve. In the first place, it is simply not true that 'Anything is possible', as there is no logical reason why even one state of affairs should ever come into existence, let alone life arising by accident. Secondly, even the most radical atheists are eventually forced to concede that there has simply never been enough time for this to happen. Writing in *Nature* magazine, Utah State University's Frank Salisbury discussed the staggering odds against the spontaneous production of a single gene. He asked his readers to imagine 10^{20} (one hundred million trillion) planets, each with an ocean two kilometres deep and fairly rich in gene-sized DNA fragments reproducing at the rate of one million times per second, with a mutation (change) occurring at each reproduction. Salisbury calculated that even under such favourable conditions it would take trillions of universes to have much chance of producing one single gene in four billion years, even if 10^{100} different DNA molecules could serve the same gene function.[15] Nobody proposing such a thing would ever get a seconder!

In *From Nothing to Nature*, Edgar Andrews paints a very different picture: 'The code of life exists because God thought it up and wrote it on the DNA molecules that control all forms of life.' Likening this to a composer using the 'code' of musical notes to create a great variety of compositions on a single musical instrument, he goes on to say, 'God has used a single substance, DNA, and a simple code of four symbols, to create the vast range of living things, from the simplest virus to the wonder of a human brain.' As he then adds, 'This could have no more been the work of chance or accident than could the *Moonlight Sonata* be played by mice running up and down the keyboard of my piano!'[16]

The Bible's version of the origin of life uses none of atheism's mathematical manipulation but says that a God of infinite power, intelligence, wisdom and imagination brought all the dazzling complexity of life into existence exactly as and when he chose to do so. Having first created the earth 'formless and empty',[17] he stocked it with vegetation, land animals, fish and

birds 'according to their various kinds'.[18] He then 'formed ...
man from the dust of the ground and breathed into his nostrils
the breath of life, and ... man became a living being'.[19]

'The man who murdered God'

If we ignore what the Bible says, and assume, for the sake of
argument, that inanimate matter could have arisen out of
nothing, and that life came into being by spontaneous generation, we are still a long way short of accounting for the vast
number of species living on our planet, and even further away
from explaining the origin of *Homo sapiens,* the most sophisticated of them all. How did we get from protons to people?
With God out of the way, one model has ruled the roost for
nearly 150 years. Until then, it had been generally believed
that the entire cosmos had a transcendent, intelligent Designer,
and that the wonders of nature reflected his wisdom, imagination and power. But in the middle of the nineteenth century
the idea of God's creative activity was pushed aside and replaced by one in which the role of Deity was replaced by the
roll of dice.

The story of how this happened has an unlikely beginning.
In 1825 a Shropshire doctor sent his son to study medicine at
Edinburgh University. With little or no interest in the subject,
the young man squandered two years there before his father
suggested a career in the ministry of the Church of England. As
this seemed as good an idea as any, he switched to Cambridge
University to read classics, mathematics and theology. Although
he was later to call his years at Cambridge 'worse than wasted'
(he did poorly in classics and made a mess of mathematics), his
theology results enabled him to graduate with a B.A. degree in
1831. With little or no stomach for becoming a clergyman, and
now at a loose end, he received an unexpected invitation to

serve as a naturalist on the Admiralty vessel H.M.S. *Beagle*, soon to embark on a five-year surveying expedition. Although he had no training in the subject (his main leisure interests were shooting and beetle-collecting) he accepted, and on 27 December 1831 the *Beagle* set sail.

As the expedition went on, he developed a growing interest in geology and zoology, and sent a stream of specimens, fossils and notes back to his close friend the Rev John Henslow, who had first interested him in the natural sciences. On his return to England in 1836 he found that Henslow had shared some of his letters and reports with high-profile historians and scientists. This led him into influential circles, including membership of London's prestigious Athenaeum Club. In the following years he worked on various writing projects, including the official journal of the *Beagle's* expedition, *Geology of Volcanic Islands* and *Geology of South America*. Eight years studying barnacles left him with a work that ran to four volumes — and 10,000 barnacles to dispose of!

During this time, he also began to fill out earlier notes he had made on another subject that had increasingly fascinated him. For some years he had questioned the fixity of species, a theory generally accepted as agreeing with the Bible's teaching that God had created a vast variety of different creatures with characteristics suited to their environment. Instead, he had a growing conviction that new species could arise naturally, by descent from pre-existing ones. Encouraged by Charles Lyell, a qualified lawyer who became the most influential (though amateur) geologist of his day, he collected his ideas into a massive manuscript, and in 1859 a condensed version was published. Its title was *The Origin of Species by Means of Natural Selection* or *the Preservation of Favoured Races in the Struggle for Life*. It is now commonly known as *The Origin of Species* or simply *Origin*. Its subject matter is usually given the broad title of 'evolution'. We all know the author's name, and on the last day of 1999 *TIME* Magazine made this dramatic assessment of his influence: 'Charles Darwin didn't want to murder God. But he did.'[20]

From doubt to dogma

As a matter of fact, there was nothing new in much of what Darwin wrote in *Origin*. Many ancient cultures believed that all living creatures, and even life itself, were the result of purely natural phenomena. The ancient Norse, for example, believed that the first living beings were the giant Ymir and the original cow Audumla, both of which were gradually formed when a warm wind from Muspellsheim, a southern land of fire, caused ice to melt.

Seven chapters of *Origin* were taken up with *microevolution*, the theory that in organisms of the same species different characteristics emerge as the result of adaptation to their particular environment. Darwin had some early thoughts about this when the *Beagle* visited the Galapagos Islands in the Pacific Ocean, where he noted many varieties of turtles and what later became known as 'Darwin's finches'. Although he called this his 'special theory', there was nothing revolutionary about it, as the development of new varieties within species had been known for at least 2,000 years. Today, nobody questions gradual changes occurring within species by perfectly natural processes, by deliberate crossbreeding or by other forms of genetic manipulation.

What really upset the apple cart was Darwin's 'general theory' of *macroevolution*, which proposed a mechanism to show how life forms could have gradually evolved from a single primitive cell. Twelve years after the publication of *Origin*, Darwin guaranteed his place in history by insisting that humans, too, are descended 'from some less highly organized form'.[21]

This was a biological bombshell, yet Darwin himself was by no means certain that he had got it right. At one stage he wrote, 'I cannot remember a single first-formed hypothesis which had not after a time to be given up or greatly modified,'[22] and in a letter to a friend he called the whole thing 'grievously too hypothetical'.[23] His publisher thought that Darwin's general theory was 'as absurd as though one should contemplate a fruitful union between a poker and a rabbit',[24] and the editor of the prestigious London-based *Quarterly Review* suggested that Darwin might be better employed writing a book on pigeons! By 1872, when the last edition during his lifetime was published, Darwin had become 'plagued with self-doubt',[25] but because the intellectual climate of his day was veering away from supernatural models to materialistic ones, his 'big idea' spread like wildfire, and within twenty years of the publication of *Origin* Darwin's general theory was all the rage. As a modern publication puts it, 'The world jumped at Darwin because it was ready for Darwin.'[26]

The modern geneticist Theodosius Dobzhansky says that *Origin* 'marked a turning point in the intellectual history of mankind' and 'ushered in a new understanding of man and his place in the universe',[27] while Julian Huxley called evolution 'the most powerful and the most comprehensive idea that has ever arisen on earth'.[28] Its message now dominates the world's philosophical, scientific and cultural landscape; as the modern author Michael Denton says, 'No other theory in recent times has done more to mould the way we view ourselves and our relationship to the world around us.'[29]

No longer limited to biology, Darwinian evolution has become a total philosophy that claims to explain the origin and development of everything within a closed universe, leaving 'God' as the irrelevant invention of those who have failed to understand the obvious. Richard Dawkins uses a gratuitous insult to drive the point home: 'It is absolutely safe to say that, if you meet somebody who claims not to believe in evolution, that person is ignorant, stupid or insane (or wicked, but I'd rather not consider that.)'[30]

The American zoologist George Gaylord Simpson explains what Darwinianism is saying: 'In the world of Darwin, man ... is in the fullest sense a part of nature and not apart from it. He is *akin,* not figuratively but literally, *to every living thing.*'[31] For the macroevolutionist, all living species, from ants to antelopes, carrots to cockatoos, eels to elephants, grass to gorillas, snakes to sparrows — and hummingbirds to humans — are the result, not of conscious, imaginative design, but of chance variations arising from one original spark of life which in some way or other appeared on our planet at an unknown point in prehistory. As the British author and researcher Ian Taylor confirms, 'The idea that life on earth originated from a single-celled organism and then progressed onwards and upwards in ever-increasing complexity to culminate in man himself is what the theory of evolution is all about.'[32]

What do you make of this? So many people accept this scenario without question that in 1996 a *Sunday Times* writer said, 'We are all docile evolutionists.'[33] This is hardly surprising. Almost every modern biology textbook begins by assuming evolution, and any student in a college, school or university who takes another line is likely to be written off as a bit of an oddity. Virtually every radio and television programme tackling 'nature' takes evolution for granted. On the surface at least, this seems to confirm what Richard Dawkins wrote in *The Blind Watchmaker:* 'Although atheism might have been logically tenable before Darwin, Darwin made it possible to be an intellectually fulfilled atheist.'[34] But is this the case? Have you been pushed into thinking that macroevolution is so scientifically sound there is no point in disputing it? If so, you have gone further than many evolutionists. Writing in the *Journal of Sedimentary Petrology* in 1996, Kenneth Hsu admitted, 'Darwinism ... is not a "natural law" formulated on the basis of factual evidence, but a dogma, reflecting the dominant social philosophy of the last century.'[35] Put more simply, macroevolution is not a fact but an article of faith. If you have signed up to it, read on!

Gently does it?

In arguing against the idea that new species come about by chance, nobody would suggest that this happens suddenly. Darwin's unique contribution to evolutionism was to come up with what he believed to be a natural mechanism that produces countless tiny changes *over a vast period of time*. The general idea goes under the name of 'natural selection', and says that organisms preying on each other slowly eliminate the weaker ones and gradually produce 'the survival of the fittest', a phrase coined by the British philosopher Herbert Spencer in 1865. At the same time, these survivors gradually develop new characteristics in order to cope with their environment, and when these become a permanent feature a new species emerges as part of what Darwin called 'progress towards perfection'.

It is important to notice that, for all his theorizing, Darwin admitted that he could not point to a single case in which natural selection had in fact changed one species into another. This was a damaging confession, and in the years following his death in 1882 his general theory gradually lost support, but in the 1930s geneticists and others gave it a massive shot in the arm. Now called Neo-Darwinism, the new line of approach switched attention to an organism's genes, and said that radical alterations (mutations) at that level would lead natural selection to retain only those new genes favourable to the organism concerned. This idea has since become so popular that Sylvia Baker, a respected writer on the subject, says, 'The modern theory of evolution ... stands or falls on this question of mutation.'[36] Nobody questions that mutations take place — but do they produce the effects evolutionists claim? Here are four impressive indications that they do not.

1. Natural mutations are extremely rare. One specialist suggests that they occur once in approximately every ten million duplications of DNA, which would be far too seldom to drive macroevolution. The number needed to do this is so great that the renowned zoologist Pierre Grassé wrote that if such a thing happened, 'Miracles would become the rule... There is no law against daydreaming, but science must not indulge in it.'[37]

2. Far from producing strong new genes that would promote evolution, mutations are almost universally harmful, weakening the genetic structure or destroying it altogether. The Canadian medical professor Magnus Verbrugge likens a random mutation to a typing error and points out, 'Typing errors rarely improve the quality of a written message; if too many occur, they may even destroy the information contained in it.'[38] After untold thousands of experiments over a century of research, geneticists have not been able to produce a single case of a mutation that was clearly and positively beneficial, other than at a very localized level.

3. The third problem underlines the first two. Assuming, as an example, that an insect's wing requires only five genes (a very low estimate) and accepting the scientific view that only one mutation in 1,000 is not harmful, the probability of even two non-harmful mutations occurring is one in one thousand million million. As Verbrugge comments, 'For all practical purposes, there is no chance that all five mutations will occur within the life cycle of a single organism.'[39] The French biologist Remy Chauvin, Professor in the Laboratory of Animal Sociology at René Descartes University in Paris, agrees: 'Since those forms of animal life which mutate very rapidly have remained the same during tens of millions of generations, mutation could not be considered the motor of evolution.'[40]

4. As mutations are by nature random mistakes, damaging the genetic code in the course of copying it, how can they be seen as an engine of Darwin's 'progress towards perfection'? Malcolm Bowden makes the point well: 'The reliance of evolutionists upon damaging mutations as the means by which evolution progresses is rather like saying that using a hammer on a number of watches will eventually improve one of them! ... The mutation theory just does not work.'[41]

These four devastating blows to the idea that mutations could trigger biological progress are linked to the question of genetic information. On the video *From a Frog to a Prince* physicist Lee Spetner says, 'All the mutations that have been examined on a molecular level show that the organism has lost information, not gained it... Experimentally, one has not found a single mutation that one can point out that actually adds information. In fact, *every mutation I have seen reduces information.*'[42] This knocks a huge hole in the idea of beneficial mutations, which takes another direct hit towards the end of the video when Richard Dawkins is asked, 'Can you give an example of a genetic mutation or an evolutionary process that can be seen to increase the information in the genome?' In response to this basic and straightforward question Dawkins turns his head this way and that for no less than eleven seconds before ignoring the question altogether and speculating on what one might have seen 'about 300 million years ago'.[43] It is a very telling fumble.

What Darwin never knew

In the nineteenth and early twentieth centuries biologists knew little about biochemistry and even less about microbiology. Scientists from Darwin's day generally settled for the idea that a living cell was a relatively simple thing that had somehow emerged from the inert ingredients of some kind of chemical 'soup', and that a vast number of small, random changes eventually produced the amazing variety of living species we now see all around us.

There are two problems here for the price of one. The first is that there is no such thing as a simple living cell; Richard Dawkins tells us that the nucleus of a cell contains 'a digitally coded database larger, in information content, than all 30 volumes of the *Encyclopaedia Britannica* put together'.[44] In *Evolution: A Theory in Crisis,* Michael Denton says that if we were to magnify a single cell a thousand million times until it was twenty kilometres in diameter, we would see 'an object resembling an immense automated factory … carrying out almost as many unique functions as all the manufacturing activities of man on earth'.[45] That is such a staggering sentence that I suggest you read it again!

A cell consists of thousands of proteins, each one made up of chains of hundreds of amino acids organized in a very precise sequence. According to evolutionists, the first living cells came into being when, over millions of years, amino acids accidentally slotted into the right sequence, then somehow locked together to form the first proteins. Yet Francis Crick admits that the probability of getting even *one* protein by chance would be one in 10^{260}.[46] and calls this number 'quite beyond our everyday comprehension'.[47] As mathematicians usually consider anything with odds greater than one in 10^{150} to be impossible for practical purposes, believing that even one protein came into being by chance is a stupendous leap of faith. As G. A. Kerkut of the Department of Physiology and Biochemistry at the University of Southampton neatly notes, evidence of this happening is 'not available'.[48]

The second problem is the fact that microbiology and biochemistry have now revealed systems that could not possibly have arisen by the gradual step-by-step process that evolution demands. Whatever his doubts about other details of his 'general theory', Darwin was confident enough to issue this challenge: 'If it could be demonstrated that any complex organ existed which could not possibly have been formed by numerous, successive, slight modifications, *my theory would absolutely break down*'[49] (emphasis added). In his runaway best seller *Darwin's Black Box*,[50] first published in 1996, the American biochemist Michael Behe demonstrates that biochemistry has done precisely that while opening up a microscopic world of which Darwin knew nothing.

Behe draws attention to systems that are 'irreducibly complex' in that all their parts are interdependent and have to be in place before they will work. As a mechanical illustration, he uses a mousetrap, consisting of a flat wooden platform, a metal hammer, a spring, a sensitive catch and a metal bar to hold the hammer back when the trap is set. None of these parts has any trapping ability, yet each is essential for the trap to function; if even one was missing, a mouse could safely dance all over it. As Behe then shows, irreducibly complex systems include vision, the human immune system and the one that causes blood-clotting.

The last of these is particularly fascinating. When any other container of fluid springs a leak, the fluid drains out without resistance, yet when the human body's pressurized fluid system is punctured, clotting slows or stops the flow of blood. This clotting is a complex, multi-step process that utilizes proteins with no other function besides clotting, and each of which depends on an enzyme to activate it. The problem for the atheist is this: which came first, the protein or the enzyme? Not the protein, which cannot function without being switched on by the enzyme. But why would the enzyme evolve if there were no protein for it to activate? What is more, the blood-clotting system (which is massively more complex than I have summarized here) could not have evolved over millions of years, as all the creatures concerned would have bled to death before the system was ever perfected. Where does this leave Darwin's admission that if this could be demonstrated, 'my theory would absolutely break down'?

'Dem bones, dem bones...'

Another major flaw in the macroevolution model appears when we delve into history. In his book *Icons of Evolution*, the American scholar Jonathan Wells lists ten items commonly offered as evidence for Darwinianism. Four of these relate to fossils, said by one atheistic spokesman to constitute '100 million facts that prove evolution beyond any doubt whatsoever'.[51] Before Darwin hit the headlines the fossil record had been interpreted quite differently, but everything changed after *Origin* had taken hold, and within twenty-five years of its publication, 'Evolution had become scientific orthodoxy and from then on any fossil find had to be interpreted to fit in with accepted evolutionary theory.'[52] Notice the 'had to' — far from providing proof that macroevolution had taken place, the meaning of fossil finds had to be tweaked to match the theory that it had.

Frustrated by the fact that fossils did not show the gradual organic chain between species that his theory demanded, Darwin decided that the explanation lay in 'the extreme imperfection of the geological record'.[53] A century and a half later we have a vastly greater number of fossils to work on, but according to David Raup, Curator of Geology at Chicago's Field

Museum of Natural History, 'The situation hasn't changed much. The record of evolution is still surprisingly jerky and, ironically, we now have *even fewer examples of evolutionary transition than we had in Darwin's time…* Darwin's problem has not been alleviated'[54] (emphasis added).

The 'Fossils prove evolution' idea gets off to the worst possible start in the so-called 'Cambrian explosion' of remains found in layers of earth said to be about 600 million years old. The problem here is that they represent nearly every major group of organisms alive today, yet suddenly 'appear' with no evolutionary ancestors to back up the theory of gradual development. Phillip Johnson describes the Cambrian explosion as 'the single greatest problem which the fossil record poses for Darwinianism',[55] while even Richard Dawkins admits, 'It is as though they were just planted there, without any evolutionary history.'[56]

Nor does the fossil evidence become more convincing as we move up the geological column. Evolutionists tell us that over a period of 100 million years invertebrates (life forms with no spinal cord or backbone) evolved into vertebrates — but not one transitional form has ever been found. We are also told that in the course of thirty million years fish evolved into amphibians, but nobody has been able to find any trace of a 'fishibian'. Nor is there any link between amphibians and reptiles. Evolutionists draw yet another blank when they try to bridge the gap between reptiles and mammals, which are clearly distinguished by the structure of the ear- and jaw-bones. Evolutionists' prize exhibit in trying to bridge the gap between reptiles and birds is *Archaeopteryx*, but the case crumbles as soon as it is examined closely and the respected evolutionist Ernst Mayr admits that an animal halfway between a reptile and a bird 'would not have the slightest chance of escaping elimination through selection'.[57] What is more, fossils of two birds found in rock strata which evolutionists claim to be seventy-five million years *earlier* than *Archaeopteryx* make it impossible for it to be their ancestor.

Of all the 'missing links', none is more important to evolutionists than the one which would show that *Homo sapiens* had ape-like ancestors — we all know the joke about the monkey in the zoo asking its mate, 'Am I my keeper's brother?' — yet here, too, they are frustrated by the facts. We can illustrate this by listing seven of the strongest claims to have hit the headlines since Darwin's time:

- In 1857 so-called *Neanderthal Man* was widely touted as the vital 'missing link' between apes and humans, but the evidence against this has become so overwhelming that it is usually left out of modern textbooks and Neanderthal Man is now classified as human — a subspecies of *Homo sapiens.*
- In 1891-1892 bones found in the Far East seemed to point to *Java Man* as an upright, man-like ape, but it has since become clear that some of the fragments are from apes and some from humans.
- In 1912 a collection of bones found in Sussex was branded *Piltdown Man*, and for forty years they were hailed as 'the sensational missing link'.[58] Today, everybody knows they were part of a gigantic hoax, a 400-year-old human skull attached to an orang-utan's jaw.
- In 1922 a single tooth said to be between 1.7 million and 5.5 million years old was unearthed by an amateur geologist working in Nebraska. The international press hailed it as powerful proof of the link between humans and apes, but six years later it was found to have belonged to a pig-like animal known as a peccary.
- In 1959 the news media dubbed a skull found in the Olduvai Gorge, East Africa, *'Nutcracker Man'* and *National Geographic* hailed it as new evidence of human

descent from the ape, but the archaeologists who made the find later withdrew their claims and it is now generally accepted as being that of an extinct ape.
• In 1974 a tiny skeleton without hands or feet, nicknamed *Lucy* and said to be over three million years old, was found in the Great Rift Valley, Ethiopia. Lucy was widely promoted in the media as having been the first ape to walk upright, but experts have long since shredded the claims made on her behalf.

Hundreds of other candidates have been proposed as the elusive 'ape-men', but none has been able to survive honest analysis. In *Beyond the Ivory Tower,* Lord Zuckerman wrote, 'If man evolved from an ape-like creature, he did so without leaving a trace of that evolution in the fossil record.'[59] The attempt to make the fossils spell 'Darwinism' is so futile that New Age spokesman Jeremy Rifkin was forced to concede, 'What the "record" shows is nearly a century of fudging and finagling by scientists to conform with Darwin's notions, to no avail. Today the millions of fossils stand as very visible, ever-present reminders of the paltriness of the arguments and the overall shabbiness of the theory that marches under the banner of evolution.'[60] Rifkin is an evolutionist, but even he admits that leaning on fossils is futile.

I have gone into greater detail about macroevolution in *Does God Believe in Atheists?,*[61] but we leave the last word here about fossil links with Dr Colin Patterson, Senior Palaeontologist at the British Museum of National History: 'I will lay it on the line — there is not one such fossil for which one could make a watertight argument... It is easy enough to make up stories of how one form gave rise to another, and to find reasons why the stages should be favoured by natural selection. But such stories are not part of science, for there is no way of putting them to the test.'[62]

Call Sir Ghillean Prance

One of the world's leading botanists, Sir Ghillean Prance has had something in the order of fifty plants named after him. After heading up the New York Botanical Garden's Institute of Economic Botany, he moved to London as Director of the Royal Botanic Gardens, Kew.

I grew up with an instinctive love of nature, and from an early age decided that my career goal was to be a botanist. I can recall long hours spent roaming the moors of Scotland or the hills and woods of the Cotswolds looking for rare plants and observing the works of nature. My curiosity ranged from looking at stars through the old family telescope to dissecting a fish I had caught. However, plants always fascinated me the most and, with the help of two elderly maiden aunts who were keen amateur botanists, I soon learned to use books to key out the identification of any plant the name of which I did not know. Even from a young age, I believed that the wonders of nature were too great to have come about by chance, and in my own simple way I prayed and thanked God for it all.

I was fortunate to be sent to Malvern College, where my interest in botany increased by the day under the enthusiastic leadership of the biology master, Bill Wilson, who sometimes took those boys interested in natural history all over southern England to look for rare plants, butterflies or birds.

College chapel was compulsory at Malvern, and during school holidays I also went with my mother to the local village church. At that time, several books about the Christian faith began to influence me, especially *Mere Christianity* and *The Screwtape Letters*, both by C. S. Lewis. In fact, I became quite a fan of this Oxford professor who became a Christian comparatively late in his career and was then able to use his intellect to explain matters of faith in a meaningful, simple, yet deep manner.

Given my love of botany and my growing knowledge about plants, it was inevitable that the next step in my career was to read botany at

university. With my moderate and uneven academic record I was fortunate to end up at Oxford, but a much bigger surprise was soon to
follow. I accepted the invitation of a fellow student to attend a service
arranged by the Christian Union (OICCU) at the University Church. I
had never heard the Christian message so clearly expounded, and
went home inspired and thinking about what I had heard for the rest
of the week. I did not need an invitation to go the next week, especially to hear the sermon — the part of the service I had usually found
so dull that I preferred thinking about the plants I had collected that
week! It was on my third Sunday at Oxford that I made a definite
commitment to the God I knew through his creation and had already
learned much about through reading and through my mother's strong
faith. Accepting the redeeming work of Jesus Christ as my personal
Saviour radically changed my life and has ever since influenced the
way in which I live.

During my first year at Oxford, I wrestled with priorities between
botany and my new-found faith. I spent much time attending Bible
studies and prayer meetings, both within my college group and with
the university's Christian Union. This built up my faith and taught me
the importance of the Bible as a guide to living, but I soon began to
wonder whether God wanted me to continue my intended career as
a botanist or go into full-time Christian service as a pastor or missionary.

I spent my next summer holiday helping at an evangelistic beach
mission in Frinton, Essex, rather than collecting plants on the moors
of Scotland — something most of my family found completely out of
character! — and it was there that I met and fell in love with Anne
Hay. We married three years later and she has been my greatest
supporter and help throughout my career.

Anne's father was the rector of a church in Norwich, a former missionary in Egypt, a fine Christian and a wise counsellor. As I discussed
with him my search for God's will for my life, his constant theme was
that God had not given me so much knowledge and talent in botany
for nothing and that I should use it in his service. I gradually realized
that to be a Christian witness in the world of science was just as

important and strong a calling from God as one to any other work, so I continued my studies in botany and, after graduation, went on to study for a doctorate in tropical botany in the Oxford Forestry Department. This led me on to a career in tropical botany and rainforest exploration.

God was good to me, for before I had begun to look for a job I was offered two, one in East Africa and the other in New York, but for work in South America. I accepted the second of these, and began by spending three months in Suriname in northern South America, followed by a year in New York working up the results of the expedition and continuing research on the plant family I had studied for my doctoral thesis. This was the beginning of twenty-five years of work for the New York Botanical Garden.

I still remember the excitement of my first encounter with the rainforest in Suriname. To enter the majestic, tall forest was like entering a cathedral, and both are indeed to the glory of God. Each tree in the rainforest looks slightly different from its neighbour because of the incredible diversity of species. To a botanist like me it was a paradise, with so many unfamiliar species of plant to learn and even some that did not yet have names and needed to be described as new species and given a scientific Latin name. The time in Suriname with an experienced botanist as expedition leader confirmed my interest in tropical botany and in tropical rainforests, and for the next twenty-five years I was a frequent visitor to the Brazilian rainforest, where I took part in or organized more than ten major expeditions. I have therefore had the privilege of seeing remarkable examples of God's creation, and of studying the way in which so many plants function and interact with various animals.

My work for the New York Botanical Garden and in Brazil led to the assembling of over 30,000 collections of plants and to the writing of many scientific and general articles, as well as several books. As a result of this success I was gradually promoted through the ranks of the garden and in 1982 ended up as the Senior Vice-President in charge of all the science programmes and also director of their then new

Institute of Economic Botany. We set up the latter to work on some
future solutions for the rainforest through sustainable rather than destructive use, and the institute has gone on from strength to strength.
In 1988, I was offered one of the world's very top jobs in botany, as
Director of the Royal Botanic Gardens, Kew. God has really honoured
the commitment I made to serve him wherever he led.

In 1973, when I was stationed in Brazil for two years to set up the
postgraduate course in botany in the Amazon region, I accompanied
the course members in ecology and environmental impact on their
one-week field trip to part of the newly constructed Trans-Amazon
highway, a project designed to resettle starving people from the
drought-stricken north-eastern region of Brazil. We were all horrified
at the environmental disaster that we encountered. The settlers had
cut down large areas of forest, but most were not able to grow their
crops well, and already some had gone back to their home states.
This trip made me realize what had begun to happen to the rainforest. I became deeply concerned about environmental issues, and
my future research became much more involved in applied issues
and in the search for alternatives to deforestation, such as the extrac-
tion of non-timber forest products.

This change of research emphasis brought my botanical work and
my Christian faith much closer together. I began to look more closely
at both the reasons for such environmental destruction and at the
wonders of God's creation as revealed in the Bible. To my surprise, I
found many biblical reasons for taking better care of God's creation,
and have been involved with Christian earth-keeping ever since. For
example, we are told that 'The earth is the LORD's and everything in
it.'[63] The creation around us belongs to God, and he calls us to be its
caretakers. So far, the human race has not done a good job, but Christians, who know the Creator and have a personal relationship with
him through Christ, should be at the forefront of protecting creation.

I have found the creation that I study to be a wonder of different
interactions of beetles, pollinating water lilies, animals dispersing seed
around the forest, intricate interaction between predators and prey,

and competition to occupy a certain niche in the environment. To me, this all reveals the miracle of the created order, which cannot possibly have come about just by chance. Nature simply cannot be reduced to the study of the molecule of DNA, as reductionist scientists such as Richard Dawkins seek to do. It is the freedom of interaction God gave to different organisms that has made creation such a wonderful and complex system, the study of which confirms rather than detracts from my certainty that there is a personal and intelligent power behind it all. That power has been revealed to us by the work of the Holy Spirit and through the redeeming work of Jesus Christ. The pity is that humans have used their freedom to rebel against God, one result of which is the horrendous environmental crisis that we face today.

None of my discovering and probing into the natural world has led me into the New Age error of worshipping creation. Instead, I have been led to the foot of the cross of Christ and through him to God, the Creator of all.

7.

Is ANDi one of us?

On 12 January 2001 the *Daily Telegraph* carried the dramatic headline: 'Scientists create first genetically modified monkey.'[1] The report that followed told of ground-breaking work carried out in the Primate Research Centre at the Oregon Health Sciences University in Portland. Professor Gerald Schatten, head of an American team of scientists, told the media that an extra marker gene, taken from a jellyfish, had been inserted into the unfertilized egg of a rhesus monkey, and that as a result ANDi (scientists' shorthand for 'inserted DNA' spelt backwards), the world's first genetically modified non-human primate, had been born on 2 October 2000.

The newspaper's Science Editor explained that the process had not been easy. Scientists genetically modified 220 eggs and then fertilized them to produce forty embryos and five pregnancies, which resulted in only three live births. When the baby monkeys were examined, only ANDi was found to contain the foreign gene. Even then it did not appear to be in use in his cells, and the team would have to wait for several years to see if ANDi passed his marker gene to his offspring. Professor Schatten cautiously suggested, 'There is a likelihood.' Outlining possible benefits from the experiment, he went on, 'Monkeys like ANDi will quickly but safely help us determine if innovative therapies are safe and effective... We're trying to help accelerate the day when innovative cures for disabling and devastating diseases are shown to be safe and effective.'

Although the experiment's claims were carefully qualified, the news of ANDi's birth triggered off a predictable furore. The campaign director of the British Union for the Abolition of Vivisection protested, 'It's shocking that this should happen at a time when there are worldwide calls to reduce or even abolish research using primates.' The pressure group Gene Watch warned, 'It's incredibly important that we take stock and don't allow it to lead to enormous animal suffering that isn't justified.' Others described the work as 'abhorrent' and accused the scientists of 'playing God', while Dr David King, co-ordinator of the Campaign Against Human Genetic Engineering, complained, 'This is yet another step on the slippery slope to designer babies. People should wake up to the fact that genetic engineering of people could be just around the corner.' This is not the place to argue about vivisection or genetic manipulation, but ANDi does raise this fundamental question: are human beings no more than the most sophisticated versions of animal life in general, and something for which no supernatural explanation is necessary?

Pantheism (the idea that god is everything and everything is god) goes beyond this and teaches that there is no difference between mankind and the rest of the universe, with human beings at one with all the rest of material reality, living or otherwise. In a 1997 *Daily Telegraph* feature, Astronomer Royal Sir Martin Rees rightly debunked astrology, yet claimed, 'The atoms in our bodies were once inside a star. We are literally stardust — or (in less romantic language) the nuclear waste from long-dead stars.'[2] The British zoo and club owner John Aspinall, who died in 2000, had no hesitation in lumping humans and nature together, with humans some way down the pecking order:

'I have an oak tree that is 500 years old. Its existence is more important than any human life because it supports 70 different species.'[3]

Most atheists would not go as far as Aspinall, but would still say that man is merely the highest form of animal, the latest arrival on the evolutionary scene. The British zoologist Desmond Morris takes this line in best-selling books such as *The Naked Ape*: 'Human beings are animals. They may prefer to think of themselves as fallen angels, but in reality they are risen apes.'[4] Although Richard Dawkins calls animals 'the most complicated and perfectly designed pieces of machinery in the known universe',[5] he says they are merely 'survival machines — robot vehicles blindly programmed to preserve the selfish molecules known as genes',[6] with human beings nothing more than 'jumped-up apes'.[7]

Poles apart

So much for the rhetoric; what is the reality? The celebrated British philosopher and radio personality Professor C. E. M. Joad once famously said that an average human body consists of enough fat for seven bars of soap, enough iron to make one medium-sized nail, enough sugar to sweeten seven cups of tea, enough lime to whitewash one chicken coop, enough phosphorous to tip 2,200 matches, enough magnesium to provide one dose of salts, enough potash to explode one toy cannon and enough sulphur to rid one average-sized dog of fleas.[8] This is all very fascinating, but hardly the whole story! Over ninety per cent of the human body consists of water and proteins, the rest being made up of inorganic salts, lipids (mainly fats), carbohydrates (sugar) and the two nucleic acids DNA and RNA. The smallest living units in the human body are some 100,000 billion cells, each one of which, according to Nobel Prize winner Linus Pauling, is 'more complex than New York City'.[9]

- The human body is amazing in its elegance and complexity, with over 200 bones, 600 muscles and 100 joints, all formed and positioned to function in perfect harmony. The human *hand* has been called 'the most perfect and precise instrument in a world bristling with the mechanical wonders of the atomic age'.[10] Powerful enough to wield a pickaxe, yet precise enough to conduct microsurgery, the human hand has over 652,000 nerve endings.
- The human *ear* has 24,000 'strings' and 20,000 'keys' (a grand piano has 240 and eighty-eight), enabling us to hear an amazing variety and range of sounds.
- The human *eye* can handle 500,000 messages simultaneously. Its tiny retina contains in the region of 130 million cells, some 124 million of them rod-shaped and distinguishing between light and darkness, and about six million cone-shaped and responding to eight million variations of colour.
- The human *heart* beats some 100,000 times a day, pumping blood through the body's 80,000 miles of blood vessels, which means that every day the blood cells travel an accumulated distance of 168 million miles, equivalent to 6,720 times around the world.
- A single drop of human *blood* contains more than 250,000 million blood cells, floating in a straw-coloured plasma containing thousands of different substances, including proteins, glucose, salts, vitamins, hormones and antibodies.
- The human *brain*, shaped somewhat like an oversized walnut, has been called 'the most complex and orderly aggregation of matter in the universe'.[11] It has about 100

billion neurones (nerve cells), roughly as many as there are trees in 2.7 million square miles of Amazonian rain forest, and each one of these cells has between 10,000 and 100,000 connections with other neurones. According to experts in the field, a human brain processes ten terabytes of data over an eighty-year lifetime, the equivalent in computer terms of 7,142,857,142,860,000 floppy discs.

• The human frame is wrapped in three integrated layers of flexible waterproofing, the *skin*, which also houses a sophisticated air-conditioning system with six miles of ducts one-fifth of an inch long, allowing water to escape from the body (in the form of sweat) yet never to enter it. It has been calculated that the number of living organisms on the skin of an average human being is roughly equivalent to the number of people currently living on our planet.

These are amazing facts, and difficult to square with evolutionist Stephen Jay Gould's notion that 'Human beings arose as … a kind of glorious cosmic accident resulting from the catenation [linking] of thousands of improbable events.'[12] Are you prepared to accept the idea that 100,000 billion cells of more than 100 different types could have accidentally arranged themselves in such way as to produce a fully operational human being? Dr C. Everett Koop, one-time Surgeon General of the United States, came to a very different conclusion: 'I never operate without having a subconscious feeling that there's no way this extraordinarily complicated mechanism known as the human body just happened to come up from slime and ooze… When I make an incision with my scalpel, I see organs of such intricacy that there simply hasn't been enough time for natural evolutionary processes to have developed them.'[13]

Hard-line evolutionists who place humankind at the top of an evolutionary tree that has five million known species of living organisms 'lower down' have another problem, because many of these have some superior features. Fish can live permanently under water and birds can fly without mechanical help. Man is easily outlived by the aldabra giant tortoise and outrun by many animals, including the cheetah, which from a standing start can reach forty-five miles an hour in two seconds. The common housefly's eyes can move ten times faster than a human's; the dolphin's hearing is vastly more acute; bats have built-in radar which enables them to fly safely in the dark; and a dog's sense of smell is to a man's what a symphony orchestra is to a tin whistle. Evolutionists commonly talk of humans being superior because of their greater brain size, but even this has to be qualified; the African elephant-snout fish has a brain weighing a lot more than a human's in relation to its body weight, while some monkeys have a brain twice as large as ours.

Yet even with this fine-tuning, few would deny that there is a radical difference between themselves and other earthly life forms. What other life form can write poetry, laugh at jokes, design computer software or solve crossword puzzles? The British writer Andrew Knowles is right: 'I am a mystery. I wake up in the morning. I find myself the sole occupant of a complex, sensitive and extremely useful body. I am also the proud owner of an intricate, imaginative and highly resourceful brain. Everything about me is unique: my face, my fingerprints, my "self". I am alive. I develop. I grow. So does a vegetable. But I am more than a vegetable. Vegetables don't fall in love, or read the paper, or go on holiday... I am a body with a brain; an animal. But — I am more than an animal. Animals don't peer through telescopes, or send birthday cards, or play chess, or cook ...'[14] Knowles is right, and there are many ways in which humanity's claim to uniqueness can be backed up. Three of them stand out a mile.

The likeness

Although they come at it from different angles, theists, atheists and agnostics are generally agreed that humans have greater dignity than any other beings. The *Second Humanist Manifesto*, published in 1973, claimed that there is 'no divine purpose or providence for the human species', yet its fifth article begins, 'The preciousness and dignity of the individual person is a central humanist value.' The word 'dignity' has links with the Latin *dignus*, meaning 'worthy', and an older Hebrew word, usually translated *gloria*, which means 'weightiness' and is used to describe something of special significance.

This claim to special value is deeply embedded in the human psyche. As R. C. Sproul puts it, 'We want our lives to count. We yearn to believe that in some way we are important. This inner drive is as intense as our need for water and oxygen. We argue about religion and politics, abortion, homosexuality, nuclear weapons and welfare programmes. We bicker about a host of things, but at one point we are all in harmony: every person among us wants to be treated with dignity and worth.'[15] At his inauguration on 20 January 2001, American President George W. Bush said that one of the nation's enduring values was 'its simple dream of dignity'.

A few days earlier the British press got all worked up over a couple who used their credit card to 'buy' six-month-old twins on the Internet, only to discover that the babies had already been sold — at half the price — to another couple who had been looking after them for two months. The Home Secretary condemned the whole idea of buying and selling babies and children as not only illegal but 'frankly revolting',[16] and public opinion was overwhelmingly on his side — but why? If babies are nothing more than Bertrand Russell's 'accidental collocations of atoms', what is wrong with buying, selling or part-exchanging them the way we do computers, cars or golf clubs?

The 'Internet twins' shared the spotlight with a report that, because of pressure on other facilities at a British hospital, seven corpses awaiting burial or cremation had been bundled in sheets and piled next to a rubbish bin in an unrefrigerated room. The *Daily Mail* carried a colour photograph of the scene on its front page, clear enough for one family to recognize the head of its deceased relative. The banner headline screamed, 'The Final Indignity', and a union official at the hospital expressed his concern at 'the lack of dignity afforded the dead'.[17] These are lofty words, but if we are nothing more than biological flukes, with no meaningful origin or destiny, why should we be treated — alive or dead — with any more dignity than dogs or dung?

Our sense of human dignity is often shown in our instinct to help those in need. As a contemporary author puts it, 'A society's maturity and humanity will be measured by the degree of dignity it affords to the disaffected and the powerless.'[18] On 8 November 1987 eleven people were killed and sixty-three injured when a terrorist bomb in Northern Ireland exploded shortly before a Remembrance Day service in Enniskillen, Co. Fermanagh. One of those injured was Ronnie Hill, a Presbyterian church elder who had taken a Bible class just before walking to the open-air service. Two days later, he lapsed into a coma from which he never recovered, yet he lived until 28 December 2000. For thirteen years, his wife maintained a daily bedside vigil, hoping against hope that he might recover. At Hill's funeral, the Bishop of Clogher called her behaviour 'a miracle of loving care'.[19] It was also a moving testimony to human dignity — his and hers.

This kind of behaviour is totally at odds with an atheistic view of man. If, as the popular scientist Jacob Bronowski put it, man is nothing more than 'a machinery of atoms',[20] why is a human being of any greater value than a snail, a snake or a sardine? If humankind began as an accident and will end in annihilation, how can any individual have 'preciousness and

dignity', or find a coherent basis for treating other human beings with respect, let alone with love, care or concern? In 1996
the BBC's George Alagiah reported on the civil war in Sierra
Leone. In dealing with some of the atrocities being committed,
he told of soldiers who came across a pregnant woman and
laid bets as to whether the unborn child was male or female.
When all the wagers had been struck they killed the woman, slit
her open and settled the bets. Hearing his report was almost
literally sickening — but why? Bronowski wrote, 'Man is not
different in kind from other forms of life... It seems self-evident
to say that man is a part of nature, in the same sense that a
stone is, or a cactus, or a camel.'[21] But if that is true, why is
what those soldiers did any worse than betting on the number
of pips in an orange, then slitting it open to find out?

There is no basis for human dignity in evolution, which involves a mechanism with no purpose or intention. The American scholar Marvin Lubenow pins this down: 'To value individual life in an evolutionary scenario is a contradiction in
concepts. In evolution, the individual has no value. It is the
population gene pool alone that has value, because it is out of
that gene pool that the alleged new species will develop as evolution proceeds over time. Since there are about six billion individuals making up the human gene pool today, it does not take
a rocket scientist to figure out how much value one individual
has. For all practical purposes, the value of the individual in an
evolutionary scenario is zero.'[22]

All this is highly relevant to the question of how we should
treat those in need. If we are all nothing more than the accidental, unplanned products of senseless evolution, 'gene machines'
in which the survival of the fittest is the only mark of progress,
why should we care for the senile, the chronically sick, the starving, or the educationally sub-normal? Surely the simplest (and
least expensive) way to help the evolutionary bandwagon along

would be to get rid of them — and the sooner the better! Can you seriously go along with that idea?

What a contrast when we presuppose the God of the Bible not merely as man's Creator, but as having created him 'in his own image'! Here is a powerful and coherent reason for believing in human dignity and for treating our fellow humans with respect and honour. As the pinnacle of creation, man has God's fingerprints all over him. He is invested with unique significance, made in God's moral and spiritual likeness and with the capacity to worship his Maker and to have a living and eternal relationship with him. The distinguished twentieth-century thinker Francis Schaeffer put it perfectly: 'No matter who I look at, no matter where he is, every man is created in the image of God as much as I am. So the Bible tells me who I am. It tells me how I am differentiated from all other things. I do not need to be confused, therefore, between myself and animal life or between myself and the complicated machines of the second half of the twentieth century. Suddenly I have value, and I understand how it is that God can have fellowship with me and give me revelation of a propositional nature... Any man, no matter who he is ... is made after the likeness of God. A man is of great value not for some less basic reason but *because of his origin*'[23] (emphasis added).

The bench-mark

The second sign of man's God-given distinction from the rest of creation is that everybody operates within some kind of ethical framework. This may differ from society to society and from one individual to another, but would you seriously deny that there is a radical difference between right and wrong? When a lawyer pleads that his client does not know the difference between right and wrong he is asking the court to believe that the accused is rationally defective, or in some other way incapable of acting as a normal human being.

People who are thinking straight are able to give meaning to words like 'temptation', 'guilt', 'wickedness', 'fault', 'blame', and 'forgiveness'. They also have a stubborn sense of responsibility. As C. S. Lewis says, 'Human beings, all over the earth, have this curious idea that they ought to behave in a certain way, and cannot get rid of it.'[24] Man has a conscience, which prompts him to do certain things and not to do others. It may be neglected, smothered or suppressed at times but, as Paul Johnson reminds us, 'It is made of psychic India rubber and springs back, however unwanted or unheeded, to wag a finger at us.'[25] No part of life escapes its influence. It pokes its nose into politics, business, the use of time and money, family life, sexual relationships and other social behaviour — and will not even leave us alone on the sports field! We have a stubborn sense of what we 'ought' to do, a mysterious moral monitor that distinguishes between good and bad, right and wrong, and tells us where our responsibility lies. This leads us to ask a hugely important question: *where does this come from?* There are four possible sources.

   1. Something beneath us — that is, nature. This is a common claim, but if the universe is no more than matter, energy, time and chance, how can it include concepts of right and wrong? It is impossible to jump from atoms to ethics, or from molecules to morality. If as human beings we are no more than shrink-wrapped bags of biological elements governed by the laws of physics, how can we possibly be under any obligation to anything, least of all to nature? The contemporary scientist Rodney Holder hits the nail on the head: 'If we are nothing but atoms and molecules organized in a particular way through the chance processes of evolution, then love, beauty, good and evil, free will, reason itself — indeed all that makes us human and raises us above the rest of the created order — lose their objectivity. Why should I love my neighbour, or go out of my way to help him? Rather, why should I not get everything I can for myself, trampling on whoever gets in my way?'[26] As a basis for morality, nature is a non-starter.

2. *Something within us.* This is where today's postmodernism raises its head, telling us that there are no transcendent standards, that all moral judgements are subjective, and that individuals should be free to 'do their own thing', regardless of its effect on themselves or others. As the American author David Wells points out, 'This is the first time that a civilization has existed that, to a significant extent, does not believe in objective right and wrong.' This may sound wonderfully 'adult' and liberating to some, but can we really live with it? Adolf Hitler thought it ethically right to slaughter six million Jews; if morality is merely a matter of private judgement, what right have we to say that he was wrong? Yet we all do so! The American writer Ernest Hemingway's creed was: 'What is moral is what you feel good after, and what is immoral is what you feel bad after.'[27] Would that make sense to both parties after a vicious mugging or a violent rape? Hugh Heffner, the so-called 'Peter Pan of soft porn' and founder of the Playboy Empire, brags of having slept with over 1,000 women — yet he told the *Daily Telegraph*, 'I'm a very ethical guy … moderation is the key.'[28] To say that Heffner has the morals of an alley cat may be slandering alley cats, but if all morality is a matter of personal preference his definition of moderation is as good as anyone's. In looking for the source of human conscience, privatized morality is a dead end.

3. Something around us — in other words, the pre-
vailing culture. There are two obvious problems here. In
the first place, why should public morality be any better
than private morality? Does quantity automatically produce quality? Do a million wrongs make a right, or turn a
relative into an absolute? And what do we make of the
fact that some of the most honoured people in history
are those who fought *against* their contemporary culture
until radically beneficial changes were made? Secondly,
if morality is a product of culture, which culture shall we
choose? Here is a 1995 news item: 'Minibuses in Tehe-
ran are to be segregated to stop male and female passengers from brushing against each other, which is a sin in
Islam. A transport official said that with 370,000 women
passengers a day being brushed ten times each, 3.7 million sins were being committed.'[29] This may seem ludi-
crous to you, but if culture calls the shots, how can you
know that it is? And how would you judge another culture that took a different line? When it comes to ethical
standards, cultures not only disagree, they sometimes
change quite dramatically (present-day Germany would
not go along with Hitler's Nazism) and for these two reasons they can never give us a defining concept of morality.

4. Something above us — a transcendent, holy, unchangeable, personal Being to whom all humankind is
accountable. As we have already seen, conscience speaks
of a moral awareness of how we 'ought' to behave. In-
debtedness is involved, and as a debt can only be owed
to a person, the universality of conscience points to a
transcendent personality. The modern theologian John
Frame is right: 'If obligations arise from personal relationships, then absolute obligations must arise from our relationship with an absolute person.'[30] Just as it is impossible to measure temperature without an absolute scale

of reference, so nobody is qualified to call anything morally good or bad, right or wrong, just or unjust, unless there is a transcendent, universal, personal, unchanging standard. The God of whom the Bible speaks fits the bill perfectly, and explains why a sense of personal accountability is built into the fabric of human life. The geneticist Francis Collins is quite sure where the evidence points: 'This moral law, which defies scientific explanation, is exactly what one might expect to find if one were searching for the existence of a personal God who sought relationship with mankind.'[31]

The alternative — any alternative — means moral chaos. The Russian novelist Fyodor Dostoevsky hit the nail on the head when he said, 'Without God, everything is permitted.'[32] You may be happy to deny God's existence, but could you honestly live with the moral consequences?

Think!

The third, and in one sense the most radical, way in which human beings are separated from all others is that we are self-conscious and rational personalities, with an insatiable need to know and to understand ourselves and the world around us. While animals have an impressive set of instincts to guide their behaviour, they appear to have no concept of meaning, whereas human beings are endlessly curious about the significance of the world and their place in it. Andrew Knowles puts it well: 'Am I really a random coincidence, adrift in a cosmic accident, meaning nothing, going nowhere? Surely I have a dimension that animals and vegetables lack? After all, a carrot is obviously oblivious to the size of Jupiter. A cow cares nothing for the speed of light. But I am in a different class. I observe and appreciate. I create and choose. I criticize. Sometimes I even criticize myself.'[33]

As we saw in chapter 7, hard-line atheists sometimes go beyond agreeing that humans are thinking beings, and claim that only atheists have used their thinking to come to intelligent conclusions, but these claims collapse like burst balloons when we ask how they came by the ability, not only to think intelligently or logically, but to think at all. In *The Blind Watchmaker,* Richard Dawkins assures us that humankind came about by a 'blind, unconscious, automatic process' that had 'no purpose at all ... and had no mind and no mind's eye'.[34] Francis Crick takes the same line and claims, 'Our minds can be explained by the interaction of nerve cells and molecules.'[35] But reducing human beings (and the brain in particular) to nothing but atoms and molecules presents a massive and obvious problem: if the brain is nothing more than an accident of biological evolution, why should we trust its ability to tell us so, or to come to logical, rational conclusions about anything? Would you take career guidance from a bowl of soup?

We should hardly be surprised that the clash between evolution and rationality caused Charles Darwin's 'horrid doubt'. How can evolution account for the laws of logic? If rational thinking is nothing more than a natural process, why should we trust it to be telling us anything of value? The atheist can only deny the existence of God by denying the very basis on which he does so. The distinguished British biologist (and atheist) J. B. S. Haldane pinpointed the problem: 'If my mental processes are determined solely by the motions of atoms in my brain, I have no reason to suppose that my beliefs are true ... hence I have no reason to suppose my brain to be composed of atoms.'[36]

The person who believes in God says that an intelligent Creator has placed us in an ordered world governed by universal, dependable laws, and has given us the rational ability to connect with that world and come to logical, intelligent conclusions about it and about ourselves. Is it not more sensible to believe that than to pin your world-view to the mindless shuffling of atoms and molecules?

Call Gary Streeter

Gary Streeter has been a Member of Parliament since 1992, and has served as a government minister. He currently represents the South-West Devon constituency. He and his wife Janet have two children and make their home in Plymouth.

I was born in Hayling Island, Hampshire, where my father was a cow-man. Four years later he bought a small farm and we moved to mid-Devon. My parents were utterly non-religious, though we used to go to a Harvest Festival service every year and occasionally went to church at Christmas.

After passing the eleven-plus examinations, I went to Tiverton Grammar School, where I got nine O levels. Two years later I left with good A-level results, and went to read law at Kings College, University of London, graduating with First Class Honours.

I had always been a naturally ambitious person, yet only went to university because learning came easily — and because milking cows early in the morning, whatever the weather, was not for me! While at university I decided to become a solicitor rather than a barrister, and when the time came I was offered posts by every law firm to which I applied. After six months in law school in London, I started my articles in Clifford Chance, which I believe is now the biggest law firm in the world.

When I went to university I considered religion utterly irrelevant, except for weak-minded people who needed some kind of crutch; it was certainly not for winners like me. Sport became very important to me, and I became captain of the university's rugby team, which was unbeaten during my final two years. At that time the team included a number of clergymen's sons. They made no aggressive efforts to get me into the 'God squad', but we used to stay up into the early hours discussing all kinds of things including religion, with me trying to persuade them that God did not exist. I am not sure that we got anywhere in these late-night battles, but I know that by the time I left university I was a convinced atheist.

My position was backed up by what I perceived to be the end product of religion, as most religious people I had met seemed to me to be pretty feeble types. I was also influenced by the contemporary culture, and took it for granted that science had disposed of God, that nobody could realistically and reasonably believe otherwise, that Christianity was a pathetic charade, and that the Bible was an old-fashioned collection of myths and fables written hundreds of years after the events it claimed to record.

Unknown to me at the time, the turning-point in my life came when, to celebrate achieving my honours degree, I gatecrashed a party at the Tiverton Motel and met Janet (another gatecrasher). We danced together and I asked for her phone number, but I was so drunk that I forgot to write it down. Amazingly, I remembered it the following morning, telephoned her, and so began a serious relationship that led to our getting married in 1978, a year and a day after we first met. Early on, I discovered that she was a committed Christian, but as I considered Christianity to be totally irrelevant, I could see no way in which her faith could possibly affect our relationship.

When I began work in London, we moved into a small bed-sit overlooking Holloway Prison. Janet soon linked up with a local Baptist church, and I began to attend with her, as I knew this was what she would have wanted. What I found there confirmed my atheistic convictions, because as far as I could see the church was full of inadequate people leaning on religion as an emotional crutch. However, because I loved my wife I decided that I could live with this farce for a couple of hours a week. (In a strange way, I was able to separate what I judged to be these people's weakness from the real strength I saw in my wife's life and character — although to this day I am not sure that I can explain this!)

After a few months, we moved to south London, where one of the first things Janet did was to look for a local church. She had seen a building with a large illuminated cross on it, so we headed there on our first Sunday, but found it closed down. On our way back home, where I was looking forward to reading the Sunday newspapers, we saw a ramshackle hut that obviously housed some kind of church. Janet immediately told me to stop the car, and moments later we were sitting in the morning service.

It made such an impression on both of us that we began attending on a regular basis, and very soon my thinking underwent a radical change. For the first time in my life I began to meet intelligent, successful, talented, impressive men with a strong, personal Christian faith. Within a few months, I realized that I needed to check that my own thinking was secure, and I decided to research Christianity so that I could persuade Janet to give it up as a meaningless charade. Among other books, I read the New Testament, *Who Moved the Stone?*, written by a fellow lawyer, Frank Morison, and *By Searching*, the biography of Isobel Kuhn, a Christian missionary.

As I read these, I gradually saw that there was something in Christianity after all. I began to believe that the biblical record of the life, character and death of Jesus Christ was historically true, but for me it was the issue of his resurrection from the dead that got my closest attention. After another few weeks of intense reading (and especially Frank Morison's sifting of the evidence) I became intellectually persuaded that the case for the resurrection of Jesus was overwhelming, and soon after that I committed my life to him.

The effect was dramatic. It was as if someone had taken the lid off the truth. I could now make sense of the universe, and of my own origin and destiny. At the same time, I found an immediate sense of responsibility to others, a rapidly developing conviction that I ought to serve my fellow human beings to the best of what I now recognized to be my God-given ability.

My world-view has now been utterly transformed. From thinking that the universe came into existence in some mechanical way, that life originated as a biological accident, that mindless evolution produced the highly sophisticated species we call humankind and that when we die our final destiny is to rot, I have come to believe that God created everything outside of himself, that he loves me, that I am accountable to him for the way I live, and that because I have put my trust in his Son, Jesus Christ, I will spend eternity in his glorious presence, not sitting idly on a cloud, but engaged in what C. S. Lewis somewhere calls 'purposeful activity'.

Although my life has been transformed, I am still on a learning curve. I have made many mistakes and live an imperfect life, yet God has given me a better marriage, making me a better husband and a better father. I am equally sure that in 1985, while I was a partner in a Plymouth law firm, he called me to serve him in the political life of this country. Within six months I was elected to the Plymouth City Council. In 1992, I was elected as the Member of Parliament for Plymouth Sutton, becoming a government whip in 1995 and a minister in 1996.

My main concern now is to work out Christian values within a political framework. While we live in a largely secular age, the closer we get to living out the biblical blueprint God has designed for us, the better it will be for every part of our society. The more I read the Bible, the more I see it to be deeply relevant to every part of our lives as individuals and as a human community.

People sometimes ask me, 'Does Christianity help you?', but I think this is the wrong question. The issue is not whether it helps or hinders me, but whether it is *true*. It seems to me that most people have not rejected it on the basis of the evidence; instead, they have simply imbibed the spirit of the age, which says we have outgrown God. I would encourage everyone who reads my story to sit down and *think*! Where have we come from? Can it possibly be true that once there was nothing, and that out of nothing came something? Can it be true that life was accidentally added to that inert 'something' and that, entirely by accident, life developed into complicated, sophisticated humankind? I think it takes more faith to believe these things than it does to believe in a loving God who created us and has a purpose for our lives. I would urge them not to sleepwalk into oblivion.

8.

Signs of significance

As an entrenched atheist, Bertrand Russell maintained that '[Man's] origin, his growth, his hopes and fears, his loves and beliefs, are but the outcome of accidental collocations of atoms,' and that 'All these things, if not quite beyond dispute, are yet so nearly certain that no philosophy which rejects them can hope to stand.'[1] At one stage he was a passionate promoter of logical positivism, which says that whatever cannot be proved scientifically, by what it calls the verification principle, is nothing more than subjective experience and should not be treated as reality or knowledge. Yet, as we saw in an earlier chapter, this is a self-destructing proposition, as the verification principle itself is incapable of verification — and today the idea is as dead as the proverbial dodo.

Russell's claim (which we noted in chapter 5) that there was not enough evidence for the existence of God is scarcely in better shape. As we have already seen, the reality and nature of the universe, the complex mystery of life and the integrity of the Bible can hardly be dismissed out of hand. Nor can the elements of humanity we discussed in chapter 7; human dignity, morality and rationality all seem to be pointers towards a transcendent, wise, holy and personal Creator — but they are by no means the only ones. Man seems to have God's fingerprints all over him, and in this chapter we will examine another four.

The big 'Why?'

Writing in *The Times*, Bernard Levin suggested, 'There are probably more people seeking some larger meaning or purpose in their lives and in life in general than there have been, certainly in the West, since the day of unquestioned faith.'[2] Committed atheists take a very different line. According to the American palaeontologist Stephen Jay Gould, 'We are here because one odd group of fishes had a peculiar fin anatomy that could transform into legs for terrestrial creatures; because comets struck the earth and wiped out dinosaurs, thereby giving mammals a chance not otherwise available (so thank your lucky stars in a literal sense); because the earth never froze entirely during an ice age; because a small and tenuous species, arising in Africa a quarter of a million years ago, has managed, so far, to survive by hook and by crook. We may yearn for a "higher" answer — but none exists.'[3] Of course this is pure speculation, and Gould has no evidence to support his guesswork.

Other articulate atheists are equally sure that humankind is ultimately pointless. George Gaylord Simpson maintains, 'Man is the result of a purposeless and natural process that did not have him in mind,'[4] while Cornell University professor William Provine claims, 'The universe cares nothing for us and we have no ultimate meaning in life.'[5] Asked in the *Observer* about the purpose of life, Richard Dawkins snorted, 'Well, there is no purpose, and to ask what it is is a silly question. It has the same status as: "What is the colour of jealousy?"'[6] This chimes in with his conviction that human beings are nothing but survival machines blindly programmed to pass on their genes, and that the preservation of bits of DNA is 'the ultimate rationale for our existence',[7] but experts in this particular field have written off this idea as 'clapped-out and wrong'.[8] Oxford professor Keith Ward writes, 'As a matter of fact, nothing more pointless, no less convincing rationale, could be imagined for the existence of bodies than this. Who could give a fig for the survival of

DNA? Not genes, which know and care for nothing. Not us, who might be interested in personal survival, but would be perfectly happy if that could be accomplished without any DNA at all. Not God, who can hardly find intrinsic worthwhileness in the existence of strings of nucleic acids. To put it bluntly, nobody cares about strings of nucleic acids at all.'[9]

Ward is right. Do the laws of physics suggest any transcendent purpose in people passing on bits of DNA? Do they suggest *any* purpose? If we are nothing more than genetically driven robots, why should we be remotely concerned about manners, courtesy, kindness, courage, sympathy or loyalty? Are these just weasel words without any real value?

Until enthusiastic communicators with atheistic presuppositions get at them, the overwhelming majority of people are convinced that there *is* some meaning to life. They ask, 'Where do I come from?', 'Why am I here?', 'Where am I going?' The Jewish philosopher Martin Buber relates the story of a somewhat stupid old man who, as he got out of bed each morning, had difficulty in remembering where he had left his clothes the night before. After many sleepless nights worrying if he would ever solve the problem, he hit on a solution. As he undressed at night he jotted down where he had placed everything. In the morning, he looked at his notes. 'Trousers — on chair' so he put them on; 'shoes — under bed', so he put them on. He carried on like this until he was fully dressed, then he stopped and asked himself, 'Now, where am I?' The list gave him no answer — but he could not avoid the question.

The atheists I have quoted maintain that there is no point in looking for any meaning to life, as the existence of humanity is a mindless mystery, a cosmic accident with no explanation or purposeful outcome. Pushed to its logical conclusion, this leads to nihilism, which in its most popular form says there is no reason why the universe exists and no goal towards which it is moving. Nothing is of real value, human beings are biological accidents, the whole business of living is an exercise in futility, and personal satisfaction at any given moment is sufficient justification for doing anything.

The arts have often reflected what the Swiss psychiatrist Gustav Jung called this 'neurosis of emptiness'.[10] Samuel Beckett produced a play called *Breath*, which lasted just thirty seconds and had no actors or dialogue. The only props were bits of rubbish and the only 'script' the sigh of human life, from a baby's cry to a dying man's last gasp. Composer John Cage presented a piece of 'music' which he called 'Four Minutes Thirteen Seconds' and which consisted of total silence for that length of time, Cage suggesting that the silence 'may then be filled by the sounds of the world itself'. Artist Yves Klein produced paintings that were nothing but canvasses filled with unrelieved blue, leaving everyone who saw them to give them whatever meaning they chose. The American journalist and broadcaster Jon Casimir summed up this nihilistic approach: 'There is no meaning of life... What is passed off as an all-important search is basically just a bunch of philosophers scrabbling about on their knees, trying to find a lost sock in the cosmic laundromat.'[11] Looking back on a brilliant career, film director Robert Altman told the *Observer* in 1955, 'If I had never lived, if the sperm that hit the egg had missed, it would have made no difference to anything.'[12]

This bleak assessment of human life has several fundamental flaws. In the first place, nihilism has no evidence that God does not exist, but begins by assuming that this is the case. Yet this approach cripples the idea before it gets to its feet. It turns personal opinion into infallible dogma, an approach that can hardly be taken seriously. Secondly, no nihilist consistently lives as if there were no rational or moral order. Does a nihilist step out in front of moving traffic, cheerfully whistling *'Que sera sera'* and not remotely bothered at the outcome? Thirdly, does the nihilist really believe that there are *no* values? On 13 March 1996, Thomas Hamilton walked into Dunblane Primary School in Scotland and killed sixteen children and a teacher. All but one of the children were five years old. Would even the most determined nihilist deny that what Hamilton did was wrong — *absolutely* wrong? Yet if it was absolutely wrong, how can the nihilist say that there are no values and that moral distinctions have no meaning? What is more, how can the nihilist deny the existence of truth, then claim to be telling the truth by doing so? The nihilist says, 'There are no absolutes.' Is that statement absolute? If so, it is false. If not, it is nonsense.

For many atheists, writing the world off as meaningless has a hidden agenda, one which gets rid of any transcendent standards and gives them licence to behave in any way they choose. The British novelist Aldous Huxley admitted that this was what fuelled his own atheism: 'I had motives for not wanting the world to have a meaning; consequently assumed it had none, and was able without difficulty to find satisfying reasons for this assumption. The philosopher who finds no meaning in the world is not concerned exclusively with a problem in pure metaphysics, he is also concerned to prove that there is no valid reason why he personally should not do as he wants to do... For myself, the philosophy of meaninglessness was essentially an instrument of liberation, sexual and political.'[13]

In *River out of Eden*, Richard Dawkins complains, 'We humans have purpose on the brain,' and calls this 'a nearly universal delusion',[14] but at least two things can be said in response. Firstly, as the very idea of purpose presupposes consciousness, how does he reconcile this with his mantra that human life is entirely driven by unconscious bits of DNA blindly pursuing mechanical goals? Purpose speaks of there being an end in mind, but if there is no mind behind the universe why is the mechanical passing on of genes of any lasting value? Do the laws of physics convince us that survival is better than extinction? Secondly, any open-minded person would at least want to consider the possibility that the idea of purpose has its roots in our creation by a God who intends us to be here and who has programmed us to know that we have been brought into being as part of his own transcendent plan. The Bible says:

> You are worthy, our Lord and God,
>   to receive glory and honour and power,
> for you created all things,
>   and by your will they were created
>   and have their being. [15]

Why should this be ruled out?

God's mimics

Another human distinctive is that we have an aesthetic dimension, an innate sense of beauty which, like goodness and truth, defies scientific analysis. We are able to assess the relative qualities of form, texture, colour, order and design. We are endlessly creative in composing music, arranging words, making pictures and designing objects which sometimes serve no practical purpose, yet are meant to express some kind of meaning or to give enjoyment to us and to others.

There is a world of difference between such prolific imagination and the apparent ingenuity of animals. As the contemporary author John Benton points out, 'Beavers may build dams, but men develop quantum mechanics, paint the *Mona Lisa* and fly to the moon!'[16] In his book *Darwinism Defended*, evolutionist Michael Ruse is forced to admit that 'Nothing even yet scratches at an explanation of how a transformed ape could produce the magnificence of Beethoven's *Choral Symphony.*'[17]

Nor is there an atheistic explanation as to why we can detect and interpret signs of creative design in the work of an artist, composer or craftsman.

In 1984 Prince Charles caused a furore in British architectural circles by describing a proposed ultra-modern extension to the National Gallery in Trafalgar Square, London, as a 'monstrous carbuncle'. Ten years later, author Christopher Booker commended the prince for his role in leading the revolt against 'the megalomaniac excesses of the modern architects' and giving public voice to 'widespread feelings of popular revulsion against the dehumanized, soulless, moonscape architecture produced by the modern movement, and which in the sixties inflicted on our cities the greatest social disaster to hit this country since the war'.[18] The same note was echoed in the first issue of *Perspective*, sponsored by Prince Charles' Institute of Architecture, which spoke of the need for 'that critical spiritual dimension'. Do we find this kind of thing in the non-human world? Is appreciation of beauty for beauty's sake seen anywhere else but among human beings?

This brings us to another question: is there any objective reality that gives content to the word 'beauty' and gives the idea of beauty or its opposite any valid meaning? If not, why should we think that a Mozart concerto is any more beautiful than the sound of a pneumatic drill, that a Constable masterpiece is an improvement on an oil slick, or that the Taj Mahal has more to commend it than a tin shack? Even when we have made allowances for subjective opinion related to factors such as age or localized culture, nobody can deny that the concept of beauty is universally recognized. Why should this be the case if the universe and everything in it is a mindless and accidental accumulation of matter and anti-matter?

The British physician John Rendle-Short makes another telling point about aesthetics: 'Compare the most beautiful of bird songs with a Beethoven symphony, or the elegant but repetitive

mating dance of the bird of paradise with a human ballet production ... the bird's efforts are always the same. You can recognize the kookaburra by his inimitable laugh even when he is
a quarter of a mile away. Certain birds make certain sounds;
spiders build a unique but constant web; animals have stereo-
typed habits — they seldom vary. But man has original ideas,
he can create new things, and does so constantly.' Rendle-Short
has no doubt as to why this is so: 'In his own small way he
mimics God the Creator.'[19] It is reported that when Albert Einstein first heard Yehudi Menuhin playing the violin as a child
prodigy he said, 'Now I know there is a God in heaven.'

Predictably, Richard Dawkins will have none of this, and
says that aesthetic values are matters of taste that vary from
person to person but have no intrinsic worth, and in *River out
of Eden*, he declares, 'Beauty is not an absolute virtue in itself.'[20] Yet how can he possibly know this without being able to
transcend the point he is making? Dawkins' rejection of beauty
as a virtue leaves Keith Ward 'speechless',[21] and he points to
beauty as one of the conscious states that human beings *do* put
value on, in things such as music, painting, poetry or nature:
'Looking at the Alps in the snow and taking pleasure in their
colour, grandeur and austere magnificence is something that
we can enjoy *just for its own sake*. Such moments of contem-
plation are, for many, among the high points of their human
experience'[22] (emphasis added). For Dawkins to deny the reality of aesthetic value outside of material facts is to fly in the face
of both reason and experience. H. R. Rookmaaker, one-time
professor of the History of Art at the Free University, Amster-
dam, sees beauty as a reflection of the character of God, and
adds, 'Our being cannot be satisfied unless the thirst for beauty
is quenched.'[23]

Appreciation of beauty is a concept that fits in perfectly with
the Bible's statement: 'The heavens declare the glory of God.'[24]

The God-shaped vacuum

Of all the factors separating humankind from other living organisms and pointing to our unique place in creation, none is more striking than our spiritual dimension. After extensive research, the modern scholar Joseph Gaer wrote, 'As far as we can determine, religion has existed in every society, from the most primitive to the most culturally advanced. The more keys modern science finds with which to open the locked doors of the past, the more we learn about the early days of man on earth, the more evidence there is that all societies in the past had one thing in common — some form of religion.'[25] There is no evidence of this in any other animals — not even the praying mantis prays! — yet no group of human beings has ever been discovered which was without religion of any kind. If we have evolved from 'lower' animals, we should expect to find at least some primitive tribes, ancient or modern, with no religion at all, but this is not the case. As the Princeton scholar Samuel Zwemer discovered, 'Religion is as old as the oldest record and is universal among the most primitive tribes today.'[26]

What does the atheist say to this phenomenon? We have space to mention just one of the major ideas which have been advanced. In the nineteenth century the German thinker Ludwig Feuerbach said that religion was merely 'the dream of the human mind'. He claimed that man built up a picture of all the virtues and powers which he himself lacked, and which could comfort, protect and sustain him in an alien world, bundled them all together, and called the result 'God'. In Feuerbach's famous phrase, 'Man is the beginning, the centre and the end of religion.'[27] Feuerbach was one of the most celebrated philosophers in Europe, and 20,000 people attended his funeral. Since then, millions of people have taken his ideas on board, but his arguments collapse under the slightest pressure.

- How can we possibly say that an object of human wishes or desires has no real, objective existence beyond the mind of the person who wishes or desires it?
- The argument that God is nothing more than wish-fulfilment on the part of the theist can boomerang. It may more easily be argued (and Aldous Huxley has already provided us with an example of this) that the non-existence of a sovereign, holy God to whom we are personally accountable is wish-fulfilment *on the part of the atheist*. After all, a holy God who knows me through and through, requires me to live a life of holiness, and makes it clear that there is to be a day of eternal judgement, has decidedly limited appeal! Is there not more than a grain of truth in the saying that an atheist cannot find God for the same reason that a thief cannot find a policeman?
- It is important to remember that Feuerbach became an atheist, not because he had satisfied himself that God did not exist, but for personal reasons. While he was a theological student at Heidelberg University, his two brothers were severely punished for leading a revolt against the university's religious teachers; Feuerbach's knee-jerk reaction was to renounce his faith and mount a determined attack on religion. He sustained this throughout his life, but he was never able to produce any philosophical, theological or rational evidence on which to build his beliefs.

Even when no one Supreme Being is in mind, humans have a stubborn sense that unseen powers can influence their lives. In his book *In Harm's Way*, a fascinating account of his experience as a war correspondent, the British journalist Martin Bell wrote, 'I came to put my faith in certain routines and rituals which may be considered superstitions, but which none the less worked for me.'[28] Among these he included the wearing of his famous white suit and (slightly less famous) green socks, and carrying items which were 'matters of life and death' because they had to do with the tokens of good fortune. These included 'a silver threepenny bit, a four-leafed, and even a five-leafed clover, a fragment of water-snake skin in an envelope, a brass pixie, countless silver crosses and Saint Christophers, and tapes of [the American singer] Willie Nelson'. Commenting on this collection of talismans, Bell went on, 'I carry them all ... and who can tell which will work and which will not? Better to be safe by accumulation than sorry by preferring one to another.'[29] Although this was blatant superstition, it confirms man's inbuilt spirituality, his sense that there is reality over and above the material. As John Houghton says, 'There is general evidence that most human beings, from whatever part of the world and from the earliest times, have exhibited a fundamental belief in a divine being or beings, and in some sort of spiritual world.'[30]

Just as impressive as the fact that man seems to have an inbuilt tendency to religion — the *Encyclopaedia of Religion and Ethics* runs to thirteen large volumes — is the fact that the idea of one supreme Deity is so prevalent. Dualism (the idea that the universe is governed by two equal, uncreated powerful forces, one good and one evil) has had surges of popularity from time to time; polytheism (belief in a multitude of distinct and separate deities) has surfaced in Hinduism and other faith systems; and pantheism (which says that everything is divine) is an ancient idea now being recycled in the New Age Movement; but belief in one supreme Deity has been by far the greatest expression of human religious belief. In his masterly study *Origin of the Idea of God*, the German scholar Pere Wilhelm Schmidt, arguably the greatest modern authority on the subject, has this to say: 'A belief in a Supreme Being is to be found among *all* the people of the primitive culture, not indeed everywhere in the same form or the same vigour, but still everywhere prominent enough to make his dominant position indubitable.'[31]

Why is this the case if religion is just something man dreamed up?

Such universal belief in one true God poses another problem for the atheist: why has it proved impossible to destroy? No other idea known to man has suffered such bitter, brutal and bloodthirsty persecution, not least in the twentieth century. For decades, Marxist-Leninist Communism poured its energies into total warfare against the Christian faith. Lenin declared, 'Every religious idea, every idea of God, every flirtation with the idea of God is unutterable vileness,'[32] and mass propaganda, brainwashing, imprisonment, torture and execution were among the weapons used in the atheistic crusade that followed. Thousands of churches were torn down or put to other use, millions of Bibles were destroyed, Christian leaders 'disappeared' without trace and countless thousands of believers were deprived of their jobs, their homes, their liberty or their lives. In the People's Republic of China, Mao Tse-tung expelled all Christian missionaries, liquidated religious organizations and slaughtered thousands of believers. In Cambodia, Pol Pot's atheism was a major force behind a brutal agenda culminating in the notorious 'killing fields', when between April 1975 and January 1977 over 1,500,000 people, one-fifth of the country's population, were massacred.

Yet in spite of these atrocities, belief in God has stubbornly outlived all of his would-be undertakers, and in some cases the scenes of its bitterest persecution have witnessed its greatest progress. At the time of the Communist Revolution in China in 1949 there were five million Christians; forty years later there were eighty million. How can the atheist explain the persistence and progress of faith in God? The best that Richard Dawkins can manage is to call religion 'a virus of the brain', a 'meme' of cultural inheritance transmitted like genes, but, as Melanie Philips pointed out in the *Observer*, 'The evidence for the existence of this meme doesn't exist.'[33] Will atoms and molecules develop religious ideas if they are left around for long enough? If not, how can we explain what has been called a 'God-shaped vacuum' in the human psyche, a historical and universal phenomenon that sets humanity apart from every other species? The eighteenth-century British politician Edmund Burke wrote that man 'is by his constitution a religious animal', and that 'Atheism is against not only our reason but our instincts.'[34] Man's instinct to reach out beyond himself to a superior spiritual power is always there, even when it is suppressed by preference or prejudice. Nobody provides a better example of this than the famous French thinker Jean-Paul Sartre, who, after a lifetime preaching a godless philosophy, called atheism 'a cruel, long-term business'[35] and finally admitted, 'Everything in me calls for God, and that I cannot forget.'[36]

The great leveller

The modern scholar Eric Kast points out one further distinction between human beings and others, namely that we alone experience 'the disease of conceptualizing death'.[37] As far as we are aware, no other living being has the slightest interest in how or when its life will end, yet from the first time we are aware of death, it hovers relentlessly over us.

One response to this is to try to push it into the background of our thinking, and we have invented a truckload of terms to avoid the dreaded 'D... word'. We say that someone has 'passed away', 'passed on', or is 'no longer with us'. More crudely (and to avoid being serious?) we speak of those who have 'kicked the bucket', 'snuffed it', 'cashed in their chips', or 'popped their clogs', and are now 'six feet under' or 'pushing up the daisies'. Some hospitals in the United States even refer to the death of a patient as 'negative patient care outcome'.

One obvious reason for this reluctance to get to serious, personal grips with the subject is that it points so powerfully to the fact that every day of life brings death closer. Life at times is so full and fruitful that we are reluctant to think of leaving behind all the rewarding experiences it brings to us. Our family relationships, friendships, material possessions, physical and intellectual abilities and achievements, our enjoyment of nature, music, literature, sport, food, drink, sex and every form of self-expression — all of these will one day be snatched from us, perhaps much sooner than we imagine, and we hate the fact. The modern theologian Alister McGrath calls concern about this 'the trauma of transience'[38] and tells of how, as a young boy, it used to affect him as he lay in bed at night and gazed out of his bedroom window: 'Although I was always impressed by the beauty of the night sky, I nevertheless found it made me feel rather melancholy. Why should something so beautiful make me feel so sad? Because I knew that the light from some of those stars had taken thousands of years to reach the earth. And I knew that I would be dead and gone long before the light now leaving those stars would ever reach earth. The night sky seemed to me to be a powerful symbol of my own insignificance and mortality. I found it unbearable.'[39]

Countless other people find themselves frustrated and confused at the whole subject. Elizabeth Clough, head of TV Channel 4's religious programmes (though she admits to being 'not religious') told the *Daily Telegraph* in 2001 of being impressed by the way in which a Christian family she knew coped so securely with a relative's death, and went on, 'When my children ask me about death, I find my answers *to my own ears* very unsatisfactory'[40] (emphasis added).

For some people, the trauma is relentless. In 1963, at the peak of his career, the popular British actor and comedian Kenneth Williams wrote these words in his diary: 'The madness screaming up inside me. So many awful thoughts — this terrible sense of doom hanging over me. I wonder if anyone will ever know about the emptiness of my life. I wonder if anyone will ever stand in a room that I have lived in and touch the things that were once a part of my life and wonder about me? How could they ever be told? How to explain that I only experienced vicariously, never first hand, that the sharing of a life is what makes a life... Now I am thinking all the while of death in some shape or another. Every day is something to be got through. All the recipes of the past are no longer valid. I've spent all my life in the mind. I have entered into nothing.'[41]

For millions of people, the 'trauma of transience' is made even worse by the uncertainty of what lies beyond. Interviewed in *TIME* Magazine one month before his death in 2001, Dr Christiaan Barnard, the South African surgeon who in 1967 performed the world's first human heart transplant, said, 'At about 79, people ask me: "Where do you go from here?" I say to them, "I'm on the waiting list." I don't know exactly where I am on that list *or where I'm going,* but I'm on it'[42] (emphasis added). Bertrand Russell taught that man began as an accident and will end in annihilation, and that worrying about life beyond the grave was pointless, because to die was 'to pass through the gate of darkness'.[43] Of course he had no evidence for this idea, which is totally at odds with the record of human history that faith in an afterlife has been a universal concept for as far back as we can trace. As the *Daily Telegraph*'s Mary Kenny puts it, 'In all cultures and at all times, human beings have conceived of a spiritual life beyond the body.'[44] Annihilationism also jars with the fact that human beings are the pinnacle of creation, with non-physical qualities and abilities that go beyond anything we find elsewhere in the living world. In his book *The Denial of Death,* the modern writer Ernest Becker shows how incompatible this is, and what a devastating blow it deals to the human ego: 'Man is literally split in two. He has awareness of his own splendid uniqueness in that he sticks out of nature with a towering majesty, and yet he goes back into the ground a few feet in order blindly and dumbly to rot and disappear for ever.'[45]

I have written extensively elsewhere about death and the afterlife.[46] The question to ask here is why there should be such a radical distinction between human beings and others on the issue of death. If sparrows, caterpillars, whales, apes, humans and the millions of other living species on our planet are all part of the so-called 'Great Chain of Being', separated by nothing more than the chance fluctuation of atoms and molecules over millions of years, why should death be such a consuming issue for just one species and of no concern whatever to all the others? If humans are nothing more than grown-up germs, at what point in the growing-up process did death begin to be a factor? And why in the world should this have ever happened?

Although the subject of death grips us all, it is one to which atheism can make no serious contribution. The modern thinker Ravi Zacharias says, 'The questions about death demand answers, but atheism has none… Life finishes with the last heart-beat: all relationships are severed, all endeavours are ended, the arm of justice is cut short, eternity in the heart has been swallowed up by the finality of experience. There is nothing to hope for, no God to meet, and no hope to anticipate — all is truly and ultimately ended.'[47] This does not automatically mean that the atheist has got it wrong, and some show great courage in accepting the logical outcome of their beliefs, yet most serious-minded people struggle with the idea that their destiny is nothing more than dust. The overwhelming consensus of human history is that another life *does* lie beyond this one — and that our future existence rests in higher hands than ours. In C. S. Lewis's words, 'We know that we are not made of mortal stuff.'[48]

The Bible explains this universal instinct. It says not only that man was made 'in the image of God',[49] but that God 'breathed into his nostrils the breath of life, and man became a living being'.[50] This is not said of anything else God made, and an important work written around 40 B.C. had no doubt as to what it means: 'God created man for eternity, and made him in

the image of his own immortality.'[51] Humankind was set apart
as something infinitely different, possessing a quality of 'never
ending' that comes from the very breath of God. Man is not 'all
dressed up and nowhere to go'. It is easy to see why annihilation at death might appeal to the atheist (no traumatic encounter with a holy God, no judgement, no punishment for
wrongdoing) but it clashes with every biblical writer who addresses the subject. One of them speaks for all the others when
he says: 'God has ... set eternity in the hearts of men.'[52]

Before we turn to atheism's strongest argument, it is worth
summarizing what we are left with when God is ruled out. In
Thinking Clearly About God and Science, one-time atheist
Robert Frost touches on many of the issues we have raised in
these last four chapters: 'The atheist must, of necessity, believe
that matter without mind created reason and logic. Matter without intelligence created understanding and comprehension.
Matter without morals created complex ethical codes and legal
systems. Matter without conscience created a sense of right and
wrong. Matter without emotion created skills in art, music,
drama, architecture, language, comedy, literature and dance.
Matter without design created in humankind an insatiable hunger for meaning and purpose.'[53] Can you seriously believe this?

Call Ram Gidoomal

*Brought up in Africa as a Hindu, Ram Gidoomal moved to England in
1967. After a very successful business career, he is now heavily involved in a number of charitable organizations, including those helping to relieve poverty and suffering in Third World countries. He was
awarded the CBE in 1998.*

Although I was born in Kenya, my family roots are elsewhere. When
the Indian sub-continent was partitioned in 1946 into the separate

countries of India and Pakistan, my parents, who were Hindus, found themselves on the Muslim side of the border, in Hyderabad Sind, Pakistan. Because of religious and political prejudices, it was a traumatic time for them and it was not long before they felt forced to emigrate. They could have moved across the newly established border into India, but decided instead to leave the palace they owned, cross the Indian Ocean, and settle in Kenya.

My father was a very successful businessman and in 1950 I was born into an extremely wealthy family living in a luxurious fifteen-bedroom house, surrounded by servants and all the trappings of material success. Concerned for my religious well-being, my father introduced me to the Hindu scriptures at a very early age, especially the *Bhagavad-Gita*, the *Mahabharata* and the *Ramayana*. I was fascinated by them all and read them with great interest. By the time I was twelve years old I was actively searching for the meaning of life and asking what seemed to me to be the most important question of all: why do we exist?

In many ways it was a blissful childhood, but things were soon to change. Overwhelmed by his business and family responsibilities, my father took his own life, leaving my mother a widow at just twenty-two years of age. Another blow was soon to follow. When Kenya gained its independence my entire family was deported, and in 1967 the dejected Gidoomals arrived in England. We had been forced to leave all our wealth in Kenya and our extended family of fifteen were crammed into four rooms above a newsagent's shop in Shepherd's Bush, London.

Those early days were very hard going as we tried to get to grips with our reduced circumstances. We had been disowned by India because we had opted for British citizenship, forced to leave Muslim Pakistan because we were Hindus, and kicked out of Kenya because we were not African. Now we found ourselves caught up in warnings about racial conflict, with a government minister predicting 'rivers of blood' if the immigration of Asians and others was not severely curbed. Many of us became ill in the bitterly cold weather of that first winter, and we were racked by insecurity and uncertainty as to what the future might hold.

My uncle, now the father figure in our extended family, had emigrated to England a year earlier. He had started a small business in an Asian community and now we all pitched in in an attempt to survive, saving every penny we could by doing all the work ourselves. I especially remember getting up at the crack of dawn to deliver newspapers, while my brother-in-law left for the London markets at 5 a.m. to buy Asian food for resale in our local community.

Just as we were beginning to make some kind of progress we took another, potentially fatal, blow. My uncle returned to Kenya to try to settle our family affairs and rescue the considerable assets we had been forced to abandon there, but when he got back to Mombasa he found that some of our land had been confiscated and much of our wealth written off. Increasingly depressed about the prospect of returning to the cold, unwelcoming atmosphere in England, he eventually cracked under the pressure, and quietly committed suicide. I had lost two 'fathers' in the same way.

Several interesting results flowed from my uncle's death. Not only did my brothers and I now take over positions of authority within the family, we were also able to make the most of British cultural and social freedoms without any family restraint from an older generation. The local pub, Queen's Park Rangers football, discotheques and youth clubs soon became an enjoyable part of our adolescent lifestyle. Determined to get a good education, I passed my O and A Levels and won a place to study physics at Imperial College, London. On the way, I had mastered the English language, adding this to Sindhi and Hindi, Swahili (which I had learned in Kenya) and Gujarti and Kutchim, which most of my school friends spoke.

To begin with, life at college was a miserable experience. For the first time in my life I had to do all my own chores, such as shopping and washing my clothes. My room in the hall of residence was a place of loneliness and isolation, and when I tried to mix with other students the environment felt alien and hostile. When I did get talking with others (usually easier after a few beers) I found the conversation disappointingly trivial; nobody seemed interested in the things that were important to me. After three months I had had enough and moved back to the family's cramped accommodation in Shepherd's Bush.

Yet for all my unhappiness at college, it was there that my life was transformed. I was sitting in a pub one day when a group of Christian musicians came in and began to give an informal concert, interspersing songs with their own personal testimonies. Two particular songs — 'He's got the whole world in his hands' and 'Put your hands in the hands of the Man of Galilee' — made a great impression on me, and when the concert was over I invited them back to my room to argue things out (I had substituted 'argue' for 'discuss' on one of their response slips!). After we had talked for hours they gave me a Bible to read and though we often met over the next few weeks to argue about religion, they eventually gave me up as a lost cause.

For the next six months, as I struggled to read the Bible on my own, it gradually became clear to me that its teaching was focused not on abstract principles but on a person — Jesus Christ. The more I studied, the more I was struck with the fact that here was a true, historical figure, unlike most of those in the Hindu scriptures. What is more, his teaching seemed powerfully relevant to the issues I was facing in my life at that time. The most fundamental (and uncomfortable) of these was the question of my own personal sin.

As a Hindu, I had been brought up to believe that a seemingly endless cycle of birth, death and rebirth was the solution to the problem of sin, yet now I could see that the whole system was shrouded in uncertainty. How could these millions of reincarnations make any difference? How could they remove my sin? How could I ever live a good enough life to overcome my bad karma (the sum of my wrong actions)? How could I be certain I would ever be released? Jesus, on the other hand, said with clarity and certainty, 'I am the way and the truth and the life. No one comes to the Father except through me.'[54] I was deeply conscious of my own spiritual bankruptcy and of the losing struggle to pay my karmic debt. Yet Jesus was making a tremendous promise: 'Here I am! I stand at the door and knock. If anyone hears my voice and opens the door, I will come in and eat with him, and he with me.'[55] The offer certainly seemed to address my need. If I handed my life over to Christ he would forgive all my sin, give me the power to live a life pleasing to God, and guarantee my eternal security in heaven. Yet it all seemed too easy, and my trading instincts made me think that there had to be a catch somewhere!

One night, I opened the window in my room, got on my knees and prayed, 'Lord Jesus, I confess that I have got to a point in my life where I just can't continue on my own. I need help. Lord, I am opening the door. You come in and take charge of my life.' Simplistic as this may sound to some, it marked the beginning of a radically different life, one which I have found to be rationally, spiritually and emotionally satisfying.

Inevitably, such a sudden conversion produced serious tensions. The first came over the issue of idol worship, which had always been an integral part of family life. First thing in the morning, and again at 6.30 in the evening, we would bow down to the idols in our Hindu house temple and seek their help. At college, I would pray to my gods and perform various Hindu rituals, even though they seemed irrelevant and ineffective. As soon as I became a Christian I abandoned all idol worship, and immediately faced opposition from the other members of my family. Yet nothing could shake my knowledge that Jesus Christ gave the dynamic liberation from bondage, fear and shame that the Hindu gods were powerless to bestow.

Another tension came over the question of marriage. After I had obtained an honours degree in physics, I had many overtures to contract an arranged marriage — one offering an annuity for life if I would marry the girl on offer! With my new perspective on life, I turned them all down and eventually fell in love with Sunita, a fellow Sindhi born in Britain. As our relationship matured we were both accused of unethical behaviour, not least because I came from the business caste, while she came from the professional caste. The tensions this created have still not been completely dissolved, but our strong faith (Sunita later became a Christian) has enabled us to counter the criticism with tolerance and tact.

The third major tension was to produce equally lasting results. My first job after college was as an analyst with Lloyds Bank International, but two years later I moved to Switzerland (where my three children were later to be born) to take a leading post in a multinational family business that was soon handling an annual turnover running into hundreds of millions of pounds. The buzz of hectic business activity had always been a powerful driving force in my life, and by 1989 I was really 'flying'. Then, on a business trip to India, I paid a brief visit to Bombay's shanty towns and was appalled by the devastating poverty I saw. As a Hindu, my response might have been to imagine that this was the outworking of the law of karma and to think that these people must in some way have deserved this, but now their shocking need produced a massive conflict of conscience. How could a follower of Jesus, with his very simple lifestyle, enjoy so many of life's riches and not do something to alleviate the poverty of others? My first reaction was to think that perhaps I should work even harder, make even more money, and thus have more to give away, but then came the conviction that God was saying, 'Ram, I don't want your money, I want you.'

When I got back to England I handed in my notice and eventually left the company altogether. In the meantime, I founded Christmas Cracker, an enterprise aimed at helping to relieve poverty and suffering in Third World countries. The project now involves thousands of young people and others and has already raised well over £4,000,000. I am also involved in South Asian Development Partnership, a charity helping in community relations and in health and social issues affecting South Asians in the United Kingdom, and in South Asian Concern, which exists to encourage, equip and enable Christians to be more effective in leadership, mission and outreach amongst South Asians.

These and many other community and charitable commitments bring me a deeper and more enduring sense of satisfaction and self-worth than even the most successful of my business enterprises. The

Bible nowhere teaches that wealth is wrong, but Jesus said that it must be seen in its right perspective: 'What good is it for a man to gain the whole world, yet forfeit his soul?'[56] True success is to be seen in spiritual, not material terms. To end life as a billionaire, yet remain unreconciled to God, is to be nothing more than a tragic failure. In the Bible's own words, 'For what is seen is temporary, but what is unseen is eternal.'[57]

My greatest concern is to see Asians across the world come to know Jesus Christ as the true and living way. Borrowing some of their own religious terms, my message to those from a Hindu culture would be this: because Christ was the incarnation, or avatar, not simply of a lesser god but of the supreme God himself, he had no previous karmic debt. He was without sin, and his death was a sacrifice potent enough to take away, for ever, all the bad karma of those who put their trust in him.

9.

Where was God on September 11?

Few adults who were alive at the time will ever forget where they were when they heard that United States President John F. Kennedy had been assassinated in Dallas, Texas, on 22 November 1963. Nearly thirty-eight years later another event in the United States was to leave an even more traumatic impression.

For thirty years the twin towers of the World Trade Centre dominated the skyline of Manhattan, the business heart of New York City. Including the 347-foot radio mast on top of the north tower, it was the tallest building in the world. The centre's 110 storeys provided twelve million square feet of space serviced by 103 elevators, sixteen miles of staircases, 12,000 miles of electric cable and 49,000 tons of air-conditioning equipment. On the morning of 11 September 2001 thousands of office workers and others streamed into the twin towers to begin work. It must have seemed a day like any other day, but some 300 miles to the north-east co-ordinated teams of religious fanatics were preparing to shatter that illusion.

In a meticulously planned operation, they hijacked two commercial jets on scheduled flights from Boston to Los Angeles. Brutally slitting the throats of any passengers or crew members who tried to stop them, they re-routed the Boeing 767s to New

York. Flying low over Manhattan, the planes were aimed like 400-ton guided missiles at the World Trade Centre.

At 8.45 on that beautiful September morning, American Air-lines Flight 11, with ninety-two people on board, tore into the north tower, its 20,000 gallons of highly combustible aviation fuel igniting a blaze that reached an estimated temperature of 2,000 degrees Fahrenheit. About twenty minutes later — now covered live by alert television stations — United Airlines Flight 175, carrying sixty-five people, buried itself in the south tower, with the same catastrophic results.

Gaping holes appeared on the upper levels of the towers, releasing massive balls of fire and clouds of dense black smoke that smothered the city. Desks, chairs, filing cabinets, computer equipment, together with human bodies and body parts, were blown or sucked out of the building and rained down on the earth 'like ticker tape'[1] on to the streets below. Terrified workers smashed windows and threw themselves to their deaths. One witness told of seeing at least fourteen people floating down like rag dolls. A man and a woman held hands as they hurtled to their deaths.

Less than an hour after it had been hit, the south tower began to crumble. One man told of hearing the building crack 'like when you have a bunch of spaghetti, and you break it in half to boil it'.[2] Suddenly, the entire building slithered to the ground in a cloud of metal, concrete and glass, setting off 'a huge mushroom cloud of yellow dust'.[3] About thirty minutes later the north tower collapsed, adding to a dust cloud so mas-sive and dense that it blotted out the sun.

In what the *Economist* called 'this unspeakable crime',[4] one of the world's mightiest buildings had been reduced to two jagged stumps looking for all the world like the ruins of some ancient cathedral jutting out from a gigantic mountain of smoul-dering rubble which had become a hideous headstone over the bodies of nearly 3,000 men, women and children of some eighty nationalities who had been in or near the building when the terrorists struck. The event was so appalling that it virtually over-shadowed the news that a third hijacked airliner had been steered into the Pentagon in Washington, DC, killing nearly 200 people, and that a fourth, failing to reach its target, had crashed near Pittsburgh, Pennsylvania, with the loss of forty-five lives. It was the bloodiest day in the nation's history since its Civil War, which ended in 1865, and the most murderous and devastating terrorist attack the world had ever known.

In Britain, *The Times* called it 'a tragedy that stretched human powers of understanding to breaking point'. [5] The twin towers had been designed 'to represent man's belief in humanity', but one newspaper said that, with the terrorists' attack, 'The landscape of America's belief has been destroyed.'[6] *The Times'* leading article was headed, 'The day that changed the modern world,'[7] while the *Daily Mail's* Mark Almond wrote, 'History will never be the same again.'[8]

Within hours, the media were firing a fusillade of questions. How could such a thing possibly happen? Why did the United States' Intelligence services, costing $12 billion a year, not anticipate an event that must have taken many months of planning, most of it done in their own country? Who was responsible for masterminding the attack? What could — or should — be done to punish them and to prevent such a thing ever happening again?

Atheists and agnostics had another, more fundamental question, and a *Daily Telegraph* reader supplied it the next day: 'How can anyone argue that this is what his God believes to be appropriate behaviour?'[9] Within days, in several different settings, I was challenged with a fine-tuned version of the same question: 'Where was God when the terrorists attacked America?' The question is inescapable, but the argument behind it is far from original. It goes back thousands of years and can be summed up like this:

1. If God were all-powerful he could prevent evil and suffering.

2. If he were all-loving, he would want to prevent them.

3. Evil and suffering exist.

4. God is therefore impotent, loveless or non-existent.

That seems pretty watertight and I am convinced that most people who deny or doubt the existence of God do so along these lines and not primarily for scientific or philosophical reasons. The contemporary philosopher Alvin Plantinga goes so far as to say that 'This is the only argument against God that deserves to be taken seriously.'[10]

Nobody denies the fundamental fact that triggers off the whole argument: evil and suffering are universal facts of life. Here are some examples:

Natural disasters

We live in what someone has called 'a world with ragged edges'.[11] Earthquakes, volcanoes, floods, hurricanes, tidal waves, fires and other natural disasters have killed millions of people and injured countless others, often wiping out huge numbers within a few hours. Over one million died when China's Hwang-ho river burst its banks in 1887. Some 200,000 perished in an earthquake in the same country's Kansu province in 1920, and 12,000 were drowned and millions made homeless when Hurricane Mitch, dubbed 'the Storm of the Century', hit Central America in 1998. Does an all-powerful God allow his creation to get out of control in this way?

Accidents

On 14 April 1912 the British liner *Titanic*, then the largest movable object ever made by man, and said to be so well built that 'God himself couldn't sink this ship', struck an iceberg in the

North Atlantic on her maiden voyage and sank with the loss of some 1,500 lives.

On 21 October 1966 a slag-heap loosened by persistent rain slithered into the junior school in the Welsh village of Aberfan and smothered to death five teachers and 109 children.

On 26 April 1986 a nuclear reactor in the Ukrainian town of Chernobyl was ripped apart by two explosions which 'may yet cause up to 300,000 deaths'[12] and the effects of which could take up to 200 years to remove.[13]

These three tragedies represent countless others: aeroplanes crash; trains are derailed; road vehicles collide; ships are lost at sea; buildings collapse; bridges give way; trees fall; machinery malfunctions. There are times when the whole world seems like a vast Accident and Emergency Unit, and every day adds to the millions accidentally killed or injured. Is God presiding over this mayhem?

Built-in hazards

Our planet can supply all the elements we need for survival, but it is also teeming with things that can wipe us out, from poisonous vegetation to ferocious beasts and from deadly snakes to killer sharks, to say nothing of countless bacteria and viruses capable of disfiguring, dismembering or destroying us. Even the air we breathe is sometimes contaminated with life-threatening agents of one kind or another. Has God deliberately put all these hazards in place?

Human conflict

It has been estimated that in the last 4,000 years there have been less than 300 without a major war. The twentieth century was expected to be one of unparalleled peace and prosperity, but in 1967 Britain's Secretary of Defence called it 'the most violent century in history'. He could have repeated the claim at the end of the century; thirty million people were slaughtered in World War I, while the figures for World War II are so vast that they have never been accurately computed. Countless others were ruthlessly put to death during the rise of Marxist-Leninist Communism in Russia and Eastern Europe. At one point, opponents of Mao Tse-tung's Communist Revolution in China were being exterminated at the rate of 22,000 a month.[14] Pol Pot slaughtered over 1,500,000 Cambodians in about twenty-two months. In the six weeks from 7 April 1994 over 500,000 Rwandans were massacred in the savage civil war between Hutus and Tutsis. How can a loving God allow such wholesale carnage?

The ravages of time

As if these dangers and disasters were not enough, we are all fighting a losing battle against physical, mental and psychological deterioration — and even in an age of organ transplants, microsurgery, genetic manipulation and 'wonder drugs', nobody can buck the trend. When business tycoon Sumner Redstone, cited in *Forbes* magazine as America's eighteenth richest man, told the *Daily Telegraph* in July 2001, 'Death is not on my agenda,'[15] he was toying with the truth. Living is the process of dying, and regular exercise, disciplined eating, fitness programmes and the best of medical attention can only delay the inevitable, which will come to over 260,000 people today. Is this miserable picture being painted by a loving God who does 'whatever pleases him'?[16]

God's tombstone?

These are five of atheism's strongest arguments, and I have examined them in some detail in *Does God Believe in Atheists?*,[17] but for over sixty years one event has been used more than any other to challenge the idea of an all-powerful, all-loving God. In *The Chambers Dictionary* the word 'holocaust' is defined as 'a large slaughter or destruction of life',[18] but since 1945 it has become virtually synonymous with one event: 'the Holocaust' has become universal shorthand for the mass murder of Jews by the Nazi regime during World War II.

When the German dictator Adolf Hitler set about building his infamous Third Reich his plans included the establishment of an Aryan 'super-race'. To achieve this, he decided to get rid of all who were unlikely to make any worthwhile contribution to a world free from human weakness, including what he called 'the stupid and degrading fallacies of conscience and morality'.[19] The physically frail and mentally unstable were obvious candidates for elimination, but his main targets were the Jews (Hitler called them 'human bacteria') and by the end of the war no fewer than six million of them — one-third of the world's entire Jewish race — had been exterminated. The impact on people's thinking ever since has been massive, leading one author to claim, 'The case against the existence of God can be summed up in two words: the Holocaust.'[20]

It certainly destroyed the faith of many. Although frequently battered by the guards, the Jewish author Elie Wiesel survived the concentration camp at Birkenau, and in his powerful book *Night* he describes some of its horrors — babies pitchforked as if they were bales of straw, children watching other children being hanged, and his mother and other members of his own family thrown into a huge furnace fuelled by human bodies. During one of the hanging sessions, Wiesel heard someone groan, 'Where is God? Where is he? Where can he be now?'[21] When it was all over, Wiesel's own reply was that Birkenau 'murdered my God and my soul and turned my dreams to dust'.[22]

The American lawyer Edward Tabash comes from five unbroken generations of orthodox Jewish rabbis in eastern Europe, but the Holocaust, which claimed the lives of two members of his own family, turned him into a dogmatic and passionate athe-ist prepared to challenge God head-on. In a debate in Califor-nia he said, 'If the God of the Bible actually exists, I want to sue him for negligence, for being asleep at the wheel of the uni-verse when my grandfather and uncle were gassed to death in Auschwitz.'[23]

Today, millions of atheists and others would agree, and would point to one particular reason for doing so: all Jews worthy of the name believe not merely that God is a living reality, but that they are his chosen people. This seems to make atheism's case even stronger. Where was God when his 'chosen people' were being systematically exterminated? What was he doing for the three years during which Jewish men, women and children were being gassed twenty-fours a day in the extermination camps at Auschwitz, Belsen, Dachau and elsewhere? Where was God when Nazi prison guards threw babies and small children into gutters of boiling human fat rather than waste time gassing them? Where was God when the remains of the slaughtered were scav-enged — hair cut off to make comfortable cushions for the murderers, tattooed skin peeled off and dried out to make lamp-shades, and gold tooth fillings pulled out and turned into jewel-lery? After wrestling with the issue of the Holocaust, the Jewish author Richard Rubenstein wrote, 'We stand in a cold, silent, unfeeling cosmos, unaided by any power beyond our own re-sources. After Auschwitz, what else can a Jew say about God?'[24]

Atheism's reply is 'Nothing' — but one Auschwitz survivor stated that he came to a very different conclusion. Quoted in *The Times*, he said that he never once questioned God's action (or apparent inaction) while he was an inmate: 'It never oc-curred to me to associate the calamity we were experiencing with God — to blame him or believe in him less, or cease be-lieving in him at all because he didn't come to our aid. God doesn't owe us that, or anything. We owe our lives to him. If someone believes that God is responsible for the death of six million because he doesn't somehow do something to save them, he's got his thinking reversed.'[25]

This Holocaust survivor is neither a fake nor a freak. He speaks from the heart for countless others who would say that their experience of suffering has strengthened rather than weakened their faith in God and given them a coherent insight into evil and its consequences. Before we examine why they can do this, I have some tough questions to ask those for whom the Holocaust has become God's tombstone, a ghastly memorial to the fact that the idea of a loving Creator being in control of the universe is dead and buried.

What problem?

The Holocaust raises huge questions for people who believe in God, *but why should it cause any problem for atheists?* If Bertrand Russell was right to dismiss man as 'a curious accident in a backwater',[26] why should it matter in the least whether lives are ended slowly or suddenly, gradually or quickly, peacefully or painfully? If Peter Atkins is right in saying that mankind is 'just a bit of slime on a planet'[27] why should we be remotely concerned at the murder of six million Jews? Do we get traumatized when we see slime trodden on or shovelled down a drain?

The British anthropologist Sir Arthur Keith says that Hitler 'consciously sought to make the practices of Germany conform to the theory of atheistic evolution',[28] while the American scholar Henry Morris confirms that 'Evolutionism was basic in all Nazi thought from beginning to end.'[29] This is seriously embarrassing for atheists, as their evolutionary model says that humankind is simply the result of nothing more than countless chemical and biological accidents. If this is true, how can human beings have any personal value, and why should we turn a hair if any regime decides to dispose of them by the million? Morris writes, 'In the biological theory of Darwin, Hitler found his most powerful weapon against human values,'[30] while an Auschwitz survivor says that its gas chambers 'were the ultimate consequence of the theory that man is nothing but the product of heredity and environment'.[31]

Nor should the Holocaust raise any *ethical* problems for the atheist. In a godless universe, what one 'animal' does to another 'animal' is morally irrelevant, which means that it is just as easy to commend the Holocaust as to condemn it. The Holocaust caused appalling physical, mental and emotional pain and suffering, but atheism has no way of declaring it to be radically *wrong*. In the absence of absolute, transcendent ethics the word 'wrong' is meaningless. Atheism says that we live in a godless universe in which everything can be explained by physics, chemistry and biology. But if this is the case, things we call 'good' and 'evil' are just impersonal, valueless data and have no explanation. If there is no God, there is no universal moral law, and if there is no such law, *nothing* is essentially good or evil. Richard Dawkins concedes this without blinking and says that we live in a universe in which there is 'no design, no purpose, *no evil and no good*, nothing but blind, pitiless indifference'[32] (emphasis added). Can you accept that, and brush aside the Holocaust as a meaningless event in a meaningless world? If there are no transcendent values, who has the right to say that there should be any, or what they should be?

Atheism says that morality is 'a creation of the genes',[33] so atheists should have no problem in believing that Hitler's genes drove him to do what he did. Atheists see moral values as a social contract aimed at producing what is usually called 'the greatest good of the greatest number', but Hitler would have signed up to that idea in a heartbeat! He justified the extermination of Jews, gypsies, the mentally unstable and others in the long-term interests of a superior race that would eventually dominate the world. Why should any atheist quibble at that?

These are tricky areas for the atheist because, as Ravi Zacharias points out, the Holocaust was 'the logical outworking of the demise of God'.[34] Although Hitler was raised in the Roman Catholic Church and kept his formal ties with the church for his own political ends, he abandoned any pretence of faith at an early age. He described himself as 'a total pagan',[35] and called Christianity 'the hardest blow that ever struck humanity'.[36] In *The Rise and Fall of the Third Reich*, journalist William Shirer said that Hitler's goal was to replace Christianity with 'the old paganism of the early Germanic gods and the new paganism of the Nazi extremists'.[37] Any honest atheist would admit that he does not have answers to the questions raised by the Holocaust, but an honest *and consistent* atheist should realize that he has no reason or basis to raise them in the first place. Logically, evil and suffering are problems only to people who believe in God.

The other side of the coin

Another flaw in the atheist's case is that logically speaking he has problems, not merely with the existence of evil, but with the existence of *good*. In a universe that can be explained solely in terms of physics, chemistry and biology, 'good' becomes as meaningless as 'evil'. If you are an atheist, ask yourself how goodness, love, kindness, generosity or sympathy can be explained. Atheists are clearly *capable* of all of these, but if human beings are just collections of bones, blood and tissue, what do these things *mean* and why is there any virtue in them? (Come to think of it, what does 'virtue' mean?) When Richard Dawkins admits that 'Universal love and the welfare of the species as a whole simply do not make evolutionary sense,'[38] he is confirming that there is no way to arrive at personal morality from an impersonal universe. How can we jump from atoms to ethics and from molecules to morality? If we are nothing but genetically programmed machines, how can we condemn anything as being 'evil', or commend anything as being 'good'? Why should we be concerned over issues of justice or fairness, or feel any obligation to treat others with dignity or respect?

Time and again I have heard people respond to tragedy by asking, 'How can there be a just God?', but there is a logical fallacy in the question. Where do these people get the idea of things being just or unjust from? Without a God of absolute justice, words like 'just' and 'unjust' have no moral content but are matters of personal opinion at best and meaningless at worst. The fact that we have a sense of things being right or wrong, fair or unfair, just or unjust — that this instinct is 'there' — is a strong clue that there is some transcendent standard. Alvin Plantinga says, 'Now, as opposed to 20-25 years ago, most [atheists] have conceded that in fact there isn't any inconsistency between the existence of an omnipotent, omniscient and wholly good God and the existence of the evil the world contains.'[39] Had you realized this? The fact is that the existence of evil points *towards* the existence of God, not away from it.

In his autobiography, Lord Hailsham, the former Lord Chancellor, tells how the realization of this straightened out his own thinking. After pointing out that rejecting God can never solve the problem of evil, he goes on: 'The real problem is not the problem of evil, but the problem of good, not the problem of cruelty and selfishness, but the problem of kindness and generosity, not the problem of ugliness, but the problem of beauty... It is light which is the problem, not darkness... The thing we have to explain in the world is the positive, not the negative. It is this which led me to God in the first place.'[40]

Facing facts

There is no way in which the person who believes in God can evade the issue of evil and suffering, but before we turn to the biblical response, we need to nail down some basic facts.

- Although our planet provides enough food to feed all six billion of us, millions die of starvation every year because of our exploitation or mismanagement of the earth's resources, while the selfish pollution of the atmosphere results in agony and death for many others. Can this be laid at God's door?
- Suffering is often caused by human error or incompetence. The owners of the *Titanic* reduced the recommended number of lifeboats to avoid the boat deck looking cluttered. The Aberfan enquiry pinpointed the 'bungling ineptitude' of those who built the slag-heap over a stream. The International Atomic Enquiry Agency blamed 'defective safety culture' for the Chernobyl disaster. Even if we ignore the many millions who have been killed or wounded in military conflict and in acts of personal violence, these examples are sufficient to show that man himself is directly responsible for a great deal of human suffering. Why should God be in the dock?
- A great deal of human suffering is self-inflicted. Smokers who ignore health warnings and are crippled by lung cancer or heart disease, heavy drinkers who suffer from cirrhosis of the liver and those dying of AIDS after indiscriminate sex are obvious examples. So are gluttons

whose health collapses, workaholics who drive themselves to physical or mental breakdowns, and the countless people who suffer from serious illness as a direct result of suppressed hatred, anger, bitterness and envy. Is God to blame for their behaviour?

The link between wrongdoing and its consequences is so clear that we need to get personal here. Ravi Zacharias tells of a discussion he and some friends had with one of America's biggest construction tycoons who wanted to know why God was silent when there was so much evil in the world. At one point someone asked him, 'Since evil seems to trouble you so much, I would be curious to know what you have done about the evil you see within you.' There was what Zacharias called 'a red-faced silence'.[41] How would you have responded?

The blurred reflection

What does the Bible have to say on the subject? Far from giving slick and easy answers to the questions raised by evil and suffering, it confirms that we all have to reckon with 'the mystery of lawlessness'.[42] You may feel that this is the ultimate form of evasion, but there is no logical basis for assuming that God owes us a detailed explanation for everything that goes on in the world, and leaving us with questions is not the same as leaving us in the dark. In one of the best-known passages in the New Testament, the apostle Paul writes that, in this life, 'We see in a mirror dimly.'[43] Why should this surprise us, or make us decide that God is non-existent? How could we know all the answers unless we had total knowledge of everything? To say that unless we see the whole picture there *is* no picture is not intelligence but arrogance.

In Paul's day a mirror would have been made from burnished metal, and the image somewhat blurred, but it would still have given some indication of what it was reflecting. On the issue of evil and suffering, even the strongest believer in God has to admit that there are enigmas, grey areas and unanswered questions. Yet to say that something is mysterious is not to say that we can know nothing about it, and in the remainder of this chapter we shall look at some of the Bible's teaching on the subject. There is only one place to begin.

The stained planet

Some years ago, an article in *The Times* asked, 'What's wrong with the world?' In the correspondence that followed, the shortest letter was by far the best: 'In response to your question, "What's wrong with the world?" — I am, Yours faithfully, G. K. Chesterton.' The well-known British author's confession ties in with the Bible's insistence that when looking for somebody to blame for evil and suffering, nobody is in a position to point an accusing finger at God.

When God created the world it was without blemish of any kind, reflecting his own perfect nature: 'God saw all that he had made, and it was very good.'[44] Included in this perfect world was humanity, distinct from all the rest of creation in being made 'in the image of God',[45] a phrase that tells us at least three things about man.

1. He was created as a *personal* being, capable of a living relationship with his Creator and with his fellow human beings.

2. He was created as a *moral* being, his conscience making him aware by nature of the difference between right and wrong.

3. He was created as a *rational* being, able not merely to think, draw conclusions and make sensible decisions, but specifically to make moral choices. Although moral perfection was 'stamped upon him in the very act of creation',[46] he was not a robot, programmed to do whatever God dictated. Instead, he had the ability to obey God and the freedom to disobey him.

This state of perfection went on for some time (we are not told how long), with our first parents living in a perfect environment and in a faultless relationship with each other and with their Creator, but at some point a created angel or spirit called Satan, who had rebelled against God's authority, persuaded Adam and his wife Eve to disbelieve God and disobey his clear directions. The moment they did so, 'Sin entered the world'[47] — with catastrophic results.

- Man's relationship with God, which had depended on unqualified obedience to his perfect will, was shattered. Man retained his spiritual nature, but lost his spiritual life. He remained a person, but forfeited dynamic union with his Maker.
- He lost his innocence and his moral free will, his very nature becoming infected with godless ideas, attitudes and affections.
- His own personality was wrecked. For the first time, he lost his self-esteem and knew what it was to be guilty, alienated, ashamed, anxious and afraid.
- His inter-personal relationships were poisoned by suspicion, dishonesty, mistrust and the need to justify himself.
- His body became subject to decay, disease and death, things that were never built into man's original make-up.

Two things bring the history of human rebellion right up to date. When Adam sinned, he did so as the representative head of the entire human race and, because humanity is an integrated whole, he took the entire species with him: 'Sin entered the world through one man, and death through sin, and in this way death came to all men, because all sinned.'[48] Tied in to this is the fact that Adam began to father children *after* his fall into sin and that he did so 'in his own likeness, in his own image'.[49] Like poison dumped at the source of a river, Adam's polluted and depraved human nature has been passed on to every succeeding generation, and all of humanity is caught up in its flow. You and I did not begin life in a state of moral limbo or neutrality but, like every one of our contemporaries, with sinful tendencies and desires waiting to express themselves in words, thoughts and actions. Does your own experience not confirm this?

As rebellion against a God of infinite goodness, holiness and truth is infinitely evil, we should hardly be surprised if the consequences are vast and extensive, and a second far-reaching result of sin is that the whole cosmos has been dislocated. In the Bible's graphic illustration, 'The whole creation has been groaning as in the pains of childbirth right up to the present time.'[50] The world as we now see it is not in its original condition; we live on what someone has called 'a stained planet', one ruined by sin. Earthquakes, volcanoes, floods and hurricanes were unknown before sin entered the world, and the suffering and death they cause are due to what the British author Stuart Olyott calls 'contempt for God'[51] — in other words, man's rebellion against his Maker's authority.

The big question here is why God should have taken such an obvious risk in giving man moral freedom in the first place. Whatever the answer might be, not even an all-powerful God could give man freedom and at the same time guarantee that he would use it wisely. A person who is free and yet not free is a contradiction in terms. Not even God could bestow and with-hold freedom at one and the same time. Yet to deny God's existence by saying that he could not have made a world in which human beings could disobey him and bring about per-sonal, corporate and global catastrophe is going too far, as God has infinite wisdom and love and 'His way is perfect.'[52]

How can we possibly prove that God was wrong to give man freedom of moral choice? Would creating robots have been wiser? How can we know God's reasons and purposes unless we know everything he knows? In his book *How Long, O Lord?*, the American author Don Carson writes that God's way of working 'defies our attempt to tame it by reason', then adds, 'I do not mean it is illogical; I mean that we do not know enough to be able to unpack it and domesticate it.'[53] As finite, fallen creatures we need to swallow our pride and accept that God's ways are 'beyond tracing out'.[54] Refusing to do so, and claim-ing that the existence of evil rules out our creation by a wise and loving God, is irrational, illogical and unbiblical.

An interfering God?

This still leaves the question: 'But would an all-powerful, all-loving God not intervene to prevent evil and the suffering it causes?' It is best answered by asking others.

What kind of God would do this whenever we wanted him to? In the debate mentioned earlier in this chapter, Edward Tabash called God a 'moral monster' and issued this challenge: 'If you are listening, and you are really there, show yourself right now… Do a colossal miracle… Show me something more than ancient hearsay to prove your existence.'[55] When nothing happened, Tabash claimed to have proved his case — but he missed the point that a God who allowed himself to be ordered around in this way would be surrendering the very qualities that make him God. The kind of God who jumps whenever anybody shouts, 'Jump!' may exist in fairy tales but not in the real world, and certainly not in Scripture.

As far as natural disasters are concerned, do we really want God to prevent them by manipulating the laws of physics in such a way that we would never know from one moment to another which were working and which had been suspended? If God did this, science would be replaced by guesswork and, as Francis Bridger says in his book *Why Can't I Have Faith?*, 'We should be reduced to such a state of physical, social and psychological instability that life would fall apart, paradoxically bringing even more suffering in its train.'[56]

Turning to moral issues, at what level should God intervene? We might say that he should not have allowed the worst offenders — the Hitlers, Pol Pots and Mao Ttse-tungs of this world — to do what they did. But what about the next level — say, thugs, sadists, rapists, child abusers, drug pushers and those who wreck the lives of others for personal gain; should God step in and stop them? If he did so, another 'layer' of offenders would become the worst — say, drunk drivers, shoplifters, burglars, petty thieves and the like. If we argued in this way we would eventually get to the point at which we would be demanding that God should intervene to prevent *all* evil and sin. Would you settle for that, even if it meant having your own thoughts, words and actions controlled by a cosmic puppetmaster, robbing you of all freedom and responsibility?

This kind of God would also need to control thoughts and actions that were the *indirect* causes of suffering. On my weekly day off I usually play golf, then drive to pick up my wife from another appointment. Imagine that I am delayed by those playing in front of me, then find that I am running behind schedule.

Dashing out of the clubhouse to the car park, I accidentally knock over a lady member who hits her head so violently on a concrete kerb that she sustains irreparable brain damage. At what point — and how — should God have intervened to prevent subsequent years of suffering? By causing the players in front of me to play better or to move more quickly? By making me choose an earlier starting time? By shortening the time it took me to shower and change after the game? By steering the lady into the clubhouse through a different door? Would you accept the idea of a God who controlled things in this way, robbing you of every atom of independence or choice?

Suggesting that God should intervene to prevent all evil and suffering sounds reasonable enough, but when we think it through it raises more problems than it solves. The Bible points us in a very different direction.

A case history

The Bible's fullest treatment of the issue of evil and suffering is the story of a man called Job, who lived over 3,000 years ago. Rated 'the greatest man among all the people of the East',[57] he was seriously wealthy and the father of seven sons and three daughters. What is more, he was 'blameless and upright; he feared God and shunned evil'.[58] He seemed to have everything going for him, but in one terrible day he lost over 11,000 animals, many of his servants were killed and all his ten children died when a tornado struck the house in which they were holding a party.[59] Yet after being hit by this personal holocaust, Job 'fell to the ground in worship' and said:

Naked I came from my mother's womb,
    and naked I shall depart.

> The LORD gave and the LORD has taken away;
>   may the name of the LORD be praised.[60]

This was a stupendous declaration of faith in the sovereignty of God, but it did nothing to stop Job's suffering. His own health began to deteriorate; he was covered with boils, his skin began to peel off, his eyes grew weak, his teeth began to rot and he was hit by a combination of fever, insomnia and depression. Those nearest to him turned the screw. His wife was so sure things were hopeless that she indirectly challenged him to commit suicide: 'Curse God and die!'[61] An inner circle of friends began by being sympathetic, but soon changed their tune. Emphasizing God's knowledge, holiness and justice, they told Job that his great suffering must be punishment for great sin; one of them even felt that Job was probably getting off lightly.

From then on, Job rode an emotional roller-coaster. There were times when he rejoiced at the prospect of spending eternity in God's presence: 'I know that my Redeemer lives... I myself will see him with my own eyes.'[62] At other times he wished he had been stillborn: 'Why did I not perish at birth?'[63] He questioned God's justice in allowing the ungodly to 'spend their years in prosperity and go down to the grave in peace'[64] while he, a believer, was 'reduced to dust and ashes'.[65] There were periods when he felt that God was either distant or deaf, with no concern for his pain and no inclination to answer his prayers. Throughout this time, his friends kept up such a barrage of questions, advice and accusations that Job complained, 'Will your long-winded speeches never end?'[66] A young believer by the name of Elihu was more helpful, but then came the decisive turning-point of the whole story — God spoke directly to Job.

God's response to Job's agonizing questions forms the Bible's fullest treatment of the issue of evil and suffering — yet it never mentions either! Instead of giving Job a neatly packaged

explanation, God took a very different line. Often in the form
of questions, Job was reminded of the way in which the natural
world pointed to God's overwhelming greatness and power in
contrast to man's dependence and weakness:

> Where were you when I laid the earth's foundation?[67]

> Have you ever given orders to the morning
>   or shown the dawn its place?[68]

> Can you bind the beautiful Pleiades?
>   Can you loose the cords of Orion? [69]

> Do you send the lightning bolts on their way?[70]

> Can you set up God's dominion over the earth?[71]

> Do you have an arm like God's?[72]

The closest God came to answering Job's questions directly
was to ask some of his own:

> Will the one who contends with the Almighty correct
>   him? ...
> Would you discredit my justice?
> Would you condemn me to justify yourself?[73]

God tells him nothing about the cause of pain and suffering,
but focuses instead on man's response. The torrent of words
poured out by his friends had done nothing to bring Job clarity,
comfort or courage — they had been 'words without knowledge'[74] — but now he was able to see things in their right
perspective.

- God was in absolute control of the universe, and nothing could frustrate his eternal purposes: 'I know that you can do all things; no plan of yours can be thwarted.'[75]
- He was in no position to argue with God or to question his dealings with him: 'I am unworthy — how can I reply to you?'[76]
- He was not in possession of all the facts: 'Surely I spoke of things I did not understand, things too wonderful for me to know.'[77]
- A living relationship with God was infinitely better than religious feelings or ideas: 'My ears had heard of you but now my eyes have seen you.'[78]
- He should confess that he had been wrong to question God's power, justice and love and should humbly commit himself to him: 'I despise myself and repent in dust and ashes.'[79]

There are important principles here. Job did not get a line-by-line answer to his questions, but he learned to trust God in the dark. This was not giving in to fate but, as the Irish preacher Herbert Carson movingly puts it, responding 'like a child in the darkness gripped in his father's arms'.[80] God does not spell out to us why he allowed sin to enter the universe, but we can be sure that he is in control of even the worst of its effects, without being obliged to tell us how this works out in practice.

Job's story tells us that *it is less important to know all the answers than to know and trust the one who does*. Laying hold on this alone can be a liberating experience. Some years ago my wife was being crushed by life-threatening clinical depression. Her faith had virtually evaporated and there seemed to be no relief in sight. Then, twice in one week, people wrote to her in almost identical words, the gist of their messages being that God was under no obligation to explain anything that he caused or allowed to come into our lives. This did not give us cut-and-dried answers to all our questions, but within a day or so the suffocating cloud had lifted and Joyce emerged with her faith renewed and deepened.

God's megaphone

In his well-known book *The Problem of Pain,* C. S. Lewis wrote, 'God whispers to us in our pleasures, speaks in our conscience, but shouts in our pains; it is his megaphone to rouse a deaf world.'[81] Scripture tells us that God uses suffering to underline our physical frailty and our dependence on him, to remind us that we are not immune from the consequences of sin, to teach us that there is more to life than physical health and strength, to encourage us to look to him for help in coping with the pressures and pains of living in a fallen world, to develop depth of character and to learn how to be sensitive and sympathetic to the needs of others.

Above all, God uses suffering to divert our attention from the present to the future and from the brevity of time to the vastness of eternity. So much of our time can be taken up with trivialities such as fashion, sport, deciding where to go on holiday, choosing which restaurant to eat in, or selecting wallpaper, but when a serious accident or illness strikes these things suddenly become utterly irrelevant, and we begin to think seriously (and perhaps for the first time) about the certainty of our own death and of what might lie beyond. At this point, atheism offers nothing (literally) but dust and ashes. As Herbert Carson writes in his fine book *Facing Suffering,* 'To look ahead from a purely human standpoint is to see only the next hill — the continuing pain, the persistent sorrow, the debilitating illness with its relentless progress... All we can do, if that is the limit of our horizon, is to stumble on as best we can.'[82]

The Bible gives a very different perspective and says that although God allows evil and suffering to coexist for the time being, and for purposes we can never fully understand, they will one day be eliminated and the problems they produce perfectly and permanently solved. The God who brought the present order of things into existence, and who is 'sustaining all things by his powerful word',[83] will bring this devastated and degraded world to an end and transform the entire universe into 'a new heaven and a new earth, the home of righteousness',[84] in which there will be 'no more death or mourning or crying or pain', because 'the old order of things' will have 'passed away'.[85]

When the atheist claims that an all-powerful God could overcome evil and that an all-loving God would do so, the person who believes in God agrees, *but adds that as it is not happening at present we can be certain that it will happen in the future.* The day is coming when God will make a cosmic moral adjustment. Perfect justice will not only be done, but will be seen to be done. The wicked will no longer prosper, the righteous will no longer suffer and the problem of evil will be fully, finally and obviously settled beyond all doubt and dispute. This is what enabled the apostle Paul to brush aside twenty years of almost unrelenting pain and pressure as 'light and momentary troubles'[86] and to assure his fellow believers, 'Our present sufferings are not worth comparing with the glory that will be revealed in us.'[87] The existence of evil does not eliminate the possibility of God; it is the existence of God that guarantees the elimination of evil.

This points us to two parallel truths. The first is that if we confine our thinking to time and space alone there is no way in which we can begin to get to grips with the issue of evil and suffering. Answers to questions about meaning and purpose involve vast issues; they lie outside of the little 'box' in which we naturally live and think. Just as we cannot understand the movement of the tides without knowing about the gravitational pull of the moon upon them, so our 'boxed-in' thinking can never find answers that will quieten our minds or satisfy our hearts.

The second truth is that the Christian response to evil and suffering *does* go beyond time and space and opens us up to wider thinking. It is rooted in a relationship with a personal, living God who is not an impotent spectator of human agony, but is in total and immediate control of everything that happens. What is more, he has identified himself with the trauma of human suffering and intervened personally and at indescribable cost in order to bring it to an end, to punish evil and eventually to destroy it. In the course of our final chapter we shall see exactly how he has done this.

Call John Farese

John Farese lives in Florida with his brother Paul and sister-in-law Janis and their four children. He enjoys a very productive life, is keenly interested in a variety of sports, and has a special involvement in information technology, including the maintenance of his own web site.

He has been disabled since birth, is paralysed in both arms and legs, and has been unable to sit up for many years.

I came into this world on 27 August 1956, the second of Vincent and Joan Farese's seven children. My older brother Bernie was born with spinal muscular atrophy, a severely crippling disease that meant that he was never able to walk. So was I, and a younger sister, Tina. In each case, the doctors told my parents that the child concerned would not live beyond its eighth birthday. Tina died of pneumonia when she was four years old.

I was brought up as a Roman Catholic, and quietly accepted the doctrines taught to me by my parents and the parish priest, especially the idea that a person got right with God by obeying the sacraments of the church. At one stage I was told that if I recited forty-five prayers from a particular Catholic prayer book every day for a whole year I would escape the pains of purgatory and hell, and be immediately accepted into heaven when I died. I never missed a day, but had no assurance that my discipline would pay off. One special highlight I remember was a trip to Lourdes, in France. My mother took my brother Bernie and me there to seek healing from the Blessed Virgin Mary, but we came back home in exactly the same state as before.

My early years were spent in suburban Boston, Massachusetts, but when I was fifteen my father's business relocated our family to Florida, so we all moved south. Leaving behind relatives and friends in whom I had found a sense of security was devastating to me, yet in God's providence it was to prove the best move of my life. Brought up in a city where Catholicism was a dominant factor, I had come to believe that anyone outside that tradition was beyond salvation. Yet four months after moving to Fort Lauderdale, and when I was still homesick for Boston, our next-door neighbour invited my mother to a home Bible study. Although we had a large white family Bible in our home, it was hardly ever opened, and I was shocked when my mother accepted the invitation. There was another shock when she agreed to the Bible-study leader's suggestion that her son, who was then a freshman at Florida Bible College, might come and talk about the Christian faith to my brother and me.

That visit, and others which followed, had very different sequels. Bernie and I were so impressed by what John Tardonia told us about Jesus Christ as the one and only Saviour that we both gave intellectual assent to the gospel of grace and said a 'sinner's prayer'. In Bernie's case, this marked a dramatic change. He began to pray, study the Bible and go to church, and eventually enrolled in Bible College. Even more marked was a radical change in his lifestyle, which now seemed driven by a daily desire to please God. In my case, the only change was for the worse. I had made some new friends whose lifestyle was rampantly self-centred and immoral, and I threw in my lot with them, determined not to let my disability keep me from enjoying life to the full. For the next twelve years gambling, heavy drinking, marijuana abuse, weekly visits to strip clubs and frequent engagements with call girls provided a means of escape from the pain, loneliness and emptiness I was experiencing.

Some years after Bernie and I went our separate ways, my younger brother Paul, who was a popular athlete in high school, joined me in the sex and drugs scene, until he went away to college on an athletic scholarship. During his first term, he got into so much trouble that he was on the verge of being expelled, yet when he came home for Christmas two months later there had been an amazing change. Like Bernie, he had become a committed Christian, and he was soon urging me to turn away from my dissolute lifestyle and get right with God. I knew in my heart that he was right, and even prayed with tears that God would change my life, but I loved what I was doing, and found myself unable to break my destructive habits.

At this point Bernie gave me a Bible, which I promised to read, but it sat unopened on a shelf for the next six months, while I went back to gambling, sex and drugs. Yet there was a difference. For the first time, I began to feel uncomfortable doing what had given me such undisturbed pleasure before. I kept remembering my conversations with Paul and my promise to Bernie that I would read the Bible. These nagging thoughts eventually became so strong that I took the Bible down and began to read it. I began at the first page, and in three months had read it right through — but by then I too had become a Christian. It was while I was reading the Sermon on the Mount that God opened my eyes to the truth about my sin, the inability of religion to deal with it, and the need to repent and trust in Jesus Christ as my own personal Saviour. As I did, I was given an assurance that my sins had been forgiven and that I had become a true child of God.

Like most new Christians, I found myself full of zeal. I wanted to be baptized, join a Bible-believing church, and do whatever I could to serve others. I remembered Jesus had said that he 'did not come to be served, but to serve, and to give his life as a ransom for many'[88] and that 'No servant is greater than his master.'[89] Being bedridden, I was not sure that I could contribute anything to others, but by the grace of God I now find myself able to be of energetic service in ways far beyond anything I had imagined.

In the light of my physical condition, I am often asked the age-old question, 'How can an all-powerful God of love allow you to suffer in this way? Surely the Bible says that God always does what is right?' Yes it does — and he does! Through my suffering I have come to see that God demonstrates his unfailing love to those who have come to put their trust in him. Out of his own painful experience the psalmist wrote, 'It was good for me to be afflicted, so that I might learn your decrees'[90] — and I gladly endorse every word of that testimony.

Among other things, suffering empties us of pride and self-dependence, and makes us realize our complete dependence upon God. When we reach the point where we have nowhere to turn except to God, we begin to get a clearer view of who and what he is. Day by day, I am discovering more and more of his wisdom, love and grace. I am also finding that God's power is made perfect in my weakness and that 'When I am weak, then I am strong.'[91]

Jesus went through appalling suffering, physical, mental and spiritual, yet at the end of it all he was to 'see the light of life and be satisfied'.[92] I count it a privilege to experience in some small way 'the fellowship of sharing in his sufferings'.[93] Although I am bedridden, struggle to breathe comfortably and often have to contend with painful bed sores, I count these trials as 'light and momentary troubles'.[94] For all the difficulties they cause, I know they will seem trivial in the light of the eternal bliss that awaits God's children in the world to come.

One of the psalmists cried, 'Come and listen, all you who fear God; let me tell you what he has done for me,'[95] and I gladly do the same. He has turned my mourning into laughter and my desolation into joy. He has made my heart rejoice with 'an inexpressible and glorious joy'.[96] When I struggled to escape from his grace, he drew me to himself. I bear witness that never servant had such a Master as I have, never brother such a Kinsman, never spouse such a Husband. No sinner ever had a better Saviour than Jesus, no mourner a better Comforter. I want none beside him. In life he is my life, and in death he will be the death of death. In poverty he is my riches, in sickness my health, in darkness my sun. Jesus is to me all grace and no wrath, all truth and no falsehood, and of truth and grace he is full — infinitely full.

10.

One solitary life

There is space in this book for just one further item of evidence for the existence of God, and it is absolutely fundamental. Without it, all we have said so far is just fuel for discussion; this piece of evidence demands a decision. We shall look at that decision, and the consequences at stake, in the final chapter. At this point, we shall concentrate on the evidence itself.

- 'Here is a man who was born in an obscure village, the child of a peasant woman. He grew up in another village. He worked in a carpenter's shop until he was thirty… He never owned a home. He never wrote a book. He never held an office. He never had a family. He never went to college… He never travelled 200 miles from the place where he was born. He never did one of the things that usually accompany greatness. He had no credentials but himself.'
- 'I am far within the mark when I say that all the armies that ever marched, all the navies that ever were built, all the parliaments that ever sat and all the kings that ever reigned, put together, have not affected the human race as powerfully as has that one solitary life.'

These two assessments seem to have nothing in common, yet they are both taken from a famous anonymous essay — and both refer to the same person.

On 11 October 1999 the world population officially reached six billion, bringing the running total of human beings in history to about sixty billion. The overwhelming majority of these are now unknown; some had a localized or temporary influence; comparatively few had a major effect on human history; but nobody has left a deeper mark on human culture than the subject of the essay from which I have quoted — Jesus of Nazareth, who was born in Israel about 2,000 years ago. The noted American historian Kenneth Scott Latourette wrote, 'Jesus, the seeming failure, has had more effect upon the history of mankind than any other of its race who has ever existed,'[1] while even a sceptic like the novelist H. G. Wells admitted that Jesus was 'easily the dominant figure in history' and that nobody could write a history of the human race without giving Jesus 'the first and foremost place'.[2]

Stranger than fiction

These testimonials become all the more remarkable in the light of the following facts:

- His exact date of birth is not known, yet human history is divided into the years before he was born and those since then.
- He never wrote a book, yet more books have been written about him than about any other person, and the demand for more seems insatiable.
- He never painted a picture, composed any poetry, or wrote any music, yet nobody has inspired more paintings, poetry, plays, songs, films, videos or other art forms.

One film, based almost entirely on his recorded words, has been produced in almost 500 languages and has already been seen by more people than any other in history.

• He never raised an army or led an armed rebellion, yet millions of people have laid down their lives in his cause, and thousands still do so every year.

• Except for one brief period during his childhood, his travels were limited to an area about the size of Wales, but today his influence is literally worldwide and his followers form the largest religious grouping the world has ever known.

• His public teaching lasted only three years, and was restricted to a few parts of one of the world's smallest countries, yet today purpose-built satellites and some of the world's largest radio and television networks beam his teaching around our planet.

• He set foot in just two countries, yet today an organization committed to his cause flies regularly to more countries than any of the world's commercial airlines.[3]

• He had no formal education, but thousands of universities, seminaries, colleges and schools have been founded in his name.

• During his lifetime, he was virtually unknown outside his own country, yet in the current edition of *Encyclopaedia Britannica* the entry under his name runs to some 30,000 words.

Yet we can go further, because to rank Jesus as the greatest, wisest, best or most influential man who ever lived is not to dignify him but to degrade him and to miss the whole point of who he was and what he did. When we unearth the real Jesus we find that he provides the most compelling evidence of all for the existence of God.

Bertrand Russell once wrote, 'Historically, it is quite doubtful whether Jesus ever existed at all, and if he did we do not know anything about him,'[4] but this is prejudiced piffle. At least nineteen celebrated first- and second-century authors (almost all of them sceptics) give details of his birth, life, teaching and death, all without the slightest hint that he was a fictional character. These include the distinguished Jewish diplomat and historian Flavius Josephus, the Roman historian Suetonius, Cornelius Tacitus (another eminent historian who was also Governor of Asia) and Pliny the Younger, a Roman proconsul in Asia Minor, acknowledged as 'one of the world's great letter-writers, whose letters have attained the status of literary classics'. These are sufficient to sink Russell's ridiculous claim without trace, but to discover Jesus' true identity and his relevance to our subject we must turn to the Bible, whose credentials we established in chapter 1. Everything it says about him can be summed up in three words: *he was unique.*

The chromosomes

In the first place, Jesus was unique in his *conception*. There was nothing unusual about his birth; as far we know, he left his mother's womb in the normal way. The startling thing was how he *entered* her womb, and on this the Bible could not be more emphatic; it says that he was conceived without sexual intercourse and without male sperm being inserted into the womb in any other way. Simply put, his mother Mary was still a virgin up to the time of Jesus' birth. In later years, she was to conceive other children in the normal way,[5] but during her first pregnancy she emphatically stated, 'I am a virgin'.[6] Elsewhere, the Bible makes it clear that her husband Joseph 'had no union with her until she gave birth to a son',[7] and that Jesus was conceived 'before they came together'.[8]

This one fact sets Jesus apart, as there is no other record of human parthenogenesis (the female egg dividing itself without male fertilization). In Mary's case we are simply told that she became pregnant 'through the Holy Spirit',[9] that in some mysterious way God himself superintended the procedure by which Jesus began his earthly existence.

Those who dismiss this outright as being scientifically impossible have failed to grasp the point we made in chapter 1, that rejecting miracles in this way is itself unscientific. The question to ask is not, '*Can* miracles happen?' (of course they can, once God is brought into the picture) but, '*Have* they happened?', and each case must be examined in the light of the evidence. In this particular instance, not only is the virgin conception of Jesus stated time and again in Scripture, but the two main narratives are by men whose professions called for meticulous accuracy and attention to detail — a tax official and a physician. Why would these men have risked their reputations by concocting such a story? Why did Joseph and Mary never deny it? Why would the early church invent such a fable, knowing that it would produce a storm of ridicule and contempt?

Others try to evade the issue by suggesting that this *was* a case of parthenogenesis (which has been observed in some lower mammals, though without any viable young developing), but this theory collapses because of the genetic make-up of human beings. To put it simply, the male has x and y chromosomes, while the female has x and x. This means that even if Mary's pregnancy had been triggered off by some unique biological freak, the child born as a result would have been female, as there would have been no y chromosome to produce a male. In other words, these sceptics deny the virgin conception by replacing a miraculous fact with a miraculous fantasy!

Words and actions

Jesus was unique in *the words he spoke and the things he did.*
Visiting Jerusalem as a twelve-year-old, he got into discussion
with some of the temple's religious leaders, and everyone who
heard him 'was amazed at his understanding and his answers'.[10]
There are two key words here. 'Understanding' translates the
Greek *sunesis*, which means 'the ability to understand concepts
and see relationships between them'.[11] Those who listened were
staggered at the way in which a pre-teen from the back of beyond was effortlessly trading religious philosophy with the experts, but that was not all; his answers were even more astonishing. There is nothing unusual in a boy asking awkward questions — I have sometimes been embarrassed by five-year olds!
— but for someone without any formal education to reel off
solutions to problems that baffled the nation's religious elite
was something else. Can you put your finger on anyone else in
history who did this with ease — and who did so, not clinically
or arrogantly, but in such a way that all who heard him 'were
amazed at the gracious words that came from his lips'?[12]

At the end of what has since become known as the Sermon
on the Mount people 'were amazed at his teaching, because he
taught as one who had authority, and not as their teachers of
the law'.[13] When we read the sermon we should hardly be surprised, as it lays down spiritual principles and moral standards
that are beyond comparison. Later, when his religious enemies
were closing in, temple guards sent to arrest him were awe-
struck and slunk back empty-handed to their masters complain-
ing, 'No one ever spoke the way this man does.'[14] Nearly 2,000
years later his words produce the same kind of feedback: the
American historian Bernard Ramm says, 'They are read more,
quoted more, loved more, believed more and translated more
because they are the greatest words ever spoken.'[15]

Jesus is also unique in the miracles he performed. Scripture
records other miracles, but it has been suggested that Jesus

may have performed more in a given day than are recorded in all of Old Testament history. In addition to his extensive preaching and teaching ministry he healed people 'who were ill with various diseases, those suffering severe pain, the demon-possessed, those having seizures, and the paralysed'.[16] He cured blindness,[17] deafness,[18] dumbness,[19] leprosy[20] and lameness,[21] and the record shows that he did not even have to be present at the time, but could heal at a distance — and with a word. Virtually all the healings were instantaneous and, in complete contrast to the records of so-called 'faith healers' past and present, there is no record of a failed attempt at healing, nor of a single relapse. What is more, he never advertised his services, promoted 'healing crusades', took up collections, asked for payment or peddled promotional merchandise.

On at least three occasions he brought a dead person back to life: a twelve-year-old girl within an hour or two of her death,[22] a man whose body was being carried to the cemetery[23] and another who had lain in the grave for four days.[24] He had authority over the natural elements; while crossing the Sea of Galilee by fishing boat, one word from him brought an immediate end to a storm so violent that experienced seamen had been terrified of being drowned.[25] He was able to tell local fishermen exactly where fish could be caught, even when they had nothing to show for hours of effort.[26] He rescued an embarrassing situation at a wedding reception by turning water into the day's finest wine.[27] Faced with a hungry crowd of over 5,000 people, he met their needs with just five loaves and two fish — and when his followers tidied up afterwards the leftovers filled twelve large baskets.[28] On another occasion, he did much the same thing in feeding a crowd of over 4,000.[29]

Yet one of his biographers says that even this amazing catalogue is nothing more than the tip of the iceberg: 'Jesus did many other things as well. If every one of them were written down, I suppose that even the whole world would not have room for the books that would be written.'[30] This may sound like star-struck exaggeration, but not once we grasp the whole picture, which also shows him doing all the things we would expect God to do if he were to come to earth as a human being. Do you know of anyone else in history who comes even close to this?

Character references

Jesus was unique in *his character.* There is no question that he was truly and fully human. There was nothing freakish about him, physically, intellectually, emotionally or spiritually. He was not some kind of alien or superman. He did not have wings or a halo. The Bible makes it clear that his physical development was perfectly normal, that he needed to eat,[31] drink,[32] rest[33] and sleep,[34] and that he went through the usual range of human emotions, from great joy[35] to intense grief.[36] His teaching shows a healthy sense of humour as well as a profound understanding of human fears, desires and failings: 'He knew what was in a man.'[37] He also expressed human spirituality; he prayed,[38] fasted,[39] attended public worship[40] and was an avid reader of Scripture.[41] What is more, he went through all the pressure of wrestling with temptation and knew what it was to struggle against peer pressure and the godless influences that surrounded him. The Bible specifically tells us that he was 'tempted in every way, just as we are' — then adds, 'yet was without sin'.[42]

This is a phenomenal claim. He was clearly a man of great courage, compassion, sympathy, perseverance and faith. Even when slandered and persecuted, he remained 'gentle and humble in heart'.[43] Yet to claim that he never sinned in any way takes things to another level altogether. Where is the evidence for this? I have gone into this in detail elsewhere[44] and will only summarize here. His enemies admitted it; his followers believed it (and were prepared to stake their lives on the fact); and his inner circle of friends confirmed it, even though they were best placed to find any flaws. Yet there is an even more remarkable testimony: he himself claimed it. Speaking of his relationship with God, he openly stated, 'I always do what pleases him.'[45] Faced with a highly critical crowd steeped in biblical teaching on morality and primed by corrupt religious leaders longing to humiliate him, he stunned them into silence by asking, 'Can any of you prove me guilty of sin?'[46] On another occasion he emphasized his complete mastery over temptation by claiming that the devil 'has no hold on me'.[47]

If we accept the record as it stands, Jesus never had a guilty conscience, never blushed with shame, never regretted anything he said or did, never needed to apologize, never wished he could put the clock back or turn over a new leaf, and never needed to pray for forgiveness; in the Bible's own words, he was 'holy, blameless, pure, set apart from sinners'.[48] Can you think of anyone — past or present — who can hold a candle to this? Even those with no religious (let alone Christian) axe to grind have had to make unlikely concessions here. The famous nineteenth-century British historian and sceptical rationalist William Lecky called Jesus 'the highest pattern of virtue' and 'the strongest incentive to its practice' and admitted that his life had 'done more to regenerate and soften mankind than all the disquisitions of philosophers and all the exhortations of moralists'.[49] The nineteenth-century British philosopher John Stuart Mill was a passionate atheist, but he rated Jesus 'the ideal representative guide of humanity',[50] while one of Mill's contemporaries, the French humanist Ernest Renan confessed, 'His beauty is eternal, and his reign shall never end. Jesus is in every respect unique, and nothing can be compared with him.'[51]

The man for all sinners

Jesus is also separated from the rest of humankind in that *his death* was unique.

After several rigged trials, in which perjured witnesses and self-serving judges pulled the strings, Jesus was sentenced to death on a trumped-up treason charge, and within hours of the verdict he was executed by crucifixion, the cruellest known method in the ancient world, and one which has now been banned for nearly 1,500 years. This was a traumatic ending to a remarkable life, but crucifixion was far from unusual. Alexander the Great (356 – 323 B.C.), King of Macedonia, once crucified a thousand of his enemies; Persian rulers often used the threat of crucifixion to deter uprisings; the Romans routinely crucified provincial rebels in New Testament times, and Jesus himself was one of a batch of three men crucified simultaneously.

Then what is so special about the end of his earthly life? Certainly not death itself, which is universal and inescapable. It has been said that the whole world is a hospital, and every person in it a terminal patient. Nobody has to ask, 'Is there death after life?' But *why* do we die? Why is death the ultimate fact of life for every human being, of every race, colour and creed?

The Bible gives a crystal-clear explanation. It begins by telling us that man was originally created morally and spiritually flawless and in perfect harmony with his Creator and with all the rest of creation. Yet, as we saw in chapter 9, this perfect situation was dependent on our first parents' total and unqualified obedience to God, and when they disobeyed their relationship with God was shattered. God had warned them that the moment they sinned they would die, and although they lived physically for some time afterwards his warning was carried out to the letter. This is because the basic meaning of 'death' is not termination but *separation*. The moment they sinned, they died spiritually, in that their souls became separated from God. Instead of revelling in his presence, they became guilty, ashamed and afraid, and 'hid from the LORD God among the trees of the garden'.[52] At the same time, the 'second instalment' of the death penalty kicked in, and their bodies became subject to disease, decay and deterioration, with physical death (the separation of the soul from the body) as the eventual and inevitable result.

As we also saw in chapter 9, this foundational truth is linked to me as I write and to you as you read by the fact that it was only *after* he had become polluted by sin that Adam fathered children, and that he then did so 'in his own likeness, in his own image'.[53] From then on, the inbred pollution has flowed through every subsequent generation. As the federal head of humanity, Adam ruined all those he represented, with the result that we share his guilt as well as his corruption and pollution. Centuries later, King David of Israel, one of the greatest men in Old Testament history, confessed, 'Surely I was sinful at birth, sinful from the time my mother conceived me.'[54] You and I are in exactly the same boat. We are all sinners and we all die. As the Bible puts it, 'Sin entered the world through one man, and death through sin, and in this way death came to all men, because all sinned.'[55] In a nutshell, the answer to the question, 'Why do we die?' is that death, spiritual and physical, is the outworking of what the Bible calls 'the law of sin and death'.[56] But that raises another question. As Jesus never sinned, he was outside of that law's jurisdiction: why then did *he* die? The answer to that question tells us two ways in which his death was unique.

1. It was voluntary

Death is not an option for any of us; as the Bible bluntly puts it, we are 'destined to die'.[57] When the American film producer Woody Allen said, 'It's not that I am afraid of dying. I just don't want to be there when it happens,'[58] he was crying for the moon. We can no more avoid death than we can escape from our shadows, and every day takes each one of us twenty-four hours closer to the last item on our life's agenda. Nobody chooses to die — not even the suicide, who merely chooses the day, the time, the place and the method. Yet Jesus deliberately *chose to die*. On one occasion he told his hearers, 'No one takes [my life] from me, but I lay it down of my own accord.'[59] When that moment eventually came, Jesus 'gave up his spirit'.[60] The phrase literally means, 'He sent his spirit away,' like a master dismissing a servant. The Bible specifically states, 'No man has power to retain the spirit, or authority over the day of death,'[61] but once again Jesus proved the exception to the rule and showed that he had complete authority over the entire process of dying. As the great theologian Augustine wrote some 400 years later, 'He gave up his life *because* he willed it, *when* he willed it and *as* he willed it.'[62]

2. It was vicarious

Jesus died on behalf of others and in their place. History records heroic cases of individuals sacrificing their own lives to rescue others, but what Jesus did was in an altogether different league. He took upon himself the death penalty for sin that others deserved. Old Testament prophets had foretold the coming of a Suffering Servant who would bear the sins of others;[63] at a last meal with his followers, Jesus quoted one such passage and told them, 'What is written about me is reaching its fulfilment.'[64] This stupendous truth is repeated throughout the New Testament. One writer says, 'Christ died for the ungodly';[65] another writes, 'He himself bore our sins in his body';[66] a third adds, 'Jesus Christ laid down his life for us.'[67]

   To see the death of Jesus as nothing more than a moving example of how to endure undeserved suffering with courage, meekness and dignity is to miss the whole point. Jesus specifically said that his death on behalf of others was 'for the forgiveness of sins',[68] but how could any example, however dramatic, bring that about? Nor will it do to limit his death to an attempt to demonstrate his love for us. If during our honeymoon in Brittany my wife had decided to show her love for me by throwing herself off the top of Mont St Michel, it would have been a tragic waste of her life, and a dreadful blow to mine. Yet the death of Jesus was not a tragedy but a triumph. Some time earlier, Jesus spoke of it as something 'which he was about to accomplish at Jerusalem'.[69] Death is commonly seen as defeat — by disease, an element or incident beyond our control, or an enemy of some kind. Yet Jesus referred to his death as a victorious accomplishment; virtually his last words as he hung on the cross were: 'It is finished.'[70] In the original Greek this is just one word — *tetelesthai* — and is one used to indicate that a bill had been paid in full. It was Jesus' announcement that his death fulfilled the specific purpose for which he had come into the world.

The Bible confirms this in a number of ways. It says that his death was an 'atoning sacrifice',[71] which means that he took upon himself the consequences of God's righteous anger against the sins of others and in so doing turned that anger away from them and made it possible for God to act favourably towards them. Elsewhere it is said to be 'a ransom for many'.[72] By nature and by choice people are 'slaves to sin',[73] but Jesus gave his own life as the ransom price to set them free from their moral and spiritual bondage. Using another metaphor, the Bible tells us that people who were by nature God's enemies were 'reconciled to him through the death of his Son'[74] and that as a result they have 'peace with God'.[75]

One New Testament writer sums it all up by saying, 'Christ … died for sins once for all, the just for the unjust, in order that he might bring us to God.'[76] In the life and death of his Son, God provided the way in which sinners can get right with God. God's holy law demands that as his creatures we must obey it in every part; it also demands that as lawbreakers we must pay its penalty in full. In his life and death, Jesus did both — and he did so on behalf of guilty, lost and helpless sinners such as the person writing this book and the one reading it.

God the sufferer

Before completing our study of the ways in which Jesus was unique we need to take on board a vitally important truth which I hinted at in chapter 9 — namely, that the death of Jesus is the way in which God not only ensured the final elimination of sin but identified himself with human suffering. A modern parable illustrates this:

> At the end of time, billions of people were scattered on a great plain before God's throne. Most shrank back from the brilliant light before them. But some groups near the front talked heatedly — not with cringing shame but with belligerence: 'Can God judge us?'
>
> 'How can he know about suffering?' snapped a pert young brunette. She ripped open a sleeve to reveal a tattooed number from a Nazi concentration camp. 'We endured terror ... beating ... torture ... death!'
>
> In another group a black man lowered his collar. 'What about this?' he demanded, showing an ugly rope burn. 'Lynched for no crime but being black!'
>
> In another crowd, a pregnant schoolgirl with sullen eyes. 'Why should I suffer?' she murmured. 'It wasn't my fault.'
>
> Far out across the plain were hundreds of such groups. Each had a complaint against God for the evil and suffering he had permitted in his world. How lucky God was to live in heaven where all was sweetness and light, where there was no weeping or fear, no hunger or hatred! What did God know of all that men had been forced to endure

in this world? For God leads a pretty sheltered life, they said.

So each of these groups sent forth their leader, chosen because he had suffered the most. A Jew, a black, a person from Hiroshima, a horribly disabled arthritic, a thalidomide child. In the centre of the plain they consulted with each other.

At last they were ready to present their case. It was rather clever. Before God could be qualified to be their judge, he must endure what they had endured. Their verdict was that God should be sentenced to live on earth — as a man! Let him be born a Jew. Let the legitimacy of his birth be doubted. Give him a work so difficult that even his family will think him out of his mind when he tries to do it. Let him be betrayed by his closest friends. Let him face false charges, be tried by a prejudiced jury and convicted by a cowardly judge. Let him be tortured. At last, let him see what it means to be terribly alone. Then let him die in agony. Let him die so that there can be no doubt that he died. Let there be a whole host of witnesses to verify it.

As each leader announced the portion of his sentence, loud murmurs of approval went up from the throng of people assembled. When the last had finished pronouncing sentence there was a long silence. No one uttered another word. No one moved. For suddenly all knew that God had already served his sentence. [77]

This powerful story points to the amazing fact that when Jesus died on the cross God himself was suffering in the place of others, and paying the penalty their sin deserved. Far from insulating himself against suffering, God is the supreme sufferer in the universe. A man whose son had been killed asked his minister, 'Where was God when my son was killed?' The minister replied, 'Exactly where he was when his own Son was killed.' God has entered into the very depths of human pain and in doing so provided a means by which the punishment for human rebellion can be turned aside and he can graciously forgive evil and bring the evildoers concerned to a living and eternal relationship with himself.

We need to note that God's justice was not compromised in the death of Jesus. When Jesus died in the place of others and on their behalf, he became as accountable for their wickedness as if he had been responsible for it, and as a result he received in his own body and spirit the full fury of God's holy anger against evil. The Bible specifically tells us that God acted in this way 'to demonstrate his justice'.[78] This was not an empty gesture, nor was there any 'back-room deal' or sleight of hand: 'He was pierced for our transgressions, he was crushed for our iniquities.'[79]

Just as clearly, the death of Jesus reveals God's amazing love. As one New Testament writer puts it, 'God demonstrates his own love for us in this: While we were still sinners, Christ died for us.'[80] In what some people call the greatest statement in Scripture, Jesus said, 'God so loved the world that he gave his one and only Son, that whoever believes in him shall not perish but have eternal life.'[81]

No serious discussion about human sin and suffering can evade the death of Jesus, in which the justice and love of God are shown in all their fulness. As Alister McGrath says, 'God suffered in Christ. He *knows* what it is like to experience pain. He has travelled down the road of pain, abandonment, suffering and death... God is not like some alleged hero with feet of clay, who demands that others suffer while remaining aloof from the world of pain himself. He has passed through the shadow of suffering himself ... and by doing so, transfigures the sufferings of his people.'[82]

On the third day...

No assessment of Jesus is complete without recognizing that *his resurrection* was unique. When a friend asked for permission to remove the body for burial, the Roman officer in charge of the execution squad pronounced Jesus dead, and had his body run through with a spear just to make sure.[83] To comply with Jewish law, the body was interred before sunset.[84] It was wrapped in linen bandages, layered with about thirty-four kilograms of aromatic spices[85] and laid in a cave.[86] The next day, local religious leaders remembered that Jesus had said something about 'rising again' after three days.[87] The whole notion seemed ridiculous, but what if his followers were to steal the body and then claim that he *had* come back to life? When they shared their fears with Pontius Pilate, the local Roman governor who had judged the case, he posted a guard of soldiers at the tomb with instructions to make it 'as secure as you know how'.[88] Pilate's official seal was attached to the huge rock covering the cave's entrance, and Roman soldiers posted a round-the-clock guard.[89]

In normal circumstances that would have been the end of the story, and Jesus would soon have been little more than a footnote in human history, but within forty-eight hours there were unsettling reports that the body was missing, while a few weeks later Jesus' followers, who had previously been hiding behind closed doors for fear of arrest, were risking their lives by making an even more sensational announcement: *Jesus had risen from the dead.* Was the story true or false? The implications are so stupendous that no sensible person can brush the issue aside — and refusing to think it through is not an option. Before reviewing some of the evidence, it is worth listing alternative theories that atheists and other sceptics have put forward.

'The tomb was not empty.'

This idea never gets out of the starting-blocks. Within a few weeks Jesus' followers were putting their lives on the line by branding his executioners as 'godless men'[90] and insisting that he *had* come back to life. If they were lying, why did the authorities not open the tomb for public inspection?

'The first visitors all went to the wrong tomb.'

This theory was first put forward in 1907, but can hardly be taken seriously. At least two of those who went to the tomb on that first morning had not only seen where the body was laid, but had been close enough to take careful note of the tomb 'and how his body was laid in it'.[91] And would Joseph of Arimathea, who had previously chosen the cave as his own private tomb, have forgotten where it was just a day or so after laying his friend to rest in it?

'The body was stolen by a person or persons unknown.'

It took 500 years for someone to come up with this idea, but it can be silenced in seconds. What possible motive could they have had? Why would they leave the grave-clothes behind and make off with a naked body? As the British scholar Sir Norman Anderson wryly comments, 'A Jew of that period could scarcely be suspected of stealing bodies on behalf of anatomical research!'[92]

'The Roman authorities removed the body.'

They obviously had the opportunity, but what would have been the point? Why post a guard in the first place? If they had moved it elsewhere, why did they not squash the resurrection rumour by producing it?

'The Jewish authorities removed the body.'

As they were hand in glove with the Roman authorities, they also had the opportunity, and their paranoia about Jesus' prophecy gave them the motive to take charge of it, at least for four days. Yet there is not a shred of evidence that they did so; and again, when his followers began preaching that he had risen from the dead, why did the authorities have them arrested, imprisoned, flogged and killed, rather than silence them once and for all by producing the body?

'Jesus' followers removed the body.'

This raises a whole host of questions. How did a few frightened fugitives break through the Roman security cordon? Would hand-picked Roman guards have fallen asleep while on duty when the penalty for doing so was execution? Would *every one of them* have nodded off? If not, would they have allowed the body-snatchers to break the seal, roll the rock away, remove the grave-clothes and make off with the body — the very thing the soldiers were there to prevent? Even if we are prepared to go along with this ridiculous notion, what possible motive could they have had to risk their lives for the sake of removing a body already in the safe keeping of one of their most influential friends?

This particular theory also runs into other problems. These first followers were to write New Testament books reflecting the years they had spent under the influence of Jesus' matchless moral teaching. Would they have invented a pack of lies as the basis for all they wrote? One of them said that if Jesus had not

risen from the dead, '… we are even found to be false witnesses of God, because we witnessed against God that he raised
Christ.'[93] Can we really believe that these men, passionately
concerned for God's honour and glory, would have deliberately attributed to God something they knew perfectly well he
had not done?

This ties in with a serious psychological problem. When the
religious authorities dragged these disciples into court and gave
them strict instructions to stop preaching Jesus' resurrection,
their response was to declare, 'We must obey God rather than
men!'[94] and to head straight back to the streets. As a result, they
were bullied, flogged and in some cases executed. Would
they have put up with this kind of treatment while knowing
that they were preaching a pack of lies? They might have
risked their lives for something they had imagined, but not for
something they had invented. Men are sometimes prepared to
die for convictions, but not for inventions. One expert after
another has concluded that for these men to behave as they
did would have been psychologically impossible.

'Jesus never died.'

The so-called 'swoon theory' was popularized in the eighteenth
century, but it never stands up. We have already seen that the
officer in charge of the execution squad made doubly sure that
Jesus was dead, and the swoon theory becomes pure farce
when we consider what it suggests. After being viciously beaten
and scourged, then nailed to a cross, Jesus lost consciousness
but remained alive, even when his body was ripped open by
the soldier's spear. At no time throughout the removal and burial
of the body did any of his handlers detect the slightest sign of
life. At some time during the following thirty-six hours Jesus
came out of coma and, like some first-century Houdini, wriggled
out of the tightly-wound grave-clothes layered with sticky,

hardening embalming material, then pushed aside the huge rock sealing the tomb, overcame the entire armed guard of soldiers (or nimbly sidestepped their sleeping bodies) and made his way stark naked into the city. By the time he met his friends a few hours later he had made such a remarkable recovery that he persuaded them, not that he had somehow stumbled back from the brink of death, but that he had overcome it for ever and burst through into a dimension of life they had never experienced. To cap it all, after a lifetime during which he had never committed a single sin, he suddenly became a monstrous, blasphemous liar, conning his friends into believing something he knew to be false. Only the grossly gullible would swallow such nonsense, and it is hardly surprising that even an entrenched sceptic like the nineteenth-century scholar David Strauss dismissed the whole swoon theory as 'impossible'.[95]

All these arguments are sufficient to sink a more recent 'Jesus never died' theory that hit the headlines in the British press in 2001. This referred to a segment of the BBC Television programme *Son of God* aired on Easter Day in which historian Gloria Moss suggested that Jesus may have been anaesthetized to lessen the pain of crucifixion, and then later revived in the tomb.

The newspapers got very excited about the idea, but trying to find evidence in the programme made finding a needle in a haystack child's play by comparison. The most it could come up with was that a plant called mandrake grew in the Middle East at the time of Jesus, that an extract from its root was sometimes used as a crude anaesthetic and that an unidentified first-century man was said to have survived crucifixion. Cobbling these bits and pieces together, presenter Jeremy Bowen suggested that extract of mandrake could have been hidden in the wine vinegar given to Jesus as he hung on the cross, and that this drugged him so deeply that he was assumed to be dead.

One can understand how this made the headlines, but it is hardly a serious contribution to history.

Facts

When we turn from fantasy to facts, powerful evidence for the resurrection of Jesus is backed by some unusual credentials.

In the first place, nobody claimed to have seen it happen. This may seem a weakness in the case, but if the disciples had cooked up the story, they would surely have included at least one dramatic eyewitness account.

Secondly, at a time when a woman's testimony was thought so worthless that it was not considered binding in Jewish law, the first post-resurrection appearance of Jesus is said to have been to a woman.[96] Would the disciples have been so careless as to build their entire message on such a flimsy foundation?

Thirdly, the narratives are not absolutely identical, something which again points strongly to their truth, rather than the opposite. If the disciples had invented the story, would they not have made sure that all the loose ends were tied up? Then what of the evidence itself? Of all the available material, we shall consider three of the most impressive items.

1. The number of witnesses

The Bible records six independent, written testimonies (three by eyewitnesses) telling of eleven separate appearances over a period of forty days.[97] Some sceptics write these off as hallucinations, but this idea breaks down because the appearances fail to conform to the relevant laws. There is no evidence that any of the witnesses were neurotic or psychotic; Jesus rarely appeared in places where he and his followers had spent time together; and he appeared to two, three, seven, eleven and, on one occasion, over 500 people at a time. What is more, none of those to whom he appeared showed any signs of wishful thinking that he was still alive; on the contrary, they were convinced that Jesus was over and done with. These facts lead a distinguished medical expert to conclude, 'The resurrection appearances break every known law of visions.'[98]

When the apostle Paul told friends at Corinth that Jesus had appeared to more than 500 people at the same time, he added, 'most of whom are still living'.[99] This means that sceptics could have questioned over 250 witnesses, every one of whom would have told the same story. Why should they have done this? Their testimonies were utterly consistent and in a somewhat higher league than modern claims that Elvis Presley is still alive and well and living in various parts of the world!

2. The sudden transformation of the disciples

The crucifixion of Jesus had left them a dejected, faithless and depressed rabble, frightened out of their wits and cowering behind locked doors, terrified that they might be next on the authorities' hit list. Yet a few weeks later they had changed into a dynamic band of believers, fearlessly preaching the resurrection and prepared to face persecution, imprisonment and execution rather than deny their convictions.[100] Can you explain this?

It was the disciples' transformation that convinced Charles Colson, special counsel to USA President Richard Nixon in the 1970s, that the biblical account of Jesus' resurrection was true. When the Nixon administration's attempt to cover up its burglary of the Democrats' Watergate offices in Washington came under scrutiny by the Department of Justice it took less than a month for three of those involved to turn state evidence. Some time later Colson wrote, 'In my Watergate experience I saw the inability of men — powerful, highly motivated professionals —

to hold together a conspiracy based on a lie… Yet Christ's followers maintained to their grim deaths by execution that they
had in fact seen Jesus Christ raised from the dead. There was
no conspiracy… Men and women do not give up their comfort
— and certainly not their lives — for what they know to be a
lie.'[101] It is impossible to explain the disciples' behaviour away;
some hugely significant, objective event must have happened
to kindle such a radical change, and this instant transformation
from cowardice to courage leads Norman Anderson to call it
'far and away the strongest circumstantial evidence for the
resurrection'.[102]

3. The growth of the Christian church

Within a few years, the enemies of the movement which these
men began accused it of having 'turned the world upside
down'.[103] By the early part of the fourth century it was recognized as the official religion of the Roman Empire, which had
tried to strangle it at birth. Some 2,000 years later it is the largest religious movement the world has ever known — and it was
founded not on some new ideas on morals, ethics or social
issues, nor on a particular ritual or style of worship, but on one
stupendous fact: the resurrection of Jesus. This can hardly be
reduced to folklore. As the American author D. James Kennedy
puts it, 'The Grand Canyon wasn't caused by an Indian drag-
ging a stick, and the Christian Church wasn't created by a
myth.'[104]

Greater than 'the greatest'

At the height of his career, the great American boxer Muhammad
Ali used to boast, 'I am the greatest!' In boxing terms, he may
well have been right, yet the claims Jesus made are infinitely

greater. As we have already seen, he fulfilled all the Old Testament prophecies about a coming Messiah, he was born of a virgin, he lived a sinless life, his teaching has never been equalled and the range and number of his miracles put him in a class of his own. Yet these facts were matched by the astonishing claims he made for himself, all without any element of conceit. Here are some of them: 'I am the light of the world. Whoever follows me will never walk in darkness, but will have the light of life';[105] 'I am the bread of life. He who comes to me will never go hungry, and he who believes in me will never be thirsty';[106] 'I am the way and the truth and the life. No one comes to the Father except through me.'[107]

These claims are breathtaking, but they are transcended by this: *he claimed to be God.* The New Testament records him doing this again and again, and I have examined these incidents elsewhere;[108] here, just one will be enough to make the point. When one of his followers said to him, 'Lord, show us the Father, and that will be enough for us,' Jesus replied, 'Don't you know me, Philip, even after I have been among you such a long time? Anyone who has seen me has seen the Father.'[109] Jesus was not claiming to *be* the Father (we pointed out the plurality of persons within the Godhead in chapter 1) but that anyone who had seen Jesus had seen, in human form, as much of God's nature and character as it was possible and necessary for a human being to see and know.

The New Testament writers are unanimous in declaring his deity. One describes him as 'the image of the invisible God';[110] another calls him 'our God and Saviour';[111] and yet another speaks of him as 'the true God and eternal life'.[112] When we put all of this together, it is easy to see why the American educator William Biederwolf wrote, 'A man who can read the New Testament and not see that Christ claims to be more than a man can look over the sky on a cloudless day and not see the sun.'[113] Jesus had no credentials but himself, and his claims present the

atheist with an enormous problem, as they were made by someone of matchless integrity and wisdom. As C. S. Lewis pointed
out, to accept the calibre of his moral teaching but refuse his
claim to be God is simply not an option: 'That is the one thing
we must not say. A man who was merely a man and said the
sort of things Jesus said would not be a great moral teacher. He
would be either a lunatic — on the level with the man who says
he is a poached egg — or else he would be the devil of hell.
You must make your choice… You can shut him up for a fool,
you can spit and kill him as a demon; or you can fall at his feet
and call him Lord and God. But let us not come up with any
patronizing nonsense about his being a great human teacher.
He has not left that open to us. He did not intend to.'[114]

Call Reza Shayad

*Reza Shayad was born in the Middle East, but received most of his
education in the United Kingdom, where he is now living and working. For reasons of personal security his real name, and that of his
wife, have been changed.*

I was raised in a loving, middle-class family and, like most children in
my country, I was encouraged to work hard at school so that one day
I could achieve something in life — and also be a good Muslim.

Islam pervaded every part of life, and many public religious activities made it impossible to escape its influence. Because I came from
a Shiite background, the twelve imams who came after Muhammad
had their birthdays or deaths celebrated or mourned with great fer-
vour. In other ceremonies such as weddings, funerals and fasting,
Islam was powerfully present.

Praying (five times a day) and fasting added to my conviction that
God was happy with me and would favour me when I came to the
Day of Judgement. If I missed one or more of my prayer times I would

make up the deficit as soon as possible, sometimes praying ten times instead of five.

It was with this as my background that I came to the United Kingdom in the 1970s for an operation and also to study. After my operation I enrolled to study English and then to do my 'O' Levels and 'A' Levels. During my second year in Britain I fell in love with a girl who had no connection with Islam. We knew that we could never marry as we were; either I had to change my religion, which was unthinkable to me, or she had to become a Muslim. After many long discussions, Mary said that, as it could hardly make such a difference when we both believed in one God and loved each other, she would change her religion.

Getting married (and making Mary a Muslim) was very simple. At a London mosque the imam told us to sit on the floor while he read from the *Qur'an* and asked Mary to repeat one particular verse after him. A fee of £5, our signatures on a marriage document, and it was all over. He then told Mary, 'You are now a Muslim, and your new name is Maryam.' I was puzzled as to how anyone could become a Muslim without knowing anything about Islam, but at least Mary and I were now united in marriage in religion.

A few days later we received a book with various Muslim instructions for my wife — praying, fasting, covering up and the like. She refused point-blank. Suddenly, the beginning of our married life became a war zone, a conflict of words about religion, which came to a head when she said, 'I don't know why I ever became a Muslim. My old religion was better than yours.' As far as I was concerned this was blasphemy.

Partly to bridge the painful division between us, I began to read the Bible, but it made no sense to me. At various times, Jehovah's Witnesses and Mormons came to my door, but neither of their religious frameworks satisfied me, and the way they condemned each other strengthened my conviction that my Islamic faith was the right one. But another thought was growing in my mind: if these people genuinely believed they had the truth, and I believed I did, somebody was wrong. Suddenly, my focus changed. More than anything else I wanted to know the answer to one question: what is the truth?

Back in my native country my family was coming under threat because of their opposition to the strictly Islamic government and they were forced to escape, leaving all their possessions behind. My brother was later able to buy a passport and take refuge in the United States, but six other family members joined me and my wife and daughter, and for five years we lived together in our two-bedroomed house. The only pay packet coming in was mine, from a part-time job in a restaurant. It was very hard going.

At one point I met someone who told me that Jesus was the Son of God. I had never heard of such a thing and I invited him to my home to talk about it. We met many times over the next year, and these meetings made a deep impression on me, but two particular things were bothering me. How could God have a Son? And how could there be a Trinity, with three persons in one Godhead? Much that Christians were telling me made a great deal of sense, but whenever I thought of Jesus as the Son of God, or of the Trinity, I found myself rejecting the entire Christian faith.

Some months later my brother came to visit us from the United States. He too had changed. Because of the persecution our family was suffering, he had become an atheist and was bitterly opposed to religion. We often talked together about these things and as I thought about our family's problems I found that I too was becoming disillusioned about religion.

Things were soon to change dramatically. Resting in my room one evening, and feeling very bitter about life in general, I said to myself, 'There is no God and all these religions are just theories made up by men.' Then I started thinking about Jesus, whose name had constantly cropped up during the many religious discussions I had had over the past six years. *He* was the problem! Once again I wrestled with the question of his identity and significance, until in desperation I shouted, 'I do not believe you are there, but if you are, and you are the Son of God and say you are the truth, then show me the truth.' My eyes were closed, and my mind bursting with thoughts. Suddenly I felt as if there was someone in the room breathing on me. I thought I must have been hearing things, but when I tried to open my eyes they would not open. Thinking I must have been overly conscious of my own breathing, I held my breath for a moment, but still there was this sensation of someone else in the room. I really got frightened, and thought I must have gone out of my mind. My tongue felt like a rock and my fists stiffened. Then suddenly I found myself praising the name of Jesus, thanking him for all he had done and repeating that he was my Lord and Saviour. After a while I jumped up, looked around, and even under the bed, thinking that I had had a dream or a nightmare. Suddenly I realized that God had met with me in that room! I looked at my watch, thinking the experience had lasted just a few minutes, but over an hour had passed.

I went downstairs and said to my family, 'Jesus is the Son of God.' They thought I had gone crazy, but they have long since changed their minds. When I told some Christian friends what had happened, they told me that my experience had been the work of God the Holy Spirit. All I knew was that my thinking had been totally transformed. My prejudices against the Christian God and Jesus Christ had been wiped out. My testimony was that of the blind man healed by Jesus 2,000 years ago: 'One thing I … know. I was blind but now I see!'[115] In all the years I have been a Christian I have never had any more experiences like this one, but I thank God for showing me the truth in such a dramatic and unforgettable way.

Some weeks later I went into a Christian church for the first time in my life, and on that same day I shared my story with those present and was baptized and received into membership. The minister faithfully taught and discipled me and I gradually grew stronger in my Christian faith through the knowledge of the Word of God. Over the years that have passed since then my brother has come to faith in Christ, as have all the members of my own family and several other Muslim contacts, although no one, as far as I know, had the same dramatic experience that marked my own conversion. I thank God for all that he means to me and has done for me, and pray that I will be a channel of his love and truth as long as I live. I have gone through some severe tests and trials as a Christian, but my Saviour has never forsaken me and I thank him for the tremendous changes he has brought about in me and in my family.

Having been a Muslim for thirty years, I feel a particular burden to share the truth with those who are under the influence of Islam. Muslims are told to pray five times a day, help the needy, fast for one month in the year (Ramadan) and, if possible, go on a pilgrimage to Mecca. Why? The answer is simple: to please Allah and to make sure that in performing these duties they will be accepted by him and secure a place in heaven. As Islam acknowledges that man's greatest need is to be delivered from the curse and consequences of their sin (the *Qur'an* states that even Muhammad sinned) every Muslim should ask, 'What has Allah (God) done to meet my greatest need?' According to Islam, the answer is 'Nothing!' Instead, it teaches that every individual must earn his own way to heaven by performing certain religious duties. Yet this suggests a God who is uncompassionate, unmerciful and unloving. Would a loving human father, seeing his son drowning, do nothing more than stand on the shore shouting instructions to him? Would his love not compel him to jump into the sea to save him, regardless of the cost?

This raises an important question. The God of which faith has intervened to meet people's greatest need? Only Christianity tells of a God of love coming to earth in the person of his Son to rescue people from their sin and bring them into a loving and eternal relationship with himself. In the Bible's own words, 'For God so loved the world that he gave his one and only Son, that whoever believes in him shall not perish but have eternal life.'[116] Nor is this one of many ways by which man can be reconciled to God. The Bible specifically excludes any other means of salvation: 'Salvation is found in no one else, for there is no other name under heaven given to men by which we must be saved.'[117] Jesus himself could not have been clearer: 'I am the way and the truth and the life. No one comes to the Father except through me.'[118] As even the *Qur'an* states that Jesus was 'faultless', and 'the truth', it would have been impossible for him to deceive us about anything, let alone about the most important issue anyone could face.

I thank God for showing me the truth of his Word and for transforming my life, and I trust that my story will help many others to find Jesus Christ as their own personal Saviour.

11.
The beginning?

For thirteen years I worked in and around the Guernsey law courts, and I have never lost my interest in the legal process. Questions asked and answered, witnesses examined and cross-examined, exhibits shown and challenged, arguments put forward and rebutted; in a complex case the cut and thrust would be endlessly fascinating except for one thing — it has to end.

No debate in human culture has lasted longer than the one about God's existence, but there comes a point at which each person engaged in it must reach a conclusion. The truth must lie one way or the other, and shelving the question as irrelevant or unanswerable changes nothing. As one's entire world-view is at stake, the issue is critical and practical; it affects the way we live and the way we die. As far as this book is concerned, the time has come for me to step aside and for you to come to your own conclusion.

Summing up

My aim in writing has been not merely to put the case for God, but to show why it is both reasonable and vital that you should accept it. Before I press this home, let me review some of the key points made in earlier chapters.

1. The written evidence for God is the Bible, the most reliable ancient literature known to man. It claims to be 'the living and enduring word of God'[1] and has all the hallmarks one would expect if this were the case. After some 2,000 years of investigation, nobody has been able to prove that it makes a single false statement, and none of the places where the precise meaning of the text is in question affects its central and unanimous message. The Bible has proved itself to be an infallible database.

2. God is *uniquely* able to declare, 'I am the LORD, and there is no other.'[2] The myriads of so-called 'gods' in history are not simply less attractive or less powerful; they are non-existent: 'There is no God but one.'[3]

3. God is spiritual. He does not have physical or other material properties: 'God is spirit, and his worshippers must worship in spirit and in truth.'[4]

4. God is transcendent. He is over and above time and space and all finite reality, 'exalted as head over all'.[5] He is distinct and separate from the entire cosmos and from everything in it, and can no more be confined to space than he can be measured by time. He is *the* great reality, the absolute in regard to which all else is relative.

5. God is personal. He is not a 'thing', a principle or a concept, but has all the essential characteristics of personality. He thinks, chooses, gives, makes and keeps promises and is 'compassionate and gracious'.[6]

6. God is holy. Time and again in the Bible he is called 'the Holy One'.[7] He has no flaws, weaknesses, blemishes, shortcomings or disabilities. 'There is no one holy like the LORD,'[8] and his perfection guarantees that we live in a moral world and enables us to distinguish between right and wrong.

7. God is omnipotent: he is 'the LORD God Almighty'.[9] He has the entire cosmos under his immediate and perfect control and 'does whatever pleases him'.[10] He is a law unto himself, rules over everything and everyone, and is under no obligation to account for anything he does.

8. God loves. All his actions, even those we find difficult to understand, flow from the fundamental fact that 'God is love.'[11] Love is of his very essence, and this provides a rationale for all human love.

9. God created all reality outside of himself, including time, space, galaxies, solar systems, every form of energy and matter, nuclear structure, the laws by which nature operates and every form of life from mammoths to microbes: 'The living God ... made heaven and earth and sea and everything in them.'[12]

10. Humankind is the jewel in the crown of God's creation. Unlike anything else in the entire created order, man was made 'in the image of God',[13] given powers of thought, feeling and will that go far beyond brute instincts. This explains our ability to think rationally, to express ourselves in language, to recognize moral values and to express love in personal relationships. It also explains our spiritual dimension, the instinct to look for a reality beyond us.

11. Although 'God made mankind upright',[14] morally and spiritually perfect, man was created not as a robot, but with the gift of free will. For some time he chose to live in obedient fellowship with his Maker but eventually rebelled against God's authority, forfeiting his free will, bringing disease, decay and death upon himself and his successors and throwing the entire cosmos out of joint. Now, *we are sinners by nature and by choice*; we have all 'sinned and fall short of the glory of God'.[15] This places us under God's righteous judgement and there is nothing that we can independently do to repair the damage. Even our best efforts, religious or otherwise, are like 'filthy rags'[16] in terms of pleasing God or avoiding his anger against sin. Left to ourselves, we are 'without hope and without God in the world'.[17]

12. In *the person of Jesus Christ*, God has dramatically intervened in the human disaster. Jesus was not merely human, but 'the image of the invisible God',[18] the one in whom 'all the fulness of the Deity lives in bodily form'.[19] In his life, he fulfilled all the demands of God's holy law, then chose to die in the place of guilty sinners, taking upon himself the physical and spiritual death penalty their sin deserved. Three days later he was 'declared with power to be the Son of God, by his resurrection from the dead'[20] and he is now 'alive for ever and ever'.[21]

Nowhere in this book have I claimed to produce proof that God exists, nor, to use a common phrase, have I tried to 'ram religion down your throat'. Instead, I have laid out some of the evidence that points strongly in God's direction. The twelve 'exhibits' I have just listed are part of the data you now need to consider. What do you make of them? How should you respond? The next section applies particularly to agnostics, though much of what it says is equally relevant to atheists.

Bet your life!

The word 'genius' is often tossed around somewhat carelessly, but it can safely be used of Blaise Pascal, the French mathematician, physicist, inventor, philosopher and literary stylist, who was born in Clermont-Ferrand in 1623. Although 'one of the great minds of Western intellectual history',[22] he never went to school. His mother died when he was three years old, and from then on he was taught at home by his father, a notable lawyer, magistrate and tax commissioner. By the time he was eleven

Blaise had worked out a number of Euclid's basic propositions. As a teenager, he devised the world's first calculating machine and wrote a remarkable book on conic sections, including material that is fundamental to modern geometry. He never reached his fortieth birthday, but by the time he died he had produced the theory of probability, which led to the modern science of statistics, made significant contributions to hydrostatics, hydrodynamics and differential calculus, and discovered the principle of liquid distribution now known as Pascal's Law, and which underlies all modern hydraulic operations.

Pascal lived at a time when logic was all the rage, the leading thinkers of the day teaching that reason is the only source of all knowledge. According to them, the secrets of the cosmos, as well as the truth about man's nature and destiny, could be worked out entirely in the mind; so could the question of the existence of God. Pascal disagreed, and said that logical reasoning by itself could never settle the issue: 'We know the truth not only by reason but also by means of the heart. It is through the heart that we know the first principles.'[23] At another point he wrote, 'The heart has its reasons which are unknown to reason.'[24]

These quotations come from Pascal's *Pensées* (*Thoughts*), published eight years after his death in 1662. Originally notes written on odd scraps of paper, *Pensées* is now regarded as a classic of its kind. Pascal saw man as an enigma, 'the glory and rubbish of the universe',[25] capable of rising to great heights yet sinking to great depths. He tries to live a meaningful and happy life, yet often finds himself a bored and anxious failure. In 'the terrifying immensity of the universe' he feels 'a mere atom, a mere passing shadow, to return no more'.[26] He is not sure of his origin, identity or destiny; yet he knows that he must soon die and 'fall for ever into nothingness or into the hands of a wrathful God'.[27]

The most famous of these 'thoughts' (strictly speaking, a collection of them) has become known as 'Pascal's Wager', and was directed, not at those who denied God's existence, but at those who were undecided about it. Although a committed Christian believer, Pascal made no attempt to prove the existence of God, nor even to produce evidence pointing in that direction. Instead, he argued along these lines:

- God either exists or he does not.
- Reason alone is incapable of settling the question.
- Unbelievers can hardly accuse Christians of having no rational grounds for their beliefs when they have none for their own.
- The question is so important that sitting on the fence is not a sensible option.

Then came the well-known wager. It is somewhat complex in parts, but this is the bottom line: 'God is or he is not... *You must wager. It is not optional...* Which will you choose then? ... Let us weigh up the gain and the loss in wagering that God is. Let us estimate these two chances. *If you win, you win everything; if you lose, you lose nothing*' [28] (emphasis added).

If you began reading this book as an agnostic, and still remain one, I urge you to hear what Pascal has to say. You may not be sure of God's existence, but you are presumably not sure of his non-existence (or you would be an atheist). Then you must agree that a God who is the Creator and Sustainer of the universe, who reveals himself in the Bible, who came to earth in the person of Jesus Christ to bring people back into a living relationship with himself, and to whom you must one day give account, *is at the very least a possibility.* Since the issue is tremendously important and reason alone is incapable of settling the issue, what should you do? Pascal says it makes sense to believe in God even without satisfactory evidence. He says you should stop sitting on your hands and gamble on God's existence, because, 'If you win, you win everything; if you lose, you lose nothing.' Think this through:

- If God does *not* exist, and you *do not believe* in him, you will obviously gain nothing in this life, and presumably be annihilated at the end of it.
- If he does *not* exist but you *believe* he does, you may possibly lead a happier and more focused life, and you will certainly lose nothing, because your destiny after death would not be affected.
- If God *does* exist, and you do *not believe* in him, you will lose everything: in this life you will continue to 'grope in darkness with no light'[29] and after death you will be 'thrown outside, into the darkness, where there will be weeping and gnashing of teeth'.[30]
- On the other hand, if God *exists* and you *do believe* in him, you have everything to gain: in this life, you will know what it is to have God as your 'refuge and strength',[31] enabling you 'to will and to act according to his good purpose',[32] and after death you will 'dwell in the house of the LORD for ever',[33] receiving 'the crown of glory that will never fade away'.[34]

To put it simply, you have less to lose by believing wrongly than by disbelieving wrongly. This may sound like bribery and a crude appeal to self-interest, but this criticism ignores God's nature. If he is your Creator, who in his 'great goodness'[35] and 'unfailing love'[36] gives you 'life and breath and everything else',[37] he has the right to claim what the Bible calls 'the obedience that comes from faith'.[38] Failing to 'give unto the LORD the glory due to his name'[39] means that *every* day you are adding to an unpaid debt.

This is the single most important issue you could possibly face, and Jesus made it clear that avoiding it is not an option: 'He who is not with me is against me.'[40] Even the atheistic thinker Anthony Flew agrees that refusing to make Pascal's Wager 'amounts in effect to a bet against the existence of God'.[41] Then get to grips with it! Are you honestly satisfied with a world-view that is purely a matter of personal opinion? Do you seriously think that ignoring the question is possible, or that putting it off is sensible? Perhaps you should read chapter 2 again and see why the Bible can be trusted and why agnosticism is not a rational option. Have you grasped the significance of the identity, death and his resurrection of Jesus? If not, read chapter 10 again.

Are you qualified to brush aside all the other evidence? The Bible says, '[God] did not leave himself without witness,'[42] and in Pascal's words, 'There is enough light for those whose only desire is to see.'[43] The natural world alone displays so much of God's 'eternal power and divine nature' that to ignore this is to leave yourself 'without excuse'.[44] What do you make of the universal instinct that human life has meaning, value and purpose? As being made in the image of God would explain this, would it not make sense to decide in God's favour?

Can you shrug off the testimony of countless millions of people from every walk of life who claim to have a dynamic, life-enhancing relationship with God? Can you be sure that they are all lying or deluded? Do you have an alternative explanation for their unanimous witness to the dramatic changes in their lives? After Pascal's death a note was found sewn into his clothing. Part of it read: 'God of Abraham, God of Isaac, God of Jacob. Not the God of philosophers and scholars. Absolute certainty: Beyond reason. Joy. Peace. Forgetfulness of the world and everything but God. The world has not known thee, but I have known thee. Joy! Joy! Joy! Tears of joy!'[45] Can you brush this aside as being mumbo-jumbo? On such a vastly important issue is it sensible to insist on doing nothing until all your questions are answered? If you acted like that in everyday life, you would never get out of bed in the morning!

Although Pascal had no doubt that the evidence for God was 'more than compelling'[46] (he majored on the Bible's claims, miracles and prophecy), his wager was aimed at persuading agnostics to get off the fence: 'Wager then, without hesitation, that God is'.[47] Why not ask God to help you do this? There is nothing strange in praying to a God whose existence you doubt. As the agnostic philosopher Anthony Kenny points out, 'It is surely no more unreasonable than the act of a man adrift in the ocean … who cries for help though he may never be heard.'[48]

I have come across many people in your position whose journey into faith began with their praying along these lines: 'O God, I am not even sure if you exist, but if you do, please reveal yourself to me and enable me to put my trust in you.' If you are an agnostic, but genuinely searching for the truth, I encourage you to do the same. You have everything to gain and nothing to lose!

Believing and believing

'I believe in a cold bath before breakfast every morning. Not just during a heatwave, or when the weather is pleasantly warm, but even in the depths of winter, when there is snow on the ground and icicles are hanging from the guttering. Out of bed, pyjamas off, straight in.' Whenever I share this intimate titbit with an audience it produces a corporate shudder, with some people no doubt thinking, 'He is crazy!' Then comes the punchline: 'I have never actually had one!' The point of the story is to open listeners' minds to the fact that the word 'believe' can mean different things — and produce very different results. I believe in food, yet could die of starvation reading a menu in the most expensive restaurant in London. I believe in medicine, yet I could die surrounded by bottles of an effective cure for my illness.

Throughout this book I have shown that while there is no single, overwhelming proof that God exists, there is good and sufficient evidence for believing that he does. G. K. Chesterton said that he was persuaded not by one thing alone but by 'an enormous accumulation' of facts.[49] These include the existence and nature of the universe, the phenomenon we call 'life', the characteristics of *Homo sapiens*, the idea of ethics or the sense of how we 'ought' to behave, the universal and deep-rooted conviction that there is a transcendent something 'out there', the Bible's reliability and self-authentication, the birth, life, death and resurrection of Jesus, and the testimonies of millions of people over thousands of years.

If you were an atheist when you began reading this book, you may now have come to see the force of at least some of these arguments. If so, I would urge you not only to follow these through but also to allow those you cannot yet accept to examine and challenge you.

You may have reached the point at which you are now prepared to accept the existence of the God revealed in Scripture. This is where my cold-bath story comes in, because while you have taken a huge step in the right direction, the response God requires goes far beyond merely believing that what the Bible says about him is true. As H. R. Rookmaaker puts it, 'A positive answer to the question of whether God exists is only a small step toward truly following him.'[50]

The New Testament spells this out very clearly. When in the course of a discussion with Jesus a religious leader agreed that 'God is one and there is no other but him,'[51] Jesus commended him for answering 'wisely' but then went on to tell him, 'You are not far from the kingdom of God.'[52] This was a classic case of 'Good news, bad news.' The good news was that the man was on the right track; he acknowledged that there was one, true, living God. The bad news was that even this conviction left him no better off.

This is backed up by a New Testament writer who says to someone relying on his convictions, 'You believe that there is one God. Good! Even the devils believe that — and shudder.'[53] Here again, there is good news and bad news. To agree that only one God exists is good, but in one sense this only puts the person concerned on a par with evil spirits. When two demon-possessed men met Jesus in Gadara they shouted, 'What do you want with us, Son of God?'[54] At Capernaum, a man possessed by an evil spirit cried out, 'What do you want with us, Jesus of Nazareth? Have you come to destroy us? I know who you are — the Holy One of God.'[55] In a head-on clash with Jesus, Satan set up two particular temptations with the challenge, 'If you are the Son of God …'[56] As 'If' in this context obviously means 'Since', it is clear that in terms of acknowledging the facts even Satan 'believes'. His 'inside information' about the identity of Jesus was the basis for tempting him in the particular way he did.

Mind, heart and will

There are two clues to understanding what the Bible means when it tells us to believe in God. The first is that God is not an idea, but a living reality. He is not a proposition to be accepted, but a person to be met. The second is that in biblical language the word 'believe' means 'trust', something involving the mind, the heart and the will and calling for submission, love and commitment.

1. A change of mind

The Bible says that while faith in God includes being 'certain of what we do not see', [57] it is not an irrational leap in the dark, a rash decision made without a reasonable basis. It means believing in a God who has given us good and ample reason for doing so.

My study faces the front drive leading to my home. If I were to see a van labelled 'Parcel Force' draw up outside, and the driver bring a package to my door, I would immediately accept it. Of course, it is logically possible that the van has been stolen, that the driver is a hit man with instructions to eliminate me, and that the package is a time bomb that will explode thirty seconds after the driver has hurried back to the van. Yet with no evidence for all of this, and no reason to doubt that things are exactly as they seem to be, I would have no hesitation in opening the package. Do you have any logical reason for not accepting the 'package' I have tried to deliver in the course of this book? Can you demonstrate that the evidence for God's existence has been rigged and should be rejected? Can you prove that the 'package' is an illusion? If not, what evidence would you accept as showing that it was genuine?

On the other hand, what evidence do you have that the Bible is a collection of myths and fables, that material reality has always existed, that life came about by accident, that pure chance accounts for the diversity of species, that there are no transcendent standards and that Jesus was peddling nonsense?

2. A change of heart

Accepting God's existence is a step in the right direction — but only the first step. God also requires a change of heart with regard to your own spiritual and moral condition. We are all

past masters at self-justification, at making excuses for our fail-
ures. When our consciences bother us we tend to blame our
background, our parents, our spouses, our circumstances, peer
pressure, stress, tiredness, even our genes — anything that will
get us off the hook. This may seem to work for a while, but the
Bible confirms that we are bluffing and lying: 'If we claim to be
without sin, we deceive ourselves and the truth is not in us.'[58]
People with symptoms of serious disease will never be healed
by pretending that they are perfectly fit; nor can anyone get
right with God without admitting their sin and turning to him
for forgiveness and cleansing.

A friend of mine who was the minister of a large church in
central London got into conversation with a man who flatly
rejected what the Bible taught. At the front of the church were
two panels, one spelling out the Apostles' Creed, which includes
the words: 'I believe in God the Father Almighty, Maker of
heaven and earth, and in Jesus Christ, his only Son our Lord...
I believe in the Holy Spirit...' Waving dismissively at the panel,
the man said, 'I have great problems with those statements.' In
response, my friend pointed to another panel, and said, 'Don't
you have greater problems with those?' Written on this panel
were the Ten Commandments, including, 'I am the LORD your
God... You shall have no other gods before me... Honour your
father and your mother...You shall not commit adultery. You
shall not steal. You shall not give false testimony... You shall
not covet...'[59] How do *you* react to them? Do you have problems with any of them? Are you satisfied with your behaviour
as well as your beliefs? What does your conscience tell you?
Even if you feel you have a tolerably good track record you are
still faced with three serious problems.

Firstly, *God's law is an integrated whole*, not a disjointed
collection of unrelated rules, and 'Whoever keeps the whole
law and yet stumbles at just one point is guilty of breaking all of
it.'[60] Just as one broken link severs an entire chain, and one

crack ruins a whole window, so even one sin renders you guilty of breaking God's law. If I were caught for violating the Road Traffic Act by exceeding the speed limit, I would get nowhere by pointing out that my brake lights were in working order or that my tyres had sufficient tread. You may not be guilty of murder, adultery or child abuse, but what about things like pride, dishonesty, impurity, envy, greed, selfishness and jealousy? As God condemns 'everyone who does not continue to do *everything* written in the Book of the Law',[61] the question you need to ask yourself is not, 'Have I kept most of God's law?' but, 'Have I *constantly* kept *all* of it?'

Secondly, the Bible talks about *sins of omission* as well as sins of commission, and says that anyone 'who knows the good he ought to do and doesn't do it, sins'.[62] I have often heard people claim that they do their best to live by the so-called 'Golden Rule, 'In everything, do to others what you would have them do to you'[63] — but I have never yet met anybody who claims to have kept it. Have you *always* done *all* the good things you possibly could? Even if you have sometimes tried to live in this way, do you seriously think that a righteous God will bend the rules and accept determination and effort as a substitute for obedience?

Thirdly, trying to shelter behind the claim to have done better than others is futile, as Jesus said that 'the first and great commandment' is: 'Love the Lord your God with all your heart and with all your soul and with all your mind and with all your strength.'[64] As this is 'the first and greatest commandment'[65] (and a brilliant summary of the first four of the Old Testament's Ten Commandments) breaking it is the first and greatest sin. If you are still an atheist, where does that leave you? Denying God's existence is hardly a technicality; it is a deliberate breach of the first and greatest commandment, a capital offence against the Creator and Ruler of the universe. Nor is it any defence to be a 'practical atheist', someone who lives *as if* there was no God —

never genuinely giving him thanks, seeking his forgiveness, or asking for his help to live a godly life. Do you imagine that a holy God before whose eyes 'everything is uncovered and laid bare'[66] can be fooled with this sort of thing, or that he will just shrug it off?

Turning to God with the heart means not only admitting one's guilt, but also seeing sin for what it really is — rebellion against God, a violation of his holy law and a personal insult to his majesty and honour. The person who truly sees this no longer tries to play down his guilt, make excuses for his behaviour, or treat sin light-heartedly. Instead, he is broken-hearted and disgusted and longs to be forgiven and cleansed.

3. A change of will

When his critics were looking for ways to avoid the impact of his teaching, Jesus told them, 'Whoever is willing to do what God wants will know whether what I teach comes from God.'[67] Accepting the facts (a change of mind) and acknowledging one's spiritual condition and need (a change of heart) are not enough. There must also be a genuine willingness to live differently. The mind is concerned with what we know, the heart with what we feel and the will with what we do, but these are not in water-tight compartments. There is no space to develop this here, but we dare not miss the point that *willingness to obey God is a vital factor in discovering the truth about him:* 'Whoever is willing to do ... will know...' A willingness to live in a way that is pleasing to God will unlock the truth more quickly and surely than a thousand pages of logical argument. You should therefore be asking not only, 'Am I willing to know the truth about God?' but 'Am I willing to surrender my self-centred independence and accept his authority in every part of my life?'

Those who suggest that Christianity is a crutch for weaklings have obviously not thought this through. Christianity is not for wimps, people content to let themselves be pushed around by the latest popular opinions about life and lifestyle. It is for those who are deliberately willing to live in ways controlled 'not by the sinful nature but by the Spirit'.[68] Are you willing to do this?

New birth; new beginning

Bringing about such a change of mind, heart and will needs something so radical that Jesus said, 'I tell you the truth, no one can see the kingdom of God unless he is born again.'[69] The implications could not be more serious or far-reaching. Unless you experience this new birth you will live and die without God, and if you die without God you will spend eternity exposed to his awesome, righteous and unrelenting anger. The stakes could not be higher. When Jesus added, 'Flesh gives birth to flesh, but the Spirit gives birth to spirit,'[70] he showed that only God could bring this change about. Although being born again is the only way to be brought into a living relationship with God, you can neither earn it, demand it, nor contribute to it in any way; in the Bible's own words, 'It does not ... depend on man's desire or effort.'[71]

Yet the Bible's message is one of hope, not despair. It tells us that God is 'not wanting anyone to perish, but everyone to come to repentance,'[72] and that he has demonstrated this in the death of Jesus in the place of sinners. Now, he offers to all who trust Jesus as Saviour and accept him as Lord the forgiveness of sins, moral and spiritual strength to cope with life's problems and pressures, and the certainty of spending eternity in his glorious, sinless, painless, deathless presence. All of this is confirmed in promises like these:

Seek the LORD while he may be found;
    call on him while he is near.

Let the wicked forsake his way
    and the evil man his thoughts.
Let him turn to the Lord, and he will have mercy on him,
    and to our God, for he will freely pardon. [73]

Ask and it will be given to you; seek and you will find; knock and the door will be opened to you. [74]

You will seek me and find me when you seek me with all your heart. [75]

Whoever is thirsty, let him come; and whoever wishes, let him take of the free gift of the water of life. [76]

If you are about to close this book as an atheist or an agnostic, I urge you to think again. Even if you have unanswered questions or honest doubts, take God at his word! Call upon him! Ask him to do for you what you can never do for yourself! Why stay as you are, 'without God and without hope in the world', [77] when you are being offered a new beginning?

And now...

If you have become a Christian as a result of reading this book, or are seriously considering this, here are some steps you will find helpful:

- If you can, get in touch with the person who gave you this book, or with another committed Christian. He or she will be delighted to talk things over with you and to help you think through any questions or difficulties you may have.
- Begin attending a local church that clearly believes and teaches the biblical truths you have been reading in these pages.
- Get hold of a good modern translation of the Bible and read it regularly. In this book I have almost exclusively used the New International Version, but the New King James Version or the New American Standard Bible would be fine. You may find it helpful to begin with the New Testament.
- Send for a free copy of *Read Mark Learn*, John Blanchard's book of guidelines for personal Bible study. Write to:

Dr John Blanchard,
c/o Evangelical Press,
Faverdale North Industrial Estate,
Darlington DL3 0PH
England

Notes

Introduction

1.   Friedrich Nietzsche, 'The Madman', a section of 'Gay Science' in *The Portable Nietzsche,* ed. Walter Kaufman, Viking, p.125.
2.   Cited by Ludovic Kennedy, *All in the Mind,* Hodder & Stoughton, p.254.
3.   *The Times,* 13 January 2000.
4.   See *Sunday Telegraph,* 24 October 1999.
5.   *Daily Express,* 23 March 2000.
6.   Bernard Palmer, *Cure for Life,* Summit Publishing Ltd, p.72.

Chapter 1 — Cards on the table

1.   Frederic G. Kenyon, *Our Bible and the Ancient Manuscripts,* Harper & Brothers, p.23.
2.   Frederic G. Kenyon, *The Bible and Archaeology,* Harper & Row, p.288.
3.   Cited by Brian Edwards, *Nothing But the Truth,* Evangelical Press, p.135.
4.   Robert Dick Wilson, *A Scientific Investigation of the Old Testament,* Moody Press, pp.70-71.
5.   Cited by Edwards, *Nothing But the Truth,* p.294.
6.   William Ramsay, *The Bearing of Recent Discovery on the Trustworthiness of the New Testament,* Hodder & Stoughton, p.222.
7.   *Ibid.,* p.89.
8.   *TIME,* 30 December 1974.
9.   See Dave Hunt, *In Defense of the Faith,* Harvest House Publishers, p.74.

10. See Peter W. Stoner, *Science Speaks*, Moody Press, pp.67-96 for this and other illustrations.

11. Simon Greenleaf, *The Testimony of the Evangelicals: Examined by the Rules of Evidence Administered in the Courts of Justice*, Baker Book House, p.2.

12. Henry M. Morris, *The Biblical Basis for Modern Science*, Baker Book House, p.87.

13. Exodus 4:1-7.

14. Exodus 15:22-25.

15. 1 Kings 17:7-16.

16. 1 Kings 17:17-24.

17. 2 Kings 6:1-7.

18. Matthew 8:23-27.

19. Matthew 8:28-34.

20. Luke 17:11-19.

21. Matthew 14:13-21.

22. *The Chambers Dictionary*, Chambers, p.1069.

23. John Polkinghorne, *Quarks, Chaos and Christianity*, Triangle, pp.82-3.

24. Edgar Andrews, *God, Science and Evolution*, Evangelical Press, p.48.

25. *The Times*, 13 July 1984.

26. 1 Samuel 3:9.

27. Micah 1:6.

28. Matthew 25:46.

29. Revelation 20:14.

30. Acts 16:30.

31. 1 Peter 1:23.

Chapter 2 — For the undecided

1. *The Times*, 15 February 1994.

2. See William James, *The Will to Believe*, Dover, pp.1-30.

3. C. Stephen Evans, *The Quest for Faith*, Inter-Varsity Press, p.28.

4. Cited by Peter C. Moore, *Disarming the Secular Gods*, Inter-Varsity Press, p.111.

5. 1 Peter 1:23.

6. Harold Lindsell, *God's Incomparable Word*.

7. 1 Peter 4:11.

8. 1 Thessalonians 2:13.

9.   R. C. Sproul, *Reason to Believe,* Zondervan Publishing House, pp.31-2.
10. 2 Timothy 3:16.
11. Genesis 1:1.
12. Romans 5:12.
13. Revelation 7:9.
14. Isaiah 9:7.
15. Malachi 4:1.
16. John 5:39.
17. Luke 24:27.
18. Acts 17:6, New King James Version.

Chapter 3 — 'Goodbye, God'?

1.   A. J. Ayer, *Language, Truth and Logic,* pp.115-16.
2.   *Daily Telegraph,* 13 August 1996.
3.   Isaac Asimov, 'An Interview with Isaac Asimov on Science and the Bible', in *Free Enquiry 2,* Spring 1982, p.9.
4.   Etienne Borne, *Atheists,* Hawthorn Books, p.8.
5.   Madalyn Murray O'Hair, *What on Earth is an Atheist?* Arno Press, p.43.
6.   Ludovic Kennedy, *All in the Mind,* Hodder & Stoughton, 1999, p.vii.
7.   *Ibid.,* pp.xiii-xiv.
8.   *Daily Telegraph,* 12 April 1996.
9.   *Independent,* 2 March 1993.
10. *Soul of Britain,* BBC2, 11 June 2000.
11. Peter Williams, *The Case For God,* Monarch Books, p.12.
12. Kennedy, *All in the Mind,* p.262.
13. *The Listener,* 2 March 1978.
14. Ronald H. Nash, *Faith and Reason,* Zondervan Publishing House, p.53.
15. B. C. Johnson, *The Atheist Debater's Handbook,* Prometheus Books, p.23.
16. *Soul of Britain,* BBC2, 11 June 2000.
17. George Smith, *Atheism: The Case Against God,* Prometheus Books, p.7.
18. Robert A. Morey, *The New Atheism and the Erosion of Freedom,* P & R Publishing, p.46.
19. Martin Robinson, *The Faith of the Unbeliever,* Monarch Books, p.78.

20. Michael Scriven, *Primary Philosophy,* McGraw-Hill, p.103.
21. Nash, *Faith and Reason,* p.18.
22. Psalms 14:1; 53:1.
23. Matthew 15:18.
24. Proverbs 4:23.
25. Romans 1:21-22.
26. Spiros Zodhiates, *The Complete Word Study Dictionary: New Testament,* AMG Publishers, p.948.
27. *Ibid.,* p.282.
28. S. Fox, *New Scientist,* 1969, p.450.
29. *Daily Telegraph,* 12 April 1996.
30. Daniel 2:21.
31. C. S. Lewis, *Broadcast Talks,* cited in Frederick P. Wood, *Facing Facts and Finding Faith,* Marshall, Morgan & Scott, p.24.
32. *Life and Letters of Charles Darwin,* ed. Frances Darwin, Johnson reprint, p.285.
33. *The Times,* 13 January 2000.
34. *The Times,* 17 January 2000.
35. 1 John 1:5.
36. Romans 1:21.
37. John 3:19.
38. John 14:6.

Chapter 4 — The science thing

1.   George Washington Carver, *Scientists of Faith,* ed. Dan Graves, Kregel Publications.
2.   Cited in *God and the Scientists,* CPO-Design and Print, p.21.
3.   Vernon Wright, *The Relevance of Christianity in a Scientific Age,* Young Life, p.9.
4.   J. P. Moreland, *Scaling the Secular City,* Baker Book House, p.3.
5.   *Concise Oxford Dictionary,* Oxford University Press, p.939.
6.   *Soul of Britain,* BBC2, 11 June 2000.
7.   Andrews, *God, Science and Evolution,* Introduction.
8.   Johannes Hauri, cited by Samuel Zwemer, *The Moslem Doctrine of God,* p.21.
9.   See John Blanchard, *Does God Believe in Atheists?* Evangelical Press, pp.422-46.
10. *Daily Mail,* 16 May 1995.
11. *Proceedings of the National Institute of Science of India,* 27A (196): 564.

12. Bertrand Russell, *Religion and Science,* Oxford University Press, p.243.

13. *Daily Telegraph Science Extra,* 11 September 1999.

14. *Daily Telegraph,* 31 August 1993.

15. Moreland, *Scaling the Secular City,* p.197.

16. Keith Ward, *God, Chance and Necessity,* Oneworld Publications, pp.108-9.

17. J. S. Jones, *The Language of the Genes,* HarperCollins, p.xi.

18. Stephen Hawking, *Black Holes and Baby Universes,* Bantam Books, p.90.

19. *Sunday Telegraph,* 18 February 2001.

20. *Ibid.*

21. John Eccles, 'Science Can't Provide Ultimate Answers', *US News and World Report,* February 1985.

22. *Sunday Telegraph,* 17 April 1996.

23. John Houghton, *The Search for God,* Lion Publishing, pp.213-14.

24. *Soul of Britain,* BBC2, 11 June 2000.

25. Erwin Schrödinger, *Nature and the Greeks,* cited by David Wilkinson and Rob Frost, *Thinking Clearly About God and Science,* Monarch Publications, p.67.

26. Andrew Miller, *Real Science, Real Faith,* ed. R. J. Berry, Monarch Publications, pp.94-5.

27. Bertrand Russell, *Why I am not a Christian,* Simon & Schuster, p.50.

28. *Sunday Telegraph,* 7 April 1996.

29. *Sunday Telegraph,* 30 March 1997.

30. Michael Williams and J. P. Moreland, *Jesus Under Fire,* Paternoster Press, p.10.

31. *Daily Telegraph,* 30 September 1996.

32. *Soul of Britain,* BBC2, 11 June 2999.

33. *Ibid.*

34. *Ibid.*

35. *Ibid.*

36. *The Times,* 10 December 1994.

37. Karl Popper, *The Logic of Scientific Discovery,* Unwin Hyman Ltd, p.278.

38. Elaine Storkey, *Soul of Britain,* 11 June 2000.

39. Albert Einstein, 'Science and Religion', *Out of My Later Years,* cited by Rhoda Thomas Tripp, *The International Thesaurus of Quotations,* George Allan & Unwin, p.564.

40. Mark 1:1.

41. John 1:1.

42. Matthew 12:30.

43. Mark 12:29-30.

44. John 1:1.

45. Boris Dotsenko's story is adapted from *Scientists Who Believe,* Moody Press, by kind permission of the editor, Eric C. Barrett.

Chapter 5 — Maria got it right

1.   Charlie Broad, Professor of Moral Philosophy at Cambridge, cited by Ravi Zacharias, *Can Man Live Without God?,* Word Publishing, p.209.

2.   Cited by Peter A. Angeles, *Critiques of God,* Prometheus Books, p.296.

3.   Bertrand Russell, *Why I am not a Christian,* p.107.

4.   D. Adams, *The Hitch-Hiker's Guide to the Galaxy,* The Original Radio Scripts, Pan Books, p.39.

5.   Stephen Hawking, *A Brief History of Time,* 1995 Edition, Bantam Books, pp.139-40.

6.   *Daily Telegraph,* 28 June 1996.

7.   Cited by Gary Scott Smith, 'Naturalistic Humanism', in *Building a Christian Worldview,* vol. 1, ed. W. Andrew Hoffecker, Presbyterian and Reformed Publishing Company, p.174.

8.   William Lane Craig, *Reasonable Faith,* Crossway Books, p.103.

9.   Isaac Asimov, 'In the Game of Energy and Thermodynamics You Can't Even Break Even', *Journal of the Smithsonian Institute* (June 1990), p.6.

10. Andrews, *God, Science and Evolution,* p.35.

11. Arthur Eddington, *The Expanding Universe,* Macmillan, p.124.

12. Ward, *God, Chance and Necessity,* p.59.

13. Genesis 1:1.

14. Douglas Kelly, *Creation and Change,* Christian Focus Publications, p.45.

15. Revelation 4:11.

16. Romans 12:2.

17. Genesis 1:31.

18. David Wilkinson, *God, the Big Bang and Stephen Hawking,* Monarch Publications, p.148.

19. George Smoot and Keay Davidson, *Wrinkles in Time,* Avon Books, p.145.

20. Timothy Ferris, *The Whole Shebang*, Simon & Schuster, p.147.

21. *Stephen Hawking's Universe*, BBC2, 30 August 1997.

22. *Sunday Telegraph*, 31 August 1997.

23. G. F. W. von Leibniz, 'Nature and Grace', *Selections*, p.527.

24. Edward Tryon, *Nature* 246 (1973), p.393.

25. *Daily Telegraph*, 6 April 1998.

26. William Lane Craig, *The Kalam Cosmological Argument*, Barnes & Noble, p.149.

27. Hawking, *A Brief History of Time*, p.134.

28. See Roger Penrose, *The Emperor's New Mind: Concerning Computers, Minds and the Law of Physics*, Oxford University Press, pp.339-45.

29. Immanuel Kant, *Critique of Pure Reason*, trans. Norman Kemp Smith, St Martin's Press, p.520.

30. David Hume, *Dialogues Concerning Natural Religion*, ed. Nelson Pike, Bobbs-Merrill, p.222.

31. See Smoot and Davidson, *Wrinkles in Time*, pp.110-12, 293.

32. Isaac Newton, *Principia*, cited in Donald B. De Young, *Astronomy and the Bible*, Baker Book House, p.115.

33. Private letter to the author, 25 February 1999.

34. See Smoot and Davidson, *Wrinkles in Time*, p.296.

35. J. L. Mackie, *The Miracle of Theism*, Clarendon Press, p.141.

36. Paul Davies, *The Mind of God*, Penguin, p.200.

37. Hawking, *A Brief History of Time*, p.140.

38. Ward, *God, Chance and Necessity*, p.23.

39. Romans 12:15.

40. Hebrews 11:3.

41. 1 Corinthians 13:12.

Chapter 6 — From protons to people

1. *Daily Telegraph*, 12 February 2001.

2. *Daily Mail*, 12 February 2001.

3. *USA Today*, 12 February 2001.

4. See T. S. Kuhn, *The Structure of Scientific Resolutions*, 2nd edition, University of Chicago Press, p.69.

5. See John Gribben, *Genesis*, Oxford University Press, pp.191-2.

6. See Blanchard, *Does God Believe in Atheists?*, pp.282-310.

7. Phillip E. Johnson, *Testing Darwinism*, Inter-Varsity Press, p.75.

8. Henry M. Morris, *The God who is Real*, Baker Book House, p.18.

9. F. Crick, *Life Itself: Its Origin and Nature,* Macdonald, p.88.

10. *Ibid.,* pp.15-16.

11. Cited by Scott M. Huse, *The Collapse of Evolution,* Baker Book House, p.3.

12. Richard Dawkins, 'The Necessity of Darwinism', in *New Scientist,* No. 94, 15 April 1982, p.130.

13. Richard Dawkins, *The Selfish Gene,* Granada Publishing, p.16.

14. Richard Dawkins, *The Blind Watchmaker,* W. W. Norton, p.139.

15. F. B. Salisbury, 'Natural Selection and the Complexity of the Gene', in *Nature,* vol. 224 (217) 1969, 25 October, pp.342-3.

16. Edgar Andrews, *From Nothing to Nature,* Evangelical Press, pp.28-9.

17. Genesis 1:2.

18. e.g. Genesis 1:11.

19. Genesis 2:7.

20. *TIME,* 31 December 1999.

21. Cited by John Currid in *Building a Christian World View,* vol. 1, ed. W. Andrew Hoffeker, Presbyterian & Reformed Publishing Company, p.154.

22. Cited by Michael Denton, *Evolution: A Theory in Crisis,* Adler & Adler, p.69.

23. Cited in 'John Lofton's Journal', *Washington Times,* 8 February 1984.

24. Cited by M. Bowden, *The Rise of the Evolution Fraud,* Sovereign Publications, p.56.

25. Denton, *Evolution: A Theory in Crisis,* p.69.

26. John Ankerberg and John Weldon, *The Facts on Creation vs. Evolution,* Harvest House Publishers, p.8.

27. Theodosius Dobzhansky, *Mankind Evolving: The Evolution of the Human Species,* Bantam, p.1.

28. Cited by John Wright, *Designer Universe,* Monarch Publications, p.61.

29. Denton, *Evolution: A Theory in Crisis,* p.15.

30. Cited by Phillip E. Johnson, *Darwin on Trial,* Monarch Publications, p.9.

31. George Gaylord Simpson, 'The World into which Darwin Led Us', *Science,* vol. 131 (1960), 970, from *Bird, Origin of Species Revisited,* vol. 1, p.139.

32. Ian T. Taylor, *In the Minds of Men,* T. F. E. Publishing, p.36.

33. *Sunday Times,* 13 October 1996.

34. Dawkins, *The Blind Watchmaker*, pp.6-7.
35. Kenneth Hsu, *Journal of Sedimentary Petrology*, 56(5): 729-30.
36. Sylvia Baker, *Bone of Contention*, Evangelical Press, p.19.
37. Pierre Grassé, *Evolution of Living Organisms*, Academic Press, p.103.
38. Magnus Verbrugge, *Alive: An Enquiry into the Origin and Meaning of Life*, Ross House Books, p.12.
39. *Ibid.*, p.13.
40. René Chauvin, *La biologie de l'esprit*, Editions du Rocher, pp.23-4.
41. M. Bowden, *Science vs Evolution*, Sovereign Publications, pp.52-3.
42. *From a Frog to a Prince*, Creation Science Foundation.
43. *Ibid.*
44. Dawkins, *The Blind Watchmaker*, p.18.
45. Denton, *Evolution: A Theory in Crisis*, p.328.
46. Crick, *Life Itself: Its Origin and Nature*, p.51.
47. *Ibid.*
48. G. A. Kerkut, *Implications of Evolution*, Pergamon Press, p.150.
49. Charles Darwin, *Origin of Species*, 6th edition, New York University Press, p.154.
50. Michael Behe, *Darwin's Black Box*, The Free Press.
51. See Johnson, *Darwin on Trial*, p.54.
52. Baker, *Bone of Contention*, p.8.
53. Charles Darwin, *Origin of Species*, J. M. Dent & Sons Ltd., pp.292-3.
54. David M. Raup, 'Conflicts Between Darwinism and Palaentology', in *Field Museum of Natural History Bulletin*, vol. 50, p.25.
55. Johnson, *Darwin on Trial*, p.54.
56. Cited by Johnson, *Darwin on Trial*, p.54.
57. Ernest Mayr, *Population, Species and Evolution*, Harvard University Press, p.10.
58. Taylor, *In the Minds of Men*, p.227.
59. Lord Zuckerman, *Beyond the Ivory Tower*, Taplinger Publishing Co., p.64.
60. Jeremy Rifkin, *Algeny*, Viking Press, p.108.
61. See Blanchard, *Does God Believe in Atheists?*, pp.78-110.
62. Personal letter to Luther Sutherland dated 10 April 1979, and cited by him in *Darwin's Enigma*, Master Book Publishers, p.89.
63. Psalm 24:1

Chapter 7 — Is ANDi one of us?
1. *Daily Telegraph,* 12 January 2001.
2. *Daily Telegraph,* 28 December 1997.
3. *Sunday Telegraph,* 31 March 1996.
4. *Sunday Telegraph,* 17 April 1994.
5. Dawkins, *The Selfish Gene,* p.xi.
6. *Ibid.,* p.x.
7. *Sunday Telegraph,* 18 October 1998.
8. Cited by Andrew Knowles, *Finding Faith,* Lion Publishing, p.13.
9. Cited by Hunt, *In Defense of the Faith,* p.22.
10. *The Book of Knowledge,* vol. 4, the Waverley Book Co., p.40.
11. Asimov, 'In the Game of Energy and Thermodynamics, You Can't Even Break Even', p.10.
12. *60 Minutes,* 22 April 1994.
13. C. Everett Koop, in *Scientists Who Believe,* ed. Eric C. Barrett and David Fisher, Moody Press, pp.158-9.
14. Andrew Knowles, *Finding Faith,* p.8.
15. R. C. Sproul, *In Search of Dignity,* Regal Books, pp.18-19.
16. *Daily Telegraph,* 17 January 2001.
17. *Daily Mail,* 15 January 2001.
18. Paul Oestreicher, *Thirty Years of Human Rights* (The British Churches' Advisory Forum on Human Rights, 1980).
19. *Daily Telegraph,* 30 December 2000.
20. Jacob Bronowski, *The Identity of Man,* Penguin, p.7.
21. *Ibid.,* p.8.
22. Marvin Lubenow, *Bones of Contention,* Baker Books, p.197.
23. Francis Schaeffer, *Genesis in Space and Time,* Hodder & Stoughton, p.51.
24. C. S. Lewis, *Mere Christianity,* Macmillan, p.21.
25. Paul Johnson, *The Quest for God,* Weidenfeld & Nicolson, pp.2-3.
26. Rodney D. Holder, *Nothing But Atoms and Miracles?,* Monarch Publications, p.4
27. Cited by J. Andrew Kirk, *Loosing the Chains,* Hodder & Stoughton, p.63.
28. *Daily Telegraph,* 23 April 1996.
29. *Daily Telegraph,* 30 August 1995.
30. John M. Frame, *Apologetics to the Glory of God,* Presbyterian & Reformed Publishing Co., p.99.
31. Private letter to the author, 3 November 1998.

32. Fyodor Dostoevsky, *The Brothers Karamazov*, Penguin Books, p.733.
33. Knowles, *Finding Faith*, p.9.
34. Dawkins, *The Blind Watchmaker*, p.5.
35. *Sunday Times Magazine*, 11 February 1996.
36. J. B. S. Haldane, *Possible Worlds*, Chatto & Windus, p.62.

Chapter 8 — Signs of significance
1. Russell, *Why I am Not a Christian*, p.107.
2. Cited by Palmer, *Cure for Life*, p.10.
3. Cited by Ravi Zacharias, *Can Man Live Without God?*, Word Publishing, p.31.
4. Cited by Johnson, *Darwin on Trial*, p.14.
5. William Provine, 'Scientists, Face It! Science and Religion are Incompatible,' in *The Scientist*, 5 September 1988, p.10.
6. *Observer*, 9 April 1995.
7. Dawkins, *The Selfish Gene*, p.21.
8. *Sunday Telegraph*, 22 March 1998.
9. Ward, *God, Chance and Necessity*, pp.140-41.
10. Cited by Edyth Draper, *Draper's Book of Quotations for the Christian World*, Tyndale House Publishers, p.237.
11. Cited in *This I Believe*, ed. J. Marsden, Random House, p.48.
12. *Observer*, 19 February 1995.
13. Aldous Huxley, *Ends and Means*, Chatto & Windus, p.273.
14. Richard Dawkins, *River out of Eden*, Weidenfeld & Nicolson, p.96.
15. Revelation 4:11.
16. John Benton, *Is Christianity True?*, Evangelical Press, p.90.
17. M. Ruse, *Darwinism Defended*, Addison Wesley, p.108.
18. *Daily Telegraph*, 13 March 1994.
19. John Rendle-Short, *Reasonable Christianity*, Evangelical Press, p.72.
20. Dawkins, *River out of Eden*, p.120.
21. Ward, *God, Chance and Necessity*, p.142.
22. *Ibid.*, pp.141-2.
23. H. R. Rookmaaker, *Art and the Public Today*, L' Abri Fellowship, p.20.
24. Psalm 19:1.
25. Joseph Gaer, *What the Great Religions Believe*, Dodd, Mead & Co., p.16.

26. Samuel Zwemer, *The Origin of Religion,* Loiseaux Brothers, p.26.
27. Cited by Alister McGrath, *Bridge-Building,* Inter-Varsity Press, p.133.
28. Martin Bell, *In Harm's Way,* Penguin, p.72.
29. *Ibid.,* p.74.
30. John Houghton, *The Search for God,* Lion Publishing, p.143.
31. Wilhelm Schmidt, *Origin of the Idea of God,* cited by Zwemer, *The Origin of Religion,* pp.14-15.
32. Nikolai Lenin, *Selected Works,* vol. XL, Lawrence Wishart Ltd., pp.675-6.
33. *Observer,* 16 April 1995.
34. Edmund Burke, *Reflections on the Revolution in France,* cited in *The Portable Conservative Readers,* Penguin Books, p.27.
35. Jean-Paul Sartre, *Words,* Penguin Books, p.65.
36. Cited by Charles T. Gliksberg, *Literature and Religion,* Southern Methodist University Press, pp.221-2.
37. Cited by Os Guinness, *The Dust of Death,* Inter-Varsity Press, p.25.
38. McGrath, *Bridge-Building,* p.71.
39. *Ibid.,* pp.70-71.
40. *Daily Telegraph,* 18 January 2001.
41. Kenneth Williams, *Just Williams,* Fontana/Collins, p.130.
42. *TIME,* 4 September 2001.
43. Russell, *Why I am Not a Christian,* p.116.
44. *Daily Telegraph,* 29 May 1994.
45. Ernest Becker, *The Denial of Death,* Free Press, p.26.
46. See Blanchard, *Whatever Happened to Hell?,* Evangelical Press.
47. Ravi Zacharias, *A Shattered Visage,* Wolgemuth & Hyatt, p.102.
48. C. S. Lewis, *Spirits in Bondage,* Macmillan, p.41.
49. Genesis 1:27.
50. Genesis 2:7.
51. Wisdom of Solomon, 2:23.
52. Ecclesiastes 3:10-11.
53. Robert Frost, *Thinking Clearly About God and Science,* Monarch Publications, p.41.
54. John 14:6.
55. Revelation 3:20.
56. Mark 8:36.
57. 2 Corinthians 4:18.

Chapter 9 — Where was God on September 11?

1. *Daily Mail*, 12 September 2001.
2. *TIME*, Special undated edition.
3. *Daily Mail*, 12 September 2001.
4. *The Economist*, 15-21 September 2001.
5. *The Times*, 12 September 2001.
6. *Daily Mail*, 12 September 2001.
7. *The Times*, 12 September 2001.
8. *Daily Mail*, 12 September 2001.
9. *Daily Telegraph*, 12 September 2001.
10. Alvin Plantinga, 'A Christian Life Partly Lived', in *Philosophers Who Believe*, Inter-Varsity Press, p.12.
11. John Polkinghorne, *Science and Providence*, SPCK, p.67.
12. *The Economist*, 27 April 1991.
13. See *Los Angeles Times*, 20 June 1990.
14. See Paul Johnson, *Modern Times*, Orion Books Ltd, p.548.
15. *Daily Telegraph*, 5 July 2001.
16. Psalm 115:3.
17. See Blanchard, *Does God Believe In Atheists?*, pp.500-554.
18. *The Chambers Dictionary*, Chambers, p.798.
19. Cited by Zacharias, *A Shattered Visage*, p.59.
20. Francis Bridger, *Why Can't I Have Faith?*, Triangle Books, p.47.
21. Elie Wiesel, *Night*, Avon Books, p.9.
22. *Ibid.*
23. *Penpoint*, vol. 5, no.1, January 1994.
24. Cited by Dan Cohn-Sherbock, *Holocaust Theology*, Lamp Press, p.82.
25. Cited by Nigel McCullough, *Barriers to Belief*, Darton, Longman & Todd, p.66.
26. Cited by Peter A. Angeles, *Critiques of God*, Prometheus Books, p.296.
27. *Daily Telegraph*, 13 April 1996.
28. Arthur Keith, *Evolution and Ethics*, G. P. Putnam's Sons, p.28.
29. Henry M. Morris, *The Long War Against God*, Baker Book House, p.79.
30. *Ibid.*, p.77.
31. Viktor Frankl, *The Doctor and the Soul: Introduction to Logotherapy*, Knopf, p.xxi.
32. *Daily Telegraph*, 10 May 1995. These views are adapted from Dawkins' book *River Out of Eden*.

33. Michael Rose, *Evolutionary Naturalism,* Routledge, p.241.

34. Zacharias, *A Shattered Visage,* p.60.

35. Cited by D. James Kennedy, *Skeptics Answered,* Multnomah Books, p.116.

36. Cited by Richard Pierard, 'An Age of Ideology', in *The History of Christianity,* 1990 edition, ed. Tom Dowley, Lion Publishing, pp.589-90.

37. William Shirer, *The Rise and Fall of the Third Reich,* Simon & Schuster, p.240.

38. Dawkins, *The Selfish Gene,* p.2.

39. Alvin Plantinga, 'Tooley and Evil: A Reply', *Australian Journal of Philosophy,* 60 (1981):74.

40. Lord Hailsham, *The Door Wherein I Went,* Collins, pp.41-2.

41. Ravi Zacharias, *Deliver Us From Evil,* Word Publishing, p.168.

42. 2 Thessalonians 2:7, New King James Version.

43. 1 Corinthians 13:12, New American Standard Bible.

44. Genesis 1:31.

45. Genesis 1:27.

46. J. Gresham Machen, *The Christian View of Man,* Banner of Truth Trust, p.147.

47. Romans 5:12.

48. Romans 5:12.

49. Genesis 5:3.

50. Romans 8:22.

51. Stuart Olyott, *Things You Might Have Asked,* Evangelical Press, p.48.

52. Psalm 18:30.

53. D. A. Carson, *How Long, O Lord?,* Inter-Varsity Press, p.226.

54. Romans 11:33.

55. *Penpoint,* vol. 5, no.1, January 1994.

56. Bridger, *Why Can't I Have Faith?,* p.75.

57. Job 1:3.

58. Job 1:1.

59. See Job 1:13-19.

60. Job 1:20-21.

61. Job 2:9.

62. Job 19:25.

63. Job 3:11.

64. Job 21:13.

65. Job 30:19.

66. Job 16:3.
67. Job 38:4.
68. Job 38:12.
69. Job 38:31.
70. Job 38:35.
71. Job 38:33.
72. Job 40:9.
73. Job 40:1,8.
74. Job 38:2.
75. Job 42:1.
76. Job 40:4.
77. Job 42:3.
78. Job 42:5.
79. Job 42:6.
80. Herbert Carson, *Facing Suffering*, Evangelical Press, p.28.
81. C. S. Lewis, *The Problem of Pain*, Geoffrey Bles, p.81.
82. Carson, *Facing Suffering*, p.133.
83. Hebrews 1:3.
84. 2 Peter 3:13.
85. Revelation 21:4.
86. 2 Corinthians 4:17.
87. Romans 8:18.
88. Matthew 20:28.
89. John 13:16.
90. Psalm 119:71.
91. 2 Corinthians 12:10.
92. Isaiah 53:11.
93. Philippians 3:10.
94. 2 Corinthians 4:17.
95. Psalm 66:16.
96. 1 Peter 1:8.

Chapter 10 — One solitary life

1. K. S. Latourette, *Christianity in a Revolutionary Age,* vol. 1, The Paternoster Press, p.4.
2. H. G. Wells, *The American Magazine,* July 1922.
3. Mission Aviation Fellowship.
4. Russell, *Why I am Not a Christian.*
5. See Mark 6:3.
6. Luke 1:34.

7.   Matthew 1:25.
8.   Matthew 1:18.
9.   *Ibid.*
10. Luke 2:47.
11. Zodhiates, *The Complete Word Study Dictionary: New Testament,* p.1342.
12. Luke 4:22.
13. Matthew 7:28-29.
14. John 7:46.
15. Bernard Ramm, *Protestant Christian Evidence,* Moody Press, p.170.
16. Matthew 4:24.
17. See Matthew 9:27-30.
18. See Mark 7:31-37.
19. *Ibid.*
20. See Luke 17:11-19.
21. See John 5:1-9.
22. See Mark 5:21-43.
23. See Luke 7:11-17.
24. See John 11:1-44.
25. See Mark 4:35-41.
26. See Luke 5:1-11.
27. See John 2:1-11.
28. See Matthew 14:13-21.
29. See Matthew 15:29-39.
30. John 21:25.
31. See Matthew 21:18.
32. See John 4:7.
33. See John 4:6.
34. See Matthew 8:24.
35. See Luke 10:21.
36. See John 11:35.
37. See John 2:25.
38. See Luke 5:16.
39. See Matthew 4:2.
40. See Luke 4:16.
41. See Matthew 21:42.
42. Hebrews 4:15.
43. Matthew 11:29.

44. See John Blanchard, *Meet the Real Jesus,* Evangelical Press, pp.76-83.

45. John 8:29.

46. John 8:46.

47. John 14:30.

48. Hebrews 7:26.

49. William E. Lecky, *History of European Morals from Augustus to Charlemagne,* D. Appleton & Co., p.8.

50. Cited by Josh McDowell, *Evidence that Demands a Verdict,* Campus Crusade for Christ, p.109.

51. Cited by Frank Mead, *The Encyclopaedia of Religious Quotations,* Fleming H. Revell, p.57.

52. Genesis 3:8.

53. Genesis 5:3.

54. Psalm 51:5.

55. Romans 5:12.

56. Romans 8:2.

57. Hebrews 9:27.

58. Woody Allen, 'Death' (a play) in *Without Feathers*.

59. John 10:18.

60. Matthew 27:50.

61. Ecclesiastes 8:8, Revised Standard Version.

62. Cited by M. R. Vincent, *Word Studies in the New Testament,* Associated Publishers and Authors, p.82.

63. e.g. Isaiah 53.

64. Luke 22:37.

65. Romans 5:6.

66. 1 Peter 2:24.

67. 1 John 3:16.

68. Matthew 26:28.

69. Luke 9:31, New American Standard Bible.

70. John 19:30.

71. 1 John 2:2.

72. Mark 10:45.

73. Romans 6:6.

74. Romans 5:10.

75. Romans 5:1.

76. 1 Peter 3:18, New American Standard Bible.

77. *The Long Silence* originally appeared in the British student magazine *Voice*. The author is unknown.

78. Romans 3:25.
79. Isaiah 53:5.
80. Romans 5:8.
81. John 3:16.
82. McGrath, *Bridge-Building,* Inter-Varsity Press, p.144.
83. See John 19:34.
84. John 19:42.
85. John 19:39.
86. See Matthew 27:60.
87. See Matthew 27:63.
88. Matthew 27:65.
89. See Matthew 27:66.
90. Acts 2:23, New American Standard Bible.
91. Luke 23:55.
92. J. N. D. Anderson, *Jesus Christ: The Witness of History,* Inter-Varsity Press, p.129.
93. 1 Corinthians 15:15, New American Standard Bible.
94. Acts 5:29.
95. D. F. Strauss, *The Life of Jesus for the People,* vol. 1, Williams & Norgate, p.412.
96. See John 20:10-18.
97. See Mark 16:9; Matthew 28:9; Luke 24:15-32; 24:34,36; John 20:26; John 21:1; 1 Corinthians 15:6,7; Matthew 28:18; Luke 24:50-51.
98. A. Rendle-Short, *Why I Believe,* Inter-Varsity Press.
99. 1 Corinthians 15:6.
100. See e.g. Acts 4:1-22.
101. Charles A. Colson, *Kingdoms in Conflict,* p.70.
102. Anderson, *Jesus Christ: The Witness of History,* p.146.
103. Acts 17:6, New King James Version.
104. D. James Kennedy, *The Gates of Hell Shall Not Prevail,* Thomas Nelson Publishers, p.21.
105. John 8:12.
106. John 6:35.
107. John 14:6.
108. See Blanchard, *Meet the Real Jesus,* pp.151-81.
109. John 14:8-9.
110. Colossians 1:15.
111. 2 Peter 1:1.
112. 1 John 5:20.

113. Cited by Mead, *The Encyclopaedia of Religious Quotations*, p.50.
114. Lewis, *Mere Christianity*, pp.40-41.
115. John 9:25.
116. John 3:16.
117. Acts 4:12.
118. John 14:6.

Chapter 11 — The beginning?

1. 1 Peter 1:23.
2. Isaiah 45:5.
3. 1 Corinthians 8:4.
4. John 4:24.
5. 1 Chronicles 29:11.
6. Psalm 103:8.
7. e.g. Psalm 22:3; Isaiah 41:14.
8. 1 Samuel 2:2.
9. Jeremiah 44:7.
10. Psalm 115:3.
11. 1 John 4:8.
12. Acts 14:15.
13. Genesis 1:27.
14. Ecclesiastes 7:29.
15. Romans 3:23.
16. Isaiah 64:6.
17. Ephesians 2:12.
18. Colossians 1:15.
19. Colossians 2:9.
20. Romans 1:4.
21. Revelation 1:18.
22. *The New International Dictionary of the Christian Church*, ed. J. D. Douglas, The Paternoster Press, p.749.
23. Blaise Pascal, *Pensées and Other Writings,* trans. Honor Levi, Oxford, *Pensées* 142.
24. Blaise Pascal, *Pensées,* trans. Martin Turnell, Harvill Press, cited by Colin Brown, *Philosophy and the Christian Faith,* Inter-Varsity Press, p.59.
25. Blaise Pascal, *Selections from 'The Thoughts',* trans. Arthur H. Beattie, Appleton-Century-Crofts, p.68.
26. Blaise Pascal, *Pensées,* 11, cited by William Lone Craig, *Reasonable Faith,* Crossway Books, p.53.

27. *Ibid.*
28. Blaise Pascal, *Pensées,* 680; cited by Peter Williams, *The Case for God,* Monarch Books, p.377.
29. Job 12:25.
30. Matthew 8:12.
31. Psalm 46:1.
32. Philippians 2:13.
33. Psalm 23:6.
34. 1 Peter 5:4
35. Nehemiah 9:25.
36. Psalm 48:9.
37. Acts 17:25.
38. Romans 1:5.
39. Psalm 29:2, New King James Version.
40. Matthew 12:30.
41. Anthony Flew, 'Is Pascal's Wager the Only Safe Bet?', cited by Williams, *The Case for God,* p.393.
42. Acts 14:17, New King James Version.
43. Blaise Pascal, *Pensées and Other Writings, Pensées,* 274.
44. Romans 1:20.
45. See Linda Smith and William Raeper, *A Beginner's Guide to Ideas,* Lion Publishing, p.43.
46. Blaise Pascal, *Pensées,* trans. H. F. Stewart, Random House.
47. Pascal, *Pensées,* 680, cited by Williams, *The Case For God,* p.377.
48. Anthony Kenny, *The God of the Philosophers,* Oxford, p.129.
49. Cited by George Roche, *A World Without Heroes,* The Hillsdale College Press, p.91.
50. H. R. Rookmaaker, *The Creative Gift,* Cornerstone Books, p.150.
51. Mark 12:32.
52. Mark 12:34.
53. James 2:19.
54. Matthew 8:29.
55. Mark 1:24.
56. Matthew 4:3,6.
57. Hebrews 11.1.
58. 1 John 1:8.
59. Exodus 20:2-7.
60. James 2:10.
61. Galatians 3:10 (emphasis added).
62. James 4:17.

63. Matthew 7:12.
64. Mark 12:30.
65. Matthew 22:38.
66. Hebrews 4:13.
67. John 7:17, Good News Bible.
68. Romans 8:9.
69. John 3:3.
70. John 3:6.
71. Romans 9:16.
72. 2 Peter 3:9.
73. Isaiah 55:6-7.
74. Matthew 7:7.
75. Jeremiah 29:13.
76. Revelation 22:17.
77. Ephesians 2:12.

Index

Aberfan disaster, 161, 169
absolutes, 138, 166, 219
accidents, 160-61
accountability, personal, 126-7, 143, 220, 223
Adams, Douglas, 74
agnosticism, 11, 30-36, 40, 44, 120, 221, 223-6, 234
Alagiah, George, 122
Alexander the Great, 196
All in the Mind, 45
Allen, Woody, 197
Almond, Mark, 159
Altman, Robert, 137
amino acids, 103
Anaximander, 76
Anderson, Sir Norman, 204, 210
Andrews, Edgar, 23, 58, 76-7, 83, 94
animism, 58
annihilationism, 148, 150
Apaloo, Adzo, 85-9
'ape-men', 107-8
Archaeopteryx, 106-7
Aristotle, 21
Asimov, Isaac, 44, 76
Aspinall, John, 115-16

atheism / atheists, 26, 28, 30, 33, 40, 41, 42, 43, 44-53, 61, 62, 66, 67, 68, 69, 70, 80, 84, 92, 93, 94, 99, 116, 120, 128, 130, 135, 136, 138, 142, 143, 146, 150, 162, 164, 180, 181, 214, 221, 227, 234
  problems for, 35, 39, 81, 91, 92, 145, 149, 166, 167, 212
Atheism: the Case Against God, 47
Atheist Debater's Handbook, The, 47
Atkins, Peter, 51, 61, 66, 81, 165
Augustine (of Hippo), 198
Ayer, A. J., 44, 47

Bach, Johann Sebastian, 67
Bacon, Francis, 59-60
Baker, Sylvia 100-101
Barnard, Christiaan, 148
Bayliss, Trevor, 10
Beagle, H.M.S., 96, 97
beauty (see also man, aesthetic dimension), 140, 141, 168
Becker, Ernest, 148
Beckett, Samuel, 137

Behe, Michael, 104
Bell, Martin, 143-4
Benton, John, 139
Berry, R. J. 24
Beyond the Ivory Tower, 108
Bhagavad-Gita, 20, 151
Bible, the, 15-25, 35-9, 219
  accuracy, 15-22, 28, 54, 56,
    219, 227
  authenticity, 28, 29, 227
  authority, 35-6, 57
  external evidence for, 18-19
  God's revelation of himself in,
    35-6, 37, 39, 50
  inspiration — see authority;
    God, authorship of Scripture
  integrity, 21-2, 36, 56, 57, 134
  manuscripts, 15-18
  miracles recorded in, 22-5
  overview of, 36-9
  prophecy, 20-21, 26, 27, 38,
    39, 198, 211
  relevance, 132
  science and — see science, the
    Bible and
  verdict on atheism, 49-51
Biederwolf, William, 211
'Big Bang', the, 78-82
biochemistry, 103, 104
Black Holes and Baby Universes,
  64
Blind Watchmaker, The, 93, 99,
  128
blood-clotting, 104-5
body, the human, 116-18
Booker, Christopher, 140
Borne, Etienne, 45
Bowden, Malcolm, 102
Bowen, Jeremy, 207
Boyle, Robert, 60

Bragg, William Henry, 69
brain, the human, 51-2, 65, 117-
  18, 119, 128
Breath, 137
Bridger, Francis, 175
Brief History of Time, A, 74
British Association for the Ad-
  vancement of Science, 59
Broadcast Talks, 51
Bronowski, Jacob, 121, 122
Bruce, F. F., 27
Buber, Martin, 136
Buddha, 20
Buddhism, 59
Buerk, Michael, 10
Burke, Edmund, 146
Bush, George W., 120
By Searching, 131

Carver, George Washington, 57
Caesar, Julius, 15, 16
  Gallic War, 15, 16
Cage, John, 137
Carson, Don, 174
Carson, Herbert, 179, 180
Case for God, The, 46
Casimir, Jon, 137
cells, complexity of, 103-5, 116-
  17
Chambers Dictionary, The, 163
Charles, Prince, 140
Christ — see Jesus Christ
Chauvin, Remy, 102
Chernobyl, 161, 169
Chesterton, G. K., 171, 227
Christian church, growth of, 39,
  210
chromosomes — see genetics,
  DNA
Church of England, the, 9, 26

Clough, Elizabeth, 147
Collins, Francis, 90, 127
Colson, Charles, 209-10
Communism, 70, 145, 162
Comte, Auguste, 46
Concise Oxford Dictionary, 58
Confucius, 20
conscience, 124-7, 171, 180
consciousness, 138
Craig, William Lane, 76, 81
creation, 11, 29, 41, 51, 58, 93,
   139
   biblical record of, 77-8, 94-5,
      96, 149-50, 171-2, 196
   evidence for, 82-5
   ex nihilo, 81
Crick, Francis, 91, 92, 103, 128
crucifixion, 196, 207

Daily Express, The, 10
Daily Mail, The, 60, 90, 121, 159
Daily Telegraph, The, 62, 67, 90,
   114, 115, 125, 147, 148, 159,
   162
   Science Extra, 61
Darwin, Charles, 30, 52, 53,
   95-8, 99, 100, 102, 104, 105,
   128, 166
Darwin, Erasmus, 53
Darwinianism, 99-100, 105, 106,
   108
Darwinism Defended, 139
Darwin's Black Box, 104
Davies, Paul, 84
Dawkins, Richard, 45-6, 51, 56,
   61, 62, 66, 67-8, 93, 98-9, 102,
   103, 106, 113, 116, 128, 135,
   138, 141, 145, 166, 168

death,
   inescapable, 162, 196, 197-8
   man's awareness of, 146-50
   result of sin, 37, 172-3, 196-7
deism, 59
Denial of Death, The, 148
Denton, Michael, 98, 103
devil, the — see Satan
DNA, 91-2, 94, 101, 113, 114,
   116, 135-6, 138
Dobzhansky, Theodosius, 98
Does God Believe in Atheists?,
   92, 108, 162
Dostoevsky, Fyodor, 127
Dotsenko, Boris, 69-72
dualism, 144
Dylan, Bob, 33
Dyson, Freeman, 83

Eccles, Sir John, 64
Economist, The, 158
Eddington, Sir Arthur, 77
Einstein, Albert, 69, 141
Encyclopaedia Britannica, 189
*Encyclopaedia of Religion and
   Ethics,* 144
Entropy, Law of, 70-71
enzymes, 104-5
Evans, C. Stephen, 31
Evans, Julian, 53-6
'Everything, Theory of', 80
evil, problem of, 166-82
evolution, 11, 29, 53, 96-108,
   122, 128, 133
Evolution: A Theory in Crisis, 103
evolutionary tree, 119
evolutionism, 165

Facing Suffering, 180
faith, definition of, 229
Faraday, Michael, 60
Farese, John, 182-6
Ferris, Timothy, 80
Feuerbach, Ludwig, 142, 143
Flew, Anthony, 225
Forbes magazine, 162
fossils, 105-8
Fox, Sidney, 51
Frame, John, 126
Frenkel, Jakob, 71
From a Frog to a Prince, 102
From Nothing to Nature, 94
Frost, Robert 150

Gaer, Joseph, 142
Gallic War — see Caesar
Geology of South America, 96
Geology of Volcanic Islands, 96
genetic engineering, 114-15
genetics, 63, 64, 90-94, 100-102,
    191
Gidoomal, Ram, 150-56
God,
    attributes — see definition of
    authorship of Scripture, 35-6
    Creator, 13, 14, 34, 35, 36, 43,
        59, 61, 67, 72, 77-8, 83,
        94-5, 96, 113, 123, 128-9,
        132, 133, 134, 139, 141,
        149-50, 171-2, 196, 220,
        223, 224, 231
    'death of', 9
    definition of, 13-14, 219-20
    eternal self-existence, 13, 14,
        76, 84
    'of the gaps', 66, 77
    goodness, 173, 224
    holiness, 13, 14, 32, 134, 143,

    173, 219, 232
immanence, 13, 14
immutability, 13, 14
Judge of mankind, 13, 15,
    126-7
justice, 32, 168, 177, 179, 202
law of, 230-32
light, 52
love, 13, 14, 88, 132, 133, 174,
    179, 185, 202, 216, 220, 224
omnipotence (see also sover-
    eignty), 219-20
omniscience, 13, 14
personality, 13, 14, 126, 127,
    134, 219
plurality, 13, 14, 214
revelation of himself,
    in nature, 57, 141, 225
    in the person of Jesus Christ,
        59
    in Scripture, 35-6, 37, 39
Ruler of the universe — see
    sovereignty
sovereignty, 13, 14, 59, 78,
    143, 179, 182, 219-20, 231
spirituality, 13, 14, 219
transcendence, 13, 14, 34, 61,
    69, 72, 76, 83, 84, 95, 126,
    127, 134, 139, 219
truth, 173
uniqueness of, 13, 219, 227
wisdom, 134, 174, 185
God, Science and Evolution, 23
good and evil, existence of, 167-9
Gosling, William, 67
Gould, Stephen Jay, 118, 135
Grassé, Pierre, 101
Grayling, Anthony, 47
'Great Chain of Being', 149
Greenleaf, Simon, 21

Hailsham, Lord, 168-9
Haldane, J. B. S., 128
Hamilton, Thomas, 138
Hare, David, 44
Hawking, Stephen, 64, 74, 79, 80, 81-2, 84
Heffner, Hugh, 125
hell, 28
Hemingway, Ernest, 125
Henslow, John, 96
Herschel, William, 60
Hill, Ronnie, 121
Hinduism, 20, 59, 144, 151, 153, 154
Hitch-hiker's Guide to the Galaxy, The, 74
Hitler, Adolf, 125, 126, 163, 165, 166, 167
Holder, Rodney, 124
Holocaust, the, 125, 163-7
Homer, 16
Houghton, Sir John, 65, 144
Howatch, Susan, 45
Hoyle, Sir Fred, 75
Hsu, Kenneth, 99-100
Human Genome Project, 64, 90
humanism, 120
Hume, David, 22, 23, 82
Hunt, Dave, 20
Huxley, Aldous, 138, 143
Huxley, Julian, 9, 53, 98
Huxley, Thomas, 30

Icons of Evolution, 105
Iliad (Homer), 16
In Harm's Way, 143
Independent, The, 45, 51
individual, value of the, 122

International Council of Scientific Studies, 65
Islam, 20, 59, 126, 212-13, 216

James, William, 31
Java Man, 107
Jesus Christ, 26, 27-8, 29, 38, 39, 55-6, 131, 153-4, 156, 187-217, 221
    birth, 38, 187, 188, 190, 227
    character, 39, 131
    claims, 38, 55-6, 153-4, 195, 211
    conception, 190-91
    death, 29, 38, 39, 56, 131, 156, 195-202, 221, 227, 233
    deity, 26, 27-8, 57, 156, 211-12, 221
    historical figure, 39, 56, 131, 153, 188, 190
    humanity, 194
    identity, 39
    life, 38, 39, 55, 56, 131, 187, 227
    miracles, 38, 192-4
    prophecies concerning, 38, 198, 211
    relevance, 39, 57, 153
    resurrection, 26, 27-8, 38, 56, 131, 203-10, 221, 225, 227
    sinlessness, 156, 194-5, 217
    sufferings, 185, 200-202
    teaching, 38, 50, 70, 153, 156, 189, 192, 212, 232, 233
    uniqueness, 190, 192, 194, 195, 203
Joad, C. E. M., 116
Johnson, Paul, 45, 60, 124

Johnson, Phillip, 92, 106
Jones, Steve, 63, 64
Josephus, Flavius, 190
Journal of Sedimentary Petrology, 99
Jung, Gustav, 137
justice (see also God, justice), 168

Kant, Immanuel, 82
Kast, Eric, 146
Keith, Sir Arthur, 165
Kelly, Douglas, 78
Kennedy, D. James, 210
Kennedy, John F., 157
Kennedy, Sir Ludovic, 9, 45, 46-7, 52
Kenny, Anthony, 226
Kenny, Mary, 148
Kenyon, Sir Frederic, 16, 17
Kepler, Johannes, 60
Kerkut, G. A., 103-4
King, David, 115
Klein, Yves, 137
knowledge, human,
   limits of (see also science, limits of), 33-4, 49, 52, 61-9, 77, 88
Knowles, Andrew, 119, 127-8
Koop, C. Everett, 118
Koran, the — see *Qur'an*, the
Kuhn, Isobel, 131

Language, Truth and Logic, 47
Latourette, Kenneth Scott, 188
Le Fanu, James, 64, 67
Lecky, William, 195
Leibniz, Gottfried, 80
Lenin, 145
Levin, Bernard, 30, 135

Lewis, C. S., 51, 54, 109, 124, 132, 149, 180, 212
life,
   origin of, 68, 91-113, 133
   purpose of, 69
   quality of, 65
Life Itself: Its Origin and Nature, 92
Lindsell, Harold, 35
Linnaeus, Carolus, 60
Listener, The, 47
Livy, 15
logic, 52, 222
origin of, 62, 128, 150
logical positivism, 46-7, 62, 134
Lubenow, Marvin, 122
'Lucy', 108
Lyell, Charles, 96

MacKay, Donald, 61-2
Mackie, J. L., 84
macroevolution (see also evolution), 97-108
Mahabharata, 16, 151
man,
   aesthetic dimension, 139-41
   awareness of death, 146-50
   created 'in God's image', 123, 149-50, 171, 220, 225
   creativity, 140, 141, 150
   destiny, 15, 32, 73, 132, 148, 149, 222, 224
   dignity and worth, 120-23, 134, 165, 168
   fall into sin, 36-7, 172, 196-7, 220
   nature, 57, 65, 197, 220, 233
   origin of, 95, 118, 121, 123, 128, 132, 133, 134, 165, 222

physical attributes, 116-18
principles governing behaviour, 65
relationship to nature, 99, 115-29, 139-40, 141, 142, 146, 149
religious instinct — see spiritual dimension
self-conscious, rational being, 127-9, 134, 172, 220
sense of meaning and purpose, 135-9, 150, 225
sense of right and wrong, 123-7, 134, 138, 150, 166, 168, 171, 220, 227
spiritual dimension, 66, 142, 220
Mao Tse-tung, 145, 162
Marxism (see also Communism), 70
Maxwell, James Clerk, 60
Matthews, Robert, 80
Mayr, Ernst, 53, 106
McGrath, Alister, 147, 202
meaninglessness (see also man, sense of meaning and purpose; universe, meaning and purpose in), 138
Menuhin, Yehudi, 141
Mere Christianity, 54, 55, 109
microbiology, 103-5
microevolution, 97
Mill, John Stuart, 195
Millard, Alan, 18
Miller, Andrew, 66
Miracle of Theism, The, 84
miracles (see also Jesus Christ, miracles), 22-5, 26, 28, 38, 191, 192-4

monism, 58-9
morality — see man, sense of right and wrong
Moreland, J. P., 58, 62
Morey, Robert, 47
Morison, Frank, 54, 131
Mormon, Book of, 20
Morris, Desmond, 116
Morris, Henry, 22, 165-6
Moss, Gloria, 207
Muhammad, 216
Muhammad Ali, 210
mutations, 100-102

Naked Ape, The, 116
Nash, Ronald, 47, 48
natural disasters, 10, 160, 175
'natural selection', 100
nature (see also God, revelation of himself in nature; man, relationship to nature),
   effects of man's sin on, 173
   harmony and design in, 43, 59, 69, 75, 82-5, 88, 112-13
   laws of, 22-4, 71, 78, 84, 88, 128-9
Nature, 94
Nazism, 126, 163-7
Neanderthal Man, 107
Nehru, Jawaharlal, 61
Neo-Darwinism, 100
New Age Movement, 108, 113, 144
new birth, the, 233
New Testament — see Bible
New Testament Documents, The, 27
Newton, Sir Isaac, 35, 83
Nietzsche, Friedrich, 9

Night, 163
nihilism, 136-8
Nutcracker Man, 107-8

Observer, The, 135, 137, 145
O'Hair, Madalyn Murray, 45
Origin of the Idea of God, 144
Origin of Species..., The, 96-8, 105

Palmer, Bernard, 11
panspermia, 92-3
pantheism, 55, 58, 59, 115, 144
Pascal, Blaise, 221-3, 225, 226
Patterson, Colin, 108
Pauling, Linus, 117
Penrose, Roger, 82
Pensées (Pascal), 222
Perspective, 140
Philips, Melanie, 145
physics, laws of, 81, 124, 136, 139, 175
Piltdown Man, 107
Plantinga, Alvin, 160, 168
Plato, 70
Pliny the Younger, 190
Pol Pot, 145, 162
Polkinghorne, John, 23
polytheism, 144
Popper, Sir Karl, 68
postmodernism, 125
Prance, Sir Ghillean, 57, 109-13
Problem of Pain, The, 180
prophecy — see Bible, prophecy
proteins, 103, 104-5
Provine, William, 135

Quarks, Chaos and Christianity, 23
Quarterly Review, The, 98

Qur'an, the, 20, 213, 216, 217

Ramayana, The, 151
Ramm, Bernard, 192
Ramsay, Sir William, 19
Raup, David, 105-6
Ray, John, 60
Redstone, Sumner, 162
reductionism, 61-2, 113
Rees, Sir Martin, 115
Religion and Science, 61
Renan, Ernest, 195
Rendle-Short, John, 140-41
Rifkin, Jeremy, 108
Rise and Fall of the Third Reich, The, 167
River out of Eden, 138, 141
RNA, 116
Robinson, Martin, 48
Roman History (Livy), 15
Rookmaaker, H. R., 141, 227
Royal Society, the, 59, 60
Rubenstein, Richard, 164
Ruse, Michael, 139
Russell, Bertrand, 46, 61, 66, 73, 75, 120, 134, 148, 165, 190

Salisbury, Frank, 94
Samaria, 27
Sammons, Peter, 40-43
Sartre, Jean-Paul, 146
Satan, 172, 228
Schaeffer, Francis, 123
Schatten, Gerald, 114
Schmidt, Pere Wilhelm, 144
Schrödinger, Erwin, 66
Schultz, Charles, 36
science,
    the Bible and, 23-5, 29, 55-6, 57-72, 88

claims made on behalf of, 61
definitions of, 58
limitations of, 23-4, 62, 63-9, 77
Science Speaks, 20
scientific method, 58, 62
scientism, 61-2, 63, 67-8
Screwtape Letters, The, 109
Scripture — see Bible
Scriven, Michael, 48
Second Humanist Manifesto, 120
Selfish Gene, The, 93
Sermon on the Mount, the, 184, 192
Shayad, Reza, 212-17
Shirer, William, 167
Sikhism, 59
Simpson, George Gaylord, 99, 135
sin (see also evil, problem of), 28, 38, 55, 172-3, 175, 177, 180, 184, 196-200, 216, 220-21, 229-32
Smith, George, 47
Smoot, George, 79, 82
Socrates, 70
Son of God, 207
Soul of Britain, 45-6, 47, 67, 69
Sound of Music, The, 81
species,
fixity of, 96
origin of, 30, 95-108
variations within, 97
Spencer, Herbert, 100
Spetner, Lee, 102
spontaneous generation theory, 76, 93, 94, 95
Sproul, R. C., 36, 120
Stalin, 70

steady state theory, 75-6
Stephen Hawking's Universe, 80
Steno, Niels, 60
Stoner, Peter, 20
Storkey, Elaine, 69
Strauss, David, 207
Streeter, Gary, 129-33
Suetonius, 16, 190
suffering, 37, 38, 88, 157-86, 200-202
Sunday Telegraph, The, 64, 67, 80
Sunday Times, The, 99

Tabash Edward, 163, 174
Tacitus, Cornelius, 15, 16, 190
Talmudists, the, 17
Taylor, Ian, 99
Ten Commandments, the, 37, 230, 231
theism, 32-3, 45, 48, 84, 120, 143
Thermodynamics, Laws of, 60, 70-71, 75, 76
Thinking Clearly about God and Science, 150
Thomson, William, 60
TIME magazine, 19, 97, 148
Times, The, 9, 24, 30, 52, 135, 159, 164, 171
Titanic, the, 160-61, 169
Trinity, the — see God, plurality
truth, 33, 45, 132-3, 218
search for, 58, 67
Tryon, Edward, 81

universe, the (see also nature, harmony and design in),
future transformation of, 181

meaning and purpose in, 82-4,
  138-9, 140
nature of, 31-2, 59, 71, 74, 78,
  79, 80, 82-5, 134, 227
not in original state, 173
origin of, 29, 64, 73-89
vastness of, 74-5, 81

Vedas, the, 20
Verbrugge, Magnus, 101
verification principle — see logical positivism

Wald, George, 93
Wallace, Alfred Russell, 53
Walter, Natasha, 65
Ward, Keith, 62-3, 77, 84, 135-6,
  141
wars, 161-2, 169
Watts, Fraser, 68
Watson, James, 91
Wells, David, 125
Wells, H. G., 188

Wells, Jonathan, 105
What on Earth is an Atheist?, 45
White, A. J. Monty, 25-9
Who Moved the Stone?, 54, 131
Whole Shebang, The, 80
Why Can't I Have Faith?, 175
Wiesel, Elie, 163
Wilkinson, David, 79
Will to Believe, The, 31
Williams, Kenneth, 147-8
Williams, Peter, 46
Wilson, Robert Dick, 18-19
wish-fulfilment, 142-3
World Trade Centre, 157-9
Wright, Verna, 57
Wrinkles in Time, 79

Young Pillars, 36

Zacharias, Ravi, 149, 167, 170
Zohar, Danah, 58
Zuckerman, Lord, 108
Zwemer, Samuel, 142

Does God believe in Atheists?

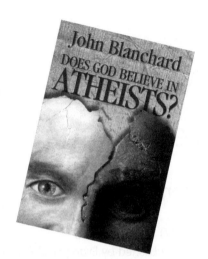

John Blanchard

ISBN 0 85234 460 0
(Also published by Evangelical Press)

'The breadth and depth of his reading is quite breathtaking, and his grasp of modern scientific and philosophical trends stunning. It is also an absolute gold-mine of "quotable quotes".'

Rev. Derek Swann
Cardiff

'A brilliant defence of belief in God.'

Rev. Andrew Anderson
International Baptist Church of Brussels

'Masterfully engages both Christian and unbeliever alike in examining the most profound question confronting mankind: does God exist?'

John Canales
Presbyterian Church of America

'No self-respecting atheist should be without it.'

Rev. Dr Nick Needham
Highland Theological College, Scotland

Meet the real Jesus

John Blanchard

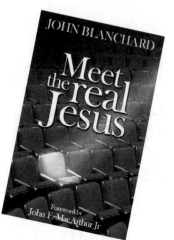

ISBN 0 85234 499 6
(Also published by Evangelical Press)

'The finest book I have ever read explaining who Jesus is.'
Brian Edwards

'In this superlative book John Blanchard has greatly increased the debt we already owe him.'
Alec Motyer

'Highly recommended... Here, instead of the fuzzy versions of the Christian faith ... are facts of the matter splendidly brought together and clearly argued.'
Rev. Dick Lucas

'Another excellent book by a great communicator ... will challenge the sceptic's unbelief and strengthen the believer's faith.'
The Irish Baptist

'Racy and readable, clear and convincing.'
Evangelical Times

'A magnificent work by a gifted man.'
Dr Adrian Rogers

A wide range of excellent books on spiritual subjects is available from Evangelical Press. Please write to us for your free catalogue or contact us by e-mail.

Evangelical Press
Faverdale North Industrial Estate,
Darlington,
Co. Durham,
DL3 0PH,
England

Evangelical Press USA
P. O. Box 84,
Auburn,
MA 01501,
USA

e-mail: sales@evangelicalpress.org

web: http://www.evangelicalpress.org